STUDY GUIDE TO ACCOMPANY

Human Physiology

by Rhoades and Pflanzer

FLORENCE C. RICCIUTI, PH.D.

SAUNDERS COLLEGE PUBLISHING
Philadelphia Fort Worth Chicago
San Francisco Montreal Toronto
London Sydney Tokyo

Printed in the United States of America

Rhoades: STUDY GUIDE to accompany HUMAN PHYSIOLOGY

ISBN # 0-03-011253-2

901 084 987654321

Table of Contents

Preface

My objectives in writing this study guide were to

1. summarize important concepts and facts;
2. organize the content in order to facilitate student learning;
3. provide a format for reviewing for examinations; and
4. test student comprehension and develop problem solving ability.

Each chapter in the study guide contains a

1) detailed outline of the text chapter;
2) list of learning objectives;
3) list of key terms and phrases; and
4) section in which student comprehension and mastery are evaluated.

The study guide outline follows the text chapter outline but contains more headings and details. In the outline major concepts are indicated by a (*). The outline can be used in class to facilitate note-taking during a lecture and to help students review for examinations.

The learning objectives, as well as the outline, emphasize the content to be mastered in a course in human physiology. The list of key terms includes most of the words and phrases in bold face in the text.

The last section consists of exercises designed to (1) evaluate mastery of concepts, (2) develop problem solving ability, and (3) organize information into tables that can be used for review.

I welcome criticisms, comments, suggestions for improvement, and would appreciate being notified of inaccurate statements and errors.

F.C.R.
New Haven, CT
March, 1989

To The Student

As you study each chapter in the text, keep the following points in mind.

1) Look over the chapter Outline and Summary to give you an overview of the material covered in the chapter.
2) Skim the chapter in the text. Do not try to absorb every detail or to memorize. This quick reading will help you become familiar with terminology, the basic concepts, and content.
3) Now, following the chapter outline in the study guide, read the chapter in the text. As you read the chapter, compare it with the outline and fill in details emphasized by your instructor during class.
4) Once you feel confident, complete the section titled "Testing Your Understanding." Answers are provided for some of the exercises in this section. For other exercises you will have to complete the table with information from the chapter. The latter type of exercise is intended to help you organize chapter material in preparation for examinations.

I hope that this guide will be useful in your study of physiology. I welcome your criticisms and suggestions for improvements.

F.C.R.
New Haven, CT
March, 1989

CHAPTER 1. THE SCIENCE OF PHYSIOLOGY

Chapter Outline

I. The History of Physiology

A. Physiological Studies in Classical and Medieval Times

1. The Observations of Aristotle
   a. Aristotle was one of the first to describe blood vessels as a system with the heart at the center.

2. The Theories of Herophilus and Erasistratus
   a. Herophilus who is considered the first physiologist in the Western tradition by some, identified the brain as the seat of the intellect.
   b. Erasistratus postulated the existence of tiny connections between veins and arteries, but he believed air was present in arteries rather than blood.

3. The "Pneumatology" of Galen
   a. Galen demonstrated that blood flowed through arteries.
   b. Galen believed that different forms of pneuma or "spirits" drove various bodily processes.

B. The Discoveries of the European Renaissance Physiologists

1. The Drawings of Versalius
   a. Versalius wrote the first modern anatomy textbook which was published in 1543 and contained many illustrations and corrected many of Galen's errors.

2. The Theories of William Harvey
   a. Harvey demonstrated experimentally the direction of blood flow in veins and the connection between arteries and veins. He recognized that the heart was a pump and not the place where blood and air met.
   b. Harvey used quantitative methods to show that the heart pumped the same blood and not a new quantity with each beat.

3. The Microscopic Studies of Malpighi
   a. Malpighi confirmed microscopically the existence of capillaries.

C. Modern Advances in Physiological Understanding

1. The Study of What We Breathe
   a. Modern understanding of air and its importance to the body can be traced to the work of 17th and 18th century physicists and chemists, like Priestly, Lavoisier, Boyle, Borelli, and others.

2. The Advancement of Cell Theory
   a. The concept of the cell theory was articulated by Schleiden and Schwann in the 19th century.
   b. The concept of cells arising only from preexisting cells and not from nonliving matter was stated first by Virchow and confirmed experimentally by Pasteur in the same century.

3. The Idea of Homeostasis
   a. The concept of homeostasis was developed by Bernard in the 19th century.

II. The Study of Physiology

A. The Scientific Method

* The scientific method involves posing questions and then searching for answers to those questions often by devising experiments and tests of reasons to validate the answers.

1. Reasoning Processes
   a. In deductive reasoning one proceeds from a general rule to a specific conclusion.

2. Steps in the Scientific Method
   a. The scientific method consists of a series of steps broadly classified as (1) observation, (2) hypothesis, (3) experiment, (4) conclusion, and, sometimes (5) testing, and (6) publication.
   b. The purpose of the experiment is to determine whether a cause-and-effect relationship exists between an observation and a variable (the hypothesized cause of the observation). Two sets of conditions are devised. One is the experiment set in which the variable is present; the other, called the control, is identical to the experimental set except the variable is omitted.
   c. The conclusion drawn from the results either validates or rejects the hypothesis.

B. Measurement, Computation, and Graphic Analysis

1. Units of Measurement
   a. Quantitative methods are invaluable for understanding bodily functions.
   b. The metric system is almost exclusively the one used for physiological measurements.

2. Scientific Notation
   a. For convenience, quantities are expressed as products of a number plus a power of ten expressed as an exponent.

3. Ratios and Proportions
   a. A ratio is an expression that compares two numbers or quantities by division.
   b. A proportion is a mathematical statement of the equality of two ratios.

4. Interpretation of Graphic Data
   a. A graph is a diagram that expresses a relationship between two or more quantities.

C. Anatomical Planes and Positions

1. Planes
   a. Imaginary planes are used to divide the body into parts.
   b. Terms of position are used to locate a structure relative to other structures.

III. General Organization of the Body

A. Cell Differentiation and Specialization

* The different groups of cells work together to maintain the life of the organism.
* Each cell manifests the form and structure best suited to the function it performs in the body.

B. Cells and Tissues

* One or more types of specialized cells become closely associated to form a tissue.
* There are four classes of tissues: epithelial, connective, nervous and muscle.

1. Epithelial Tissue
   a. Epithelial tissue consists of closely packed cells arranged in flat sheets and covering exposed body surfaces and lining body cavities, tubes and organs.

2. Connective Tissue
   a. Connective tissue is composed of cells embedded in a matrix that may contain cellular products such as fibers, soluble proteins and crystalline complexes.

3. Muscle Tissue
   a. Muscle tissue consists of elongated cells that contain contractile fibers.

4. Nervous Tissue
   a. The primary components of nervous tissue are neurons, cells specialized for receiving and conducting electrical impulses.
   b. Glial cells, a component of nervous tissue, provide neurons with structural and metabolic support.

C. Organs and Systems

* An organ is defined as a group of tissues that have been combined for the performance of a specific function or series of related functions.
* Organs and other structures that share in the performance of related tasks are grouped into systems.

D. Bodily Fluid Components

* Bodily fluids are grouped into two major compartments: intracellular fluid and extracellular fluid.
* The compartments, which are separated by the cellular plasma membrane, differ chemically.

1. Intracellular Fluid

2. Extracellular Fluid
   a. There are three types of extracellular fluids: (1) interstitial fluid; (2) plasma; and (3) lymph. These comprise the internal environment of the body.

IV. Homeostasis: Control of the Internal Environment

* Conditions in the internal environment must be maintained within certain narrow limits in order to allow cells to live and function.
* Conditions such as oxygen tension, pH, osmotic pressure, temperature and the concentrations of various metabolic substrates, hormones, and waste products are all closely regulated by the cooperative workings of tissues, organs and systems.

A. The Advantages of an Internal Environment

B. Homeostasis and Protein Conformation

* Proteins serve a variety of functions in the cell. Every protein has its own distinctive conformation that allows it to best carry out its function. The shape, and therefore the function are affected by pH, temperature, and ion concentrations.
* The molecular basis for the homeostatic process, is essentially the maintenance of protein conformation.

C. Control Systems

* Control systems operate to maintain homeostasis. They use mechanisms called sensors to detect conditions in the body and effectors to change conditions in the body.
* Two general classes of control systems are active in the body: (1) negative feedback systems; and (2) positive feedback systems.

1. Sensors and Effectors
   a. Sensors determine the level of the variable with respect to a reference point.
   b. Effectors attempt to change the level of the parameter so that it returns to the desired level.

2. The Nervous System in Homeostatic Control

   a. The nervous system, one of the major homeostatic control systems in the body, monitors temperature, arterial blood pressure, and concentration of hydrogen ions in extracellular fluids by thermoreceptors, baroreceptors and chemoreceptors.

Chapter Learning Objectives

1. Describe the contributions of Vesalius and Harvey to modern physiology.
2. Distinguish deductive from inductive reasoning and provide an example of each.
3. Outline the steps in the scientific method.
4. Using the scientific method, describe how you demonstrate that methionine is an essential amino acid.
5. Know the units of the metric system and how to convert from one unit to another, e.g., from millimeters to nanometers or nanograms to milligrams.
6. Know how to express a quantity using scientific notation.
7. Know how to express a ratio and proportion.
8. Know how to read or interpret a graphical representation of data.
9. Be able with reference to your body to use the terms describing planes and positions.
10. Describe the levels of structural organization in the body from cells to the organism.
11. Describe mechanisms in the body, which act to maintain homeostasis and why this is necessary.

Key Terms

anterior, posterior
cell
cell theory
conformation
connective tissue
control
cranial, caudal
deductive reasoning
dependent variable
direct relationship
hypothesis
independent variable
internal, external
inferior, superior
interpolation
interstitial fluid
intracellular fluid
inverse relationship
linear relationship
matrix
planes (sagittal, transverse, frontal)
positive feedback
premise
proportion
proximal, distal
ratio
reference point
scatter diagram
scientific method

effector
epithelial tissue
experiment
extracellular fluid
extrapolation
homeostasis
medial, lateral
muscle tissue
negative feedback
nervous tissue
neuron
observation
organ
scientific notation
sensor
superficial, deep
system
tissue
uncontrolled variable
variable
ventral, dorsal

Aristotle
Bernard
Galen
Harvey
Hooke
Malpighi
Pasteur
Priestley
Schleiden
Schwann

Testing Your Knowledge

I. Matching Select the correct term from the Key Terms.

__________1. proceeding from a general rule to a specific conclusion
__________2. proceeding from a specific observation to a general rule.
__________3. determined correct pattern of circulation of blood in the body.
__________4. developed concept of homeostasis
__________5. position of stomach relative to spinal cord
__________6. statement tentatively explaining observations
__________7. plane dividing body into right and left halves.
__________8. expression comparing two numbers or quantities by division
__________9. relationship in which X increases as Y decreases
__________10. position of thigh relative to foot
__________11. associated of one or more types of specialized cells
__________12. tissue composed of cells in a matrix
__________13. comprises internal environment of body
__________14. stable state of internal environment
__________15. feature of every control system

II. Calculations

1) In the table write a ratio relating the number of grams to the units listed in the table. Use scientific notation.

# grams/1 kilogram	for example 10^3g/1kg
a. /milligram	
b. /microgram	
c. /nanogram	
d. /picogram	

2) Using ratios and proportions show how you would determine the number of microliters in five gallons of soda. One quart equals 943 milliliters (ml).

III. Fill in the Table.

You weigh 120 lbs and are 5'4" tall. One gram equals 0.035 ounces and one meter equals 39.37 inches. Write your height and weight in the units indicated in the table. Use scientific notation.

Height 5'4"	Weight 120 lbs
kilometer	kilogram
meter	gram
centimeter	milligram
millimeter	microgram
micrometer	nanogram
nanometer	picogram

IV. Interpretation of Graphs.

Consider the following experiment to determine the effect of light intensity on the rate of photosynthesis as measured by the production of oxygen. The set up is illustrated in the diagram.

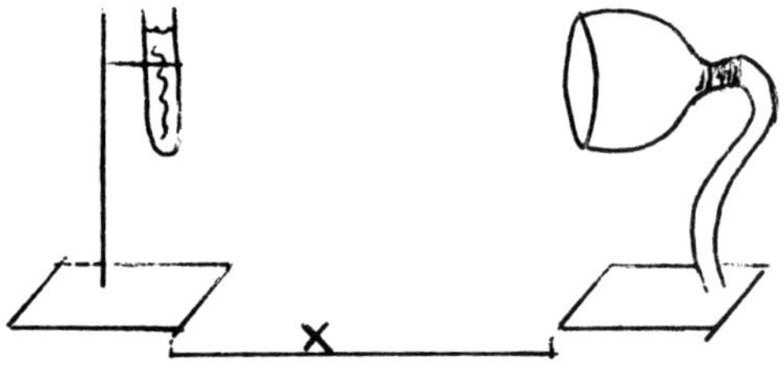

A piece of Elodea is immersed in a 5% sodium bicarbonate solution in a test tube. A 100 watt lamp is placed at variable distance X.

The rate of photosynthesis is determined by counting the number of oxygen bubbles released by the Elodea in one minute. Counts are made in triplicate and the average number per minute is plotted on the graph.

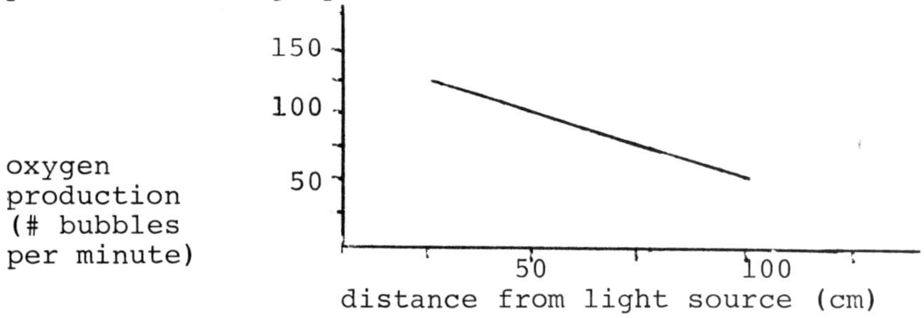

a) What is the relationship between the distance and rate of photosynthesis?
b) At 125cm, what # of bubbles would you expect to count?
c) What is the independent variable?
d) What is the dependent variable?
e) What would be a control for this experiment?

CHAPTER 2 CHEMICAL AND PHYSICAL PRINCIPLES

Expanded Chapter Outline

I. Overview: Matter and Energy in the Living Cell
   * Living organisms are composed of matter which consists largely of hydrogen, carbon, oxygen and nitrogen and 23 other essential elements.
   * The matter of a living organism is highly organized. A constant input of energy is required to maintain this state.
   * The chemical basis of matter is strikingly similar in diverse life forms.

II. Atoms and Elements

   A. Subatomic Particles
      * An atom is the smallest unit of an element that retains all the chemical properties of the element.
      * Atoms are composed of subatomic particles called protons, neutrons and electrons.

      1. Uniqueness of Elements: Protons and Atomic Number
         a. The number of protons in the atom's nucleus is called the atomic number and is unique for each element.

      2. Variation Within Elements: Neutrons, Mass Number and Isotopes
         a. The mass number is the total number of protons and neutrons in the nucleus.
         b. Isotopes of an element have the same atomic number but different mass numbers because they have different numbers of neutrons.

   B. Ions: Atoms with Electrical Charges
      * An ion results when a neutral atom gains or loses an electron.

   C. Electron Configuration and the Outer Shell
      * Electrons are located in shells which represent different energy levels and hold different numbers of electrons.
      * The number of electrons in the outer shell determines many of the chemical properties of the atom.

III. Molecules, Groups and Compounds
   * Atoms may form chemical bonds with each other by sharing, gaining or losing electrons in their outer shells.
   * Chemical bonds represent potential energy.
   * Atoms combine in definite proportions to form compounds.
   * The four types of chemical bonds in order of decreasing strength are: covalent, ionic, hydrogen and Van der Waals.

   A. Covalent Bonds: Polar and Nonpolar Molecules
      * Covalent bonds are formed when two or more atoms share electrons. The electrons may be shared equally (nonpolar) or unequally (polar) and more than one pair can be shared.
      * Carbon can form four covalent bonds.

   B. Ionic Bonds and Ionic Compounds
      * An ionic bond is formed between one atom which acquires one or more electrons and a second atom which loses electrons to the first atom. The equal and opposite electrical charges of the two atoms hold them together.

   C. Van der Waals Bonds
      * Van der Waals bonds form when negatively charged electron cloud in one atom is attracted to the positively charged nucleus of a neighboring atom.

D. Hydrogen Bonds
  * Hydrogen bonds occur among polar covalent molecules and results from the attraction between the partial positive charge of the hydrogen atom and the partial negative charge of an atom such as nitrogen or oxygen.

IV. Chemical Reactions: Basic Principles
  * Chemical reactions result from the breaking and forming of chemical bonds
  * The rate of a chemical reaction depends on temperature, concentration of reactants, and the orientation of the molecules.
  * In oxidation-reduction reactions, one reactant loses electrons which the other reactant gains.

V. Water and Aqueous Solutions

A. Polarity of the Water Molecule
  * Polar covalent bonds join the oxygen to two hydrogen atoms in a water molecule.

B. Arrangements of Water Molecules
  * Hydrogen bonds between water molecules are responsible for many of water's unique properties.

C. Water as a Solvent

1. Solutions of Ionic Compounds
   a. The ions in ionic compounds dissociate in aqueous solutions and each becomes surrounded by sphere of water molecules.

2. Solutions of Polar Covalent Compounds

3. Solutions of Nonpolar Compounds: Hydrophobic Interactions
   a. Nonpolar compounds are poorly soluble in water and cluster together in hydrophobic "pockets" to minimize their contact with water molecules.

D. Concentrations of Solutions
  * The concentration of a solution can be expressed as molality, molarity or osmolarity.

E. The pH Scale
  * pH is a logarithmic expression of the concentration of H^+ ions. Water has a pH value of 7 and is neutral.

F. Acids and Bases in Solution

1. Acids: Proton Donors
   a. An acid is any substance whose dissociation in water releases H^+ ions.
   b. Weak acids give up H^+ ions less readily and do not dissociate completely in water.

2. Bases: Proton Acceptors
   a. A base is a substance that accepts H^+ ions and thus decreases the H^+ concentration in a solution.

3. Buffers
   a. Buffers are substances that accept H^+ ions and release them to maintain and minimize changes in pH in a defined range.

VI. The Behavior of Gases

A. The Ideal Gas Laws
* The volume of a gas is affected by temperature, pressure and amount.
* The relationship between these physical parameters can be summarized in an equation, the Ideal Gas Law, which is $PV = nRT$.

B. Partial Pressures in Gaseous Solutions
* The total pressure in a container holding a solution of gases is the sum of the partial pressures of the component gases.
* The partial pressure of a gas is proportional to the amount, in moles, of the gas solution it makes up.

C. The Kinetic Theory of Gases
* Gas molecules are in continuous random motion which is affected by temperature.

VII. Gradients and the Movement of Substances
* Gradients take a variety of forms, such as pressure, electrical or concentration gradients.

A. Pressure Gradients
* The movement of blood through arteries and veins results from a pressure gradient
* The effects of pressure and resistance on flow are represented by the equation: $F = (P_1 - P_2)/R$. P_1 and P_2 represent the pressures at the starting and final points.

B. Voltage Difference and Ion Flow
* Electrical gradients result from differences in the number of positive and negative charges on either side of a membrane.
* The effects of the potential difference and resistance on the flow of ions are represented by the equation: $I = (V_1 - V_2)/R$. V_1 and V_2 represent the electrical gradient, R is the resistance of the specific channel through which ions flow and I is the ionic current.

C. Concentration Gradients: Diffusion and Osmosis

1. Diffusion of Solutes in Liquid Solvents
   a. In diffusion particles of solute move from a region of high concentration to one of low concentration by Brownian motion until a dynamic equilibrium is reached.
   b. The steeper the gradient, the greater the net movement.
   c. The rate of movement of solute molecules is expressed by Fick's Law: $J = -DA \cdot dc/dx$. J = flux; D = diffusion coefficient; A = area and dc/dx = driving force or concentration gradient.

2. Diffusion of Gases in Gaseous Solutions

3. Osmosis: Diffusion of Water Through a Membrane
   a. Osmosis is the flow of water across a barrier in response to a solute concentration gradient across the barrier.
   b. Osmotic concentration is expressed in units called osmoles which are equal n x moles. n equals the number of particles derived from each molecule of solute.

c. Osmotic pressure is related to solute concentration by the van't Hoff Law which is described by the equation rr = RTC. rr is the osmotic pressure, R is the ideal gas constant, T is temperature (K) and C is the total solute concentration expressed as osmoles of solute per liter of solution.

VIII. Macromolecules

A. Carbohydrates

1. Monosaccharides
   a. The general formula for a monosaccharide is $(CH_2O)n$, where n is the number of carbons.
   b. Monosaccharides can exist as linear chains or rings.

2. Disaccharides

3. Polysaccharides
   a. Monosaccharide units can combine to form linear or branched chains called polysaccharides

4. Many polysaccharides occur in covalent combination with proteins (glycoproteins) and lipids (glycolipids).

B. Lipids
* Lipids are composed of carbon and hydrogen and have a lower proportion of oxygen compared with carbohydrates
* Lipids are poorly soluble in water.

1. Fatty Acids
   a. A fatty acid is a long chain of covalently linked carbon atoms to which only hydrogen atoms are attached except for a COOH group at one end.
   b. Fatty acids can be distinguished by the number of carbons and the number of carbon-carbon double bonds in the chain.

2. Glycerol Compounds and Phospholipids
   a. Glycerol, a three carbon compound with three hydroxyl groups, can form bonds with the carboxylic acid groups of one, two or three fatty acids or to a phosphate group and two fatty acids to a form a phospholipid.
   b. Phospholipids have hydrophilic and hydrophobic ends.

3. Steroids
   a. The basic structure of a steroid is four interlocking rings of carbon atoms.
   b. Cholesterol, an important structural component of membranes, has hydrophilic and hydrophobic regions.

4. Glycolipids
   a. Glycolipids are composed of sphingosine and monosaccharide units.

C. Proteins

1. Amino acids
   a. All 20 amino acids have the same general structure. Four different chemical groups are bonded to the alpha carbon. Three of these, the carboxyl and amino groups are the same in all amino acids. The fourth group, or (R) is different for each amino acid and determines the properties of the amino acid.

b. The number and sequence of amino acids in a polypeptide chain determine its properties and functions.
c. Amino acids are divided into three broad groups based on the properties of their side chains at physiological pH. These groups contain amino acids with ionic, or nonionic polar, or nonpolar side chains.

2. Protein Structure
   a. There may be four different levels of organization in the structure of a protein molecule.
   b. The primary structure is the linear sequence of amino acids which are joined by covalent bonds, called peptide bonds.
   c. The secondary structure results from interactions among side chains and leads to a folding into a specific shape or conformation. Alpha-helices and beta-sheets are two classes of secondary structure.
   d. Tertiary structure is formed by the folding of the alpha-helix on itself or by stable associations between amino acids located in different parts of the chain. Proteins with tertiary structure are globular.
   e. Proteins with the quaternary structure are composed of two or more polypeptide chains held together by noncovalent interactions.
   f. The secondary, tertiary and quaternary structures are stabilized by hydrogen, ionic and S-S covalent bonds, and hydrophobic interactions between side chains.

D. Nucleotides and Nucleic Acids

1. Components of Nucleotides
   a. A nucleotide is composed of a sugar (either ribose or deoxyribose, one, two, or three phosphate groups and a purine or pyrimidine base (either adenine, guanine, cytosine, uracil or thymine).

2. Formation of Nucleotides and Their Roles in Cell Metabolism
   a. A nucleoside is composed of a base and a sugar.
   b. Nucleotides are components of nucleic acids but also have important roles in cell energy processes.

3. Nucleic Acids
   a. Nucleic acids are composed of nucleotides joined to each other by sugar-phosphate bonds.
   b. The sugar-phosphate chain is a constant feature and is the backbone of the molecule.
   c. The sequence of bases varies and the precise sequence represents genetic information.

4. The Structure of DNA
   a. DNA is a double helix composed of two complementary nucleotide chains whose bases pair with and form hydrogen bonds with each other.
   b. In DNA, adenine on one chain pairs with thymine on the other and cytosine with guanine.
   c. The chains are oriented in opposite directions.

IX. Thermodynamic Principles

* Living organisms are highly ordered and require energy input to maintain this organized state.
* The first principle of thermodynamics states that energy can neither be created nor destroyed.
* The second principle states that the disorder in the universe is always increasing.

A. Free Energy and Chemical Reactions

1. Free Energy
   a. Free energy can be used to do work in the cell and is measured in kilocalories.
   b. Chemical reactions involve changes in free energy.
   c. If the free energy change, ΔG, of a reaction is negative, the reaction is exergonic and releases free energy. If ΔG is positive, the reaction is energetically unfavorable and requires an energy input to allow it to occur.
   d. Exergonic and endergonic reactions are coupled.

B. Activation Energy and Enzyme-Catalyzed Reactions

* All reactions require a certain initial amount of energy, called activation energy.

1. The Catalytic Role of Enzymes
   a. Biological catalysts, called enzymes, lower the activation energy to allow reactions to occur under physiological conditions.

2. The Mechanics of Enzyme Action
   a. Enzymes facilitate reactions by providing binding sites (active sites) on their surfaces for reactant molecules (substrates).
   b. Although each enzyme is specific for its substrate, enzymes can be classified according to the general types of reactions they catalyze.
   c. Enzymes work by forming complexes with their substrates, and holding them in the correct orientation for the reaction to occur.

3. Enzyme Kinetics
   a. The relationship between reaction rate, enzyme turnover, number and substrate concentration is represented in the equation $V_{max} = k[E]$ in which k is the turnover number, and [E] is the enzyme concentration.
   b. The Michaelis constant, Km, is the concentration of substrate that will produce one half of the maximum reaction rate.

4. The Effects of pH and Temperature
   a. Because enzymes are proteins, they are affected by pH and temperature.

5. Enzyme Cofactors: Coenzymes
   a. A cofactor is a nonprotein component that some enzymes need to function.

C. Energy Exchange in the Cell: ATP and ADP

* ATP is the energy intermediary in the cell between endergonic and exergonic reactions.

Chapter Learning Objectives

1. Describe the structure of an atom, an ion and a molecule.
2. Distinguish covalent, polar covalent, ionic, hydrogen and van der Waals bonds as to their strength, electron configuration, and formation. Provide an example of each type.
3. Describe the effects of temperature, concentration and physical orientation of molecules on the rate of chemical reaction.
4. Describe what happens to polar covalent, ionic and nonpolar compounds in an aqueous solution.
5. Distinguish the terms osmolarity, molarity, molality and osmole.
6. Describe how a buffer acts to stabilize the pH of a solution.
7. Write the equation expressing the relationship between amount, volume and temperature on the pressure of a gas.
8. Compare pressure, electrical and concentration gradients as to (1) the direction of movement, (2) the effect of the steepness of the gradient on the movement of the substance, and (3) other factors affecting movement.
9. For a pressure gradient, write an equation relating flow, resistance and pressure differential, and for an electrical gradient, write an equation relating ionic flow, resistance and voltage difference. Compare the two equations.
10. Compare diffusion of solutes in liquid solvents, gases in gaseous solutions, and osmosis as to direction of movement of substance, sources of energy for movement and point of equilibrium.
11. Describe the relationship between osmolarity and osmotic pressure, and write an equation relating the two.
12. Given two solutions, e.g., 300 mOsm and 200 mOsm glucose solutions describe the osmolarity of each relative to the other.
13. Write the general chemical formula for a carbohydrate, and how polysaccharides are formed.
14. Compare fats, fatty acids, phospholipids and steroids as to general structural formula and properties.
15. Write the general structural formula for an amino acid and identify the function of each component.
16. Compare the four levels of structural organization seen in many proteins regarding the shape of the polypeptide/protein, the types of bonds stabilizing each level and the effect of pH and temperature on the levels.
17. Distinguish a nucleotide and nucleoside and describe how each is formed.
18. Draw and describe the structure of double helix of DNA indicating the role and or position of the sugar, phosphate, base and the types of bonds between the sugars and phosphates and between the bases.
19. Define the concept of free energy and describe how it relates to the direction of a chemical reaction.
20. Define activation energy and describe how enzymes lower it to allow a chemical reaction to occur.
21. Draw diagrams showing the lock and key and induced fit models for enzyme action.
22. Draw a graph expressing the relationship between substrate concentration and reaction rate; on the graph indicate Vmax and Km values.
23. Describe how pH and temperature affect enzyme activity.

Key Terms

acid
activation energy
active site
alpha-helix
amino acid
anion
atom
atomic number
ATP
Avogadro's number
base
beta-sheet
buffer
carbohydrate
catalyst
cation
chemical equation
cofactor
covalent bond
diffusion
electrical gradient
electron
electron shelf
element
endergonic
energy
enzyme
exergonic
fat
fatty acid

flow
flux
free energy (Δ G)
glycerol
glycolipid
glycoprotein
gradient
hydrogen bond
hydrophilic
hydrophobic interaction
hyperosmotic
hypo-osmotic
ideal gas law $PV = nRT$
ionic bond
ionic current
iso-osmotic
Km
lipid
macromolecule
mass number
molality
molarity
molecule
monosaccharide
neutron
nucleic acid
nucleotide
osmole
osmosis

osmotic pressure [rr=RTC]
oxidation
partial pressure
peptide bond
pH
phospholipid
polar covalent bond
poly-peptide
polysaccharide
product
protein
proton
purine
pyrimidine
reactant
reduction
saturated
solute
solvent
steroid
substrate
unsaturated
van der Waals bond
$V_{max} = k[E]$
$I = (V_1 - V_2)/R$
$rr = RTC$
$F = (P_1 - P_2)/R$
$J = -DA \cdot dc/dx$
Km

Testing Your Understanding

I. Matching. Select the correct term from the Key Words list for each definition.

___________1. substance that stabilizes pH
___________2. describes energy-releasing reaction
___________3. subunit of polysaccharide
___________4. lipid composed of four interlocking rings
___________5. describes fatty acid chain with double bonds between carbons
___________6. describes relationship between ionic current, resistance, and potential difference
___________7. describes relationship between osmotic pressure and osmolarity
___________8. energy barrier in chemical reaction
___________9. number of protons in nucleus
___________10. secondary structure of protein
___________11. complex of lipid and protein
___________12. weak bond between bases in DNA molecule
___________13. proton donor
___________14. bond between amino acids in peptide chain
___________15. describes solutions with same number of particles of solute

II. Fill in the Table

Biological Molecule	Elements	Subunit	Bond between subunit	3-dimensional structure
Carbohydrate				
Lipid fats phospholipid steroid				
Protein				
Nucleic acid				

III. Visual #1

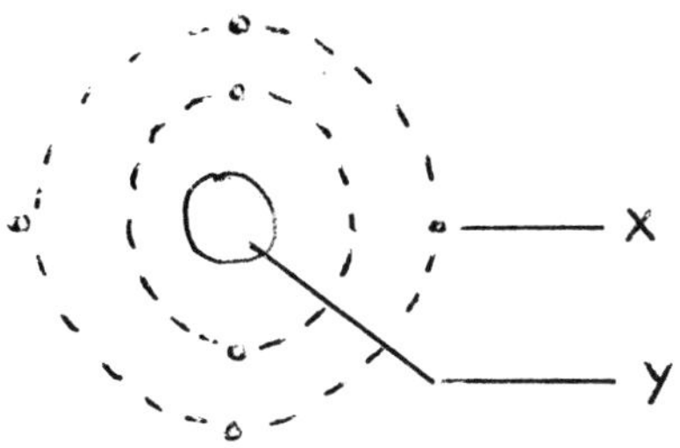

a) How many bonds can this atom form?

b) How many protons are present?

c) What is the atomic number?

d) How many neutrons are present?

e) Identify x and y

f) What type of bond(s) can this atom form?

Visual #2

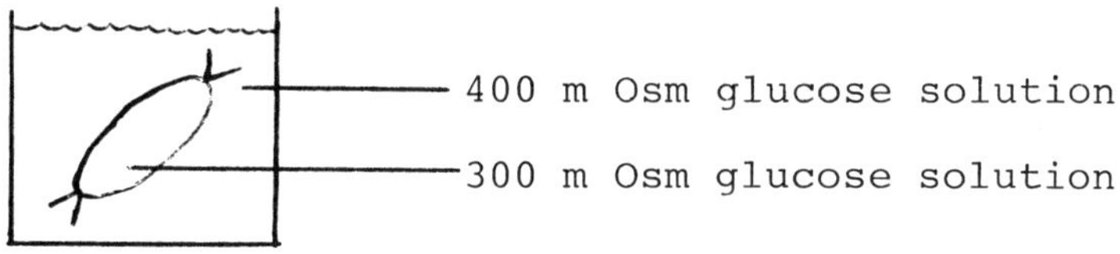

The bag is constructed from a semipermeable membrane which is permeable to water but not glucose molecules.

a) In which direction is there a net movement of water initially? ________

b) Using the terms hyperosmotic, hypo-osmotic and iso-osmotic, what is the solution in the beaker relative to the solution in the bag? ________

c) What is the solution in the bag relative to the solution in the beaker? ________

Suppose a 50 m Osm NaCl solution is added to the bag.

d) In which direction is there a net movement to water? ________

e) What is the solution in the beaker relative to that in the bag? ________

f) What is the solution in the bag relative to that in the beaker? ________

CHAPTER 3 THE STRUCTURE AND FUNCTIONS OF CELLS

Chapter Outline

I. Overview: Cell Processes and Products

* According to the cell theory, all cells come from pre-existing cells, they all have the same fundamental makeup and metabolic processes, and all organisms are composed of cells and their products.
* Eukaryotic cells have a nucleus and membrane enclosed organelles, prokaryotes do not.
* Three features of cells permit an independent existence: (1) a set of genes to control cell functions; (2) the machinery for obtaining energy; and (3) a cell membrane.
* Cell processes may be synthetic or degradative.

A. The Process of Controlling Cell Functions

* The genes in the DNA encode a set of instructions that the cell uses to make macromolecules needed to carry out its functions in the body, and to reproduce itself.

1. Directing Synthesis
   a. Information flows from genes in the DNA to RNA molecules which along with ribosomes in the cytoplasm play a major role in the production of proteins.

2. Preserving Information
   a. DNA can replicate itself to pass on information to daughter cells.

B. The Process of Obtaining Energy

* Organelles function to convert energy into a useful form to support processes like growth and reproduction.

C. The Process of Maintaining The Cell Environment

* Membranes play a major role in maintaining the intracellular environment.

1. Protecting the Interior: The Plasma Membrane
   a. The plasma membrane provides a barrier to the free movement of materials into and out of the cell.

2. Separating Cell Processes: Membranes of Organelles
   a. Membranes separate the cellular interior into compartments, called organelles.
   b. Each organelle has a defined structure and function which are intimately related.
   c. The presence of intracellular compartments permits separation of synthetic and degradative reactions, and allows for intracellular processing, sorting and packaging of synthesized molecules.

II. Cell Compartments and Their Functions

A. The Nucleus: The Library of the Cell

1. DNA: The Permanent Files
   a. Chromatin, a complex of DNA and histone, is organized into nucleosomes which exhibit higher levels of packaging, such as chromatin fibers, looped domains and chromosomes.

2. RNA: Selective Retrieval of Information
    a. There are three functional types of RNA (mRNA, tRNA, and rRNA) each of which plays a role in the production of proteins.
    b. Ribosomal RNA (rRNA) is synthesized in the nucleolus.

3. The Nuclear Envelope: A Porous Double Membrane
    a. Exchange of materials between the nucleus and cytoplasm occurs through the nuclear pores.

B. The Cytoplasm: Synthesis and Energy Release
* All the metabolic reactions occur outside the nucleus.

1. The Cytosol: A Wealth of Enzymes and Precursors
    a. The cytosol contains precursor molecules for macromolecules, enzymes and other granules and droplets.

2. Ribosomes and the Endoplasmic Reticulum: Synthesis of Proteins and Lipids.
    a. There are two functional regions of the endoplasmic reticulum (ER): the smooth and rough. The amount of each type varies with the function of the cell.
    b. The smooth ER is involved in lipid synthesis and secretion
    c. The rough ER which has attached ribosomes is involved in synthesis of proteins to be secreted from or incorporated into the membrane of the cell.
    d. Ribosomes which may be free in the cytoplasm or attached to the ER are the sites for protein synthesis.
    e. Proteins synthesized on free ribosomes are utilized within the cell. Proteins synthesized in attached ribosomes are modified by the addition of carbohydrates in the rER and then pass via a transition vesicle to the Golgi complex.

3. The Golgi Complex: Processing and Packaging
    a. In the Golgi complex macromolecules are processed and packaged into vesicles ready for transport to the cell surface and the cytosol.
    b. The amount and position of the Golgi vary with cell type.

4. Secretory Vesicles: Exocytosis and Membrane Recycling
    a. Membrane recycling involves the processes of exocytosis and endocytosis and occurs among the ER, Golgi, lysosomes and plasma membrane.

5. Lysosomes and Peroxisomes: Digestion of Food and Waste
    a. Primary lysosomes contain digestive enzymes and arise from the Golgi complex. Secondary lysosomes form after the fusion of primary lysosomes with endocytic vesicles.
    b. Lysosomal enzymes digest material in endocytic vesicles and cellular organelles and matter when necessary in a process called autophagy.
    c. Peroxisomes contain enzymes involved in detoxification reactions.

6. Mitochondria: Energy Transformation
    a. The mitochondria are the primary site for ATP synthesis.
    b. The number and position in the cell vary according to the cell's need for ATP and its function in the body.
    c. The mitochondrion has a double membrane, DNA and ribosomes.
    d. The inner membrane and matrix contain enzymes and other molecules used to make ATP.

7. The Cytoskeleton: Shape and Structure
   a. The cytoskeleton is responsible for maintaining cellular shape and positions of organelles, and for movement of materials and organelles within the cell.
   b. The cytoskeleton is composed of different types of protein fibers (microtubules, microfilaments, and intermediate filaments) which differ in their composition, structure, function and location.
   c. Myosin filaments and filaments of the microtrabecular lattice also play a role in organizing the cytoplasm.

III. The Life Cycle of the Cell
* The different types of cells in the body vary as to their patterns and rates of division.
* The cell cycle, the time period from the start of division to the start of the next division, consists of two main phases: interphase and cell division.

A. Interphase: Growth and DNA Replication
* Interphase which occupies 90% of cell cycle is divided into three stages: G1, S (synthetic stage), and G2.
* During interphase the cell carries out normal metabolic activities and duplicates DNA.
* G1 is the most variable stage timewise.

B. Cell Division: Mitosis and Cytokinesis
* Mitosis occurs in four stages: prophase, metaphase, anaphase, telophase,which can be distinguished on the basis of chromosomal appearance and activity.
* Cytokinesis is the division of the cytoplasm.

C. Abnormal Cell Cyles
* The rate of cell division is controlled in normal cells.
* Cancer cells do not respond to normal controls of cell division and growth.

IV. Research Techniques in Cell Physiology

A. Cell Cultures
* Most cells from mammalian tissues will grow and divide in a culture medium containing the required nutrients.
* Normal cells in culture have a finite lifetime and exhibit contact inhibition in contrast to cancerous cells.

B. Microscopy and Cytochemistry

1. The Light Microscope

2. The Electron Microscope

3. Cytochemical Studies
   a. Cytochemistry is used in combination with microscopy to produce a color or enhanced contrast at the sites of specific molecules.

C. Radioactivity in Cell Research
* The use of radioactive molecules allows researchers to follow the course of almost any cellular process.
* The location of radioactive molecules is best determined by the technique of autoradiography.

D. The Immune System and Cell Studies
   * Labeled antibodies specific for an antigen can be used to locate the antigen within the cell or tissue.

   1. Immunochemistry

   2. Radiolabeled Antibodies

   3. Radioimmunoassays

   4. Affinity Chromatography
      a. Because of the specificity of antigens and antibodies, antigens bound to a matrix can be used to isolate antibodies from body fluids passing through the matrix.

   5. Monoclonal Antibodies
      a. Monoclonal antibodies are produced by hybridomas formed by the fusion of antibody-producing and cancer cells.

E. Amino Acid Sequencing and HPLC

F. Fractionation of Cells
   * Cell fractionation results in the separation of the different organelles so that each can be studied in a controlled "cell-free" system.
   * Organelles are separated by differential or density gradient centrifugation.

G. Genetic Engineering
   * DNA from different organisms can be combined to form a recombinant molecule.
   * A gene can be cloned or amplified so that its function and structure can be studied.

Chapter Learning Objectives

1. Describe three advantages to the cell of the compartmentalization by membrane.
2. Describe the structure and function of each of the following structures: nucleus, nuclear envelope, nuclear pore, nucleolus, chromosome.
3. Diagram information flow in the cell.
4. Describe the structure and function of each of the following structures: smooth ER, rough ER, Golgi complex, peroxisome and mitochondria.
5. List the organelles, their contributions to and steps involved in the production, processing and packaging of a secretory protein.
6. Distinguish primary and secondary lysosomes and how each is formed.
7. List and describe the five filamentous structures comprising the cytoskeleton.
8. Describe the features of the interphase and cell divisions parts of the cell cycle.
9. Describe how each of the following research techniques is used to study physiology: cell cultures, microscopy (light, phase contrast, scanning, transmission), cytochemistry, autoradiography, immunocytochemistry, affinity chromatography, radioimmunassay, monoclonal antibodies, cell fractionation, and genetic engineering.

Key Terms

affinity chromatography
antibody
antigen
autophagy
autoradiography
cell fractionation
cell line, culture
chromatin
chromosome
cristae
cytochemistry
cytokinesis
cytoskeleton
cytosol
degradation
DNA
electron microscope
endocytosis
eukaryote
exocytosis
forming face
gene
Golgi complex
histone
homogenization
intermediate filament
interphase (G1,S,G2)
light microscope
light scanning
lipoprotein
lysosome
matrix
mature face
membrane recycling
metabolism
microfilament
microtrabecular lattice
microtubule
microvilli
mitochondria
mitosis (prophase, metaphase, anaphase, telophase)
monoclonal antibody
myosin filament
neoplasm
nuclear envelope
nuclear pores
nucleolus
nucleosome
nucleus
peroxisome
phagosome
phase contrast microscope
plasma membrane
prokaryote
radioimmunoassay
radioisotopes
recombinanant DNA
ribosome
RNA
rough ER (rER)
smooth ER (sER)
synthesis
vector

Testing Your Knowledge

I. Matching. Select the correct term from the Key Terms

__________1. complex of DNA and histones
__________2. composed of double membrane with pores
__________3. major site of ATP production
__________4. longest phase of cell cycle
__________5. site of synthesis of proteins used within cell
__________6. site of synthesis of proteins exported from cell
__________7. site of synthesis of ribosomal RNA
__________8. cell without a nucleus
__________9. contains digestive enzymes, involved in autophagy
__________10. process by which membrane vesicles leave cell
__________11. process by which membrane-enclosed materials enter cell
__________12. site of lipid synthesis
__________13. site of processing and packaging proteins for export
__________14. abnormal growth
__________15. composed of different types of protein fibers and functions in maintaining cell shape, internal movement

II. Fill in the Table

Cellular Structure	Composition	Function
nucleus		
chromosome		
nucleolus		
rER		
sER		

	Composition	Function
ribosome		
Golgi complex		
lysosome		
peroxisome		
mitochondria		
cytoskeleton		
microfilaments		
microtubules		
intermediate filaments		
myosin filaments		
microtrabecular lattice		

III. Problem

A piece of skin is placed in a medium containing a radioactively labeled amino acid and left there for hours. The tissue is homogenized, the cells fractionated, and the organelles separated using differential centrifugation.

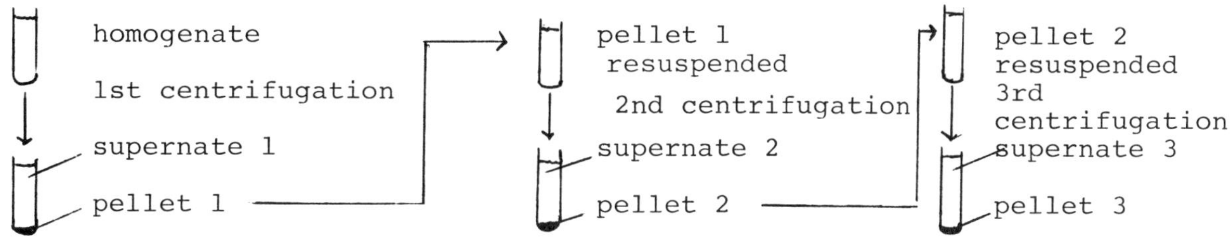

a) Which technique(s) would you use to determine the contents of pellets 1, 2, and 3.
b) In which pellet would you find digestive enzymes?
c) Which technique(s) would you use to determine the location of the radioactively labeled amino acid?
d) Where do you expect to detect radioactivity?
e) In which pellet would you find DNA?
f) Where would you find RNA?

CHAPTER 4 TRANSPORT THROUGH THE CELL MEMBRANE

Expanded Chapter Outline

I. The Components and Structure of the Membrane
   * The structural backbone of a membrane is the phospholipid bilayer in which proteins are embedded or loosely associated.
   * The functional properties of the membrane are due to the presence of specific proteins.
   * The relative quantities of lipids and proteins vary for specific membranes and usually reflect some functional aspect of the membrane around the cell or organelle.

   A. The Lipid Bilayer of Amphipathic Molecules

      1. Types and Properties of Lipids
         a. Phospholipids, cholesterol and glycolipids are found in the lipid bilayer.
         b. They have hydrophobic and hydrophilic regions.

      2. The Movement of Phospholipids within the Bilayer
         a. Phospholipids can rotate about their axes and undergo flexing motions.
         b. Cholesterol stabilizes hydrocarbon chains.
         c. Phospholipids exchange places rapidly within the same layer by lateral diffusion but "flip-flop" very slowly.

      3. Lipid Asymmetry in the Bilayer
         a. The different types of phospholipids are not distributed equally between the outer and inner halves of the bilayer.

      4. The Texture of the Plasma Membrane
         a. The membrane's fluidity is like olive oil and is important to normal functioning.

   B. Membrane Proteins

      1. Intrinsic Proteins: Amphipathic molecules
         a. Hydrophobic regions are clustered in the hydrophobic interior of lipid bilayer.
         b. Hydrophilic regions are located at aqueous interfaces.
         c. Many intrinsic proteins can undergo rapid lateral diffusion and axial rotation but probably do not "flip-flop."

      2. Extrinsic Proteins: Hydrophilic Molecules
         a. They are associated with the membrane primarily by hydrogen bonding and electrostatic interactions.

      3. Protein Asymmetry in the Membrane
         a. The asymmetrical distribution and type of protein found in membranes are related to cell and membrane function.

      4. Carbohydrate on the Surface of the Membrane
         a. Carbohydrates may be bound either to protein or lipid forming glycoproteins or glycoproteins at their hydrophilic interfaces with the environment.
         b. Carbohydrates are minor membrane components but play a role in cell-cell recognition processes and in receptor sites.

II. The Types of Movement Through the Membrane

* A cellular membrane is selectively permeable.
* Substances may pass through a membrane by active or passive transport processes.
* The lipid bilayer prevents the diffusion of polar or charged molecules except water.

A. Passive Transport: Spontaneous Movement down a Gradient

* Passive transport processes do not require cellular energy and occur in response to electrochemical gradients.

1. Simple diffusion of lipid soluble substances
   a. Molecular movement provides the energy for diffusion of a solute from a region of high concentration to a region of low concentration.
   b. The rate of diffusion of a solute through a membrane depends on the thickness of the membrane, the lipid solubility of the solute and its molecular size and charge.
   c. The relationships between rate of diffusion and molecular size, charge and lipid solubility are summarized in Overton's Rules: (1) The permeability of cell membranes to small nonpolar solutes is directly proportional to lipid solubility; (2) The permeability of cell membranes to polar solute is inversely proportional to molecular size.
   d. Diffusion trapping involves the formation of a charged molecule after the neutral form of a weak base has passed through a membrane. The charged form is not able to pass back through the membrane.

2. Simple Diffusion of Water: Osmosis
   a. Osmosis is the movement of water across a membrane from a dilute solution to a concentrated solution.
   b. Water flow through the membrane is affected by the osmolarity of the cytosol and the cell's external medium.
   c. Osmotic fragility is a term describing an erythrocyte's response to osmotic stress and represents the osmolarity of NaCl causing 50% of erythrocytes to lyse.

3. Facilitated Diffusion of Lipid-insoluble Substances
   a. The passage of some large water soluble molecules such as D-glucose and amino acids involves intrinsic membrane proteins acting as carriers.
   b. Facilitated diffusion is a rate-limited and highly specific process and can be blocked by competitive inhibitors. It involves a reversible binding of the solute with carrier proteins in the membrane.
   c. Hydrophilic channels composed of intrinsic proteins provide a way for charged ions, such as K^+ and Na^+, to cross the membrane. These channels can be regulated by "gates."
   d. Facilitated diffusion is more rapid than simple diffusion, but is rate-limited by the availability of binding sites on the carrier proteins for the solute.
   e. The solute process of facilitated diffusion and the effect of competitive inhibitors can be described by kinetic parameters such as Vmax and Km.

B. Active Transport: Energized Movement Against a Gradient

* Active transport processes require cellular energy and carrier proteins, and result in the movement of solute against the prevailing gradient.

1. Primary Active Transports
   a. Movement of the solute is directly coupled to an energy-yielding reaction.
   b. The sodium-potassium ATPase pump is an example of primary active transport. The breakdown of ATP is tightly coupled to the transport of Na^+ and of K^+ into the cell.
2. Secondary Active Transport
   a. Movement of the solute is not coupled directly to energy yielding reactions. A transport system is driven by energy stores in the electrochemical gradient for another solute, e.g., Na^+.
   b. The mechanism of Na^+-coupled transport systems is believed to involve a two-site carrier that binds both Na^+ and the solute.

C. Transport Processes and Cell Volume
1. Intracellular Osmotic Pressure and Volume
   a. Proteins, organic phosphates, metabolic intermediates and K^+ contribute to cytosolic osmotic pressure.
   b. Na^+, an impermeant solute, is the major determinant of intracellular volume.
   c. The intracellular concentration of Na^+ and indirectly the intracellular volume are regulated by the Na^+-K^+ ATPase pump.

III. Epithelial Transport

A. Characteristics of Epithelial Cells

1. Asymmetrical distribution of transport systems
   a. The transport systems are asymmetrically distributed between the apical and basolateral plasma membranes.
   b. The organization of transport systems allows for transcellular transport of water and solutes.
   c. Na^+-coupled symport systems for the entry of glucose, amino acids and phosphate are located in the apical membrane. Na^+ exits the cell through the action of the Na^+-K^+ ATPase pump located in the basolateral membrane.
   d. Transcellular transport achieves net movement from the lumen at one side of the cell to blood vessels on the other side. It can be regulated by hormones.

2. Function of Junctional Complexes
   a. Junctional complexes prevent lateral diffusion of membrane proteins in epithelial cell.
   b. Intercellular complexes like tight junctions prevent leakage between epithelial cells.
   c. The "leaky" junctions provide a paracellular pathway for water and solutes across the epithelium. Movement of ions via this pathway is passive.

3. Structural Specialization
   a. The surface areas of the apical and basolateral membranes are increased by microvilli and extensive infoldings, respectively.

<u>Learning Objectives</u>

1. Describe the fluid mosaic model for membrane structure.
2. Describe the types of movement exhibited by membrane phospholipids and cholesterol and their organization as a lipid bilayer.

3. Discuss the relationship between the molecular structure of phospholipids and cholesterol and their organization as a lipid bilayer.
4. List the two types of membrane proteins and describe their molecular structure and organization relative to the lipid bilayer.
5. Distinguish glycolipids and glycoproteins and describe their location and function in the membrane.
6. Compare simple and facilitated diffusion processes regarding specificity, role of intrinsic proteins, effect of molecular size charge and lipid solubility of solute on rate, the rates in general and source of energy.
7. Define osmosis, osmolarity and osmotic fragility. Be able to describe the effects of hyperosmotic, hypoosmotic and isoosmotic solutions on the volume of cells placed in these solutions.
8. Compare carrier and channel proteins regarding movement of solute and regulation of rate of transport.
9. Compare passive and active transport processes with respect to cellular energy requirements, role of intrinsic proteins, direction of movement of solute and effect on cellular volume.
10. Compare primary and secondary active transport processes and give an example of each.
11. Describe how cell volume is maintained.
12. Describe the functional and structural specializations seen in membranes of epithelial cells and how each specialization contributes to transcellular transport of water and solutes.

<u>Key Terms</u>

active transport
amphipathic
antiport
asymmetry
backflux
carrier protein
channel protein
cholesterol
competitive inhibition
diffusion
diffusion trapping
electrochemical gradient
extrinsic protein
facilitated diffusion
"flip flop"
fluid mosaic model
"gate"
glycolipid
glycoprotein
intrinsic protein
junctional complex
Km
"leaky"
lipid bilayer
Na^+-K^+ ATPase pump
nonpermeant solute
osmolarity
300 mOsm solution
osmosis
osmotic fragility
Overton's Rules
paracellular transport
passive transport
permeability coefficient
permeant solute
phospholipid
selectively permeable membrane
specificity
symport
transcellular transport
Vmax

<u>Testing Your Knowledge</u>

I. <u>Matching</u>. Select the correct term from the Key Terms.

__________1. movement of molecules down concentration gradient
__________2. movement of molecules against concentration gradient
__________3. having hydrophilic and hydrophobic regions
__________4. involves carrier proteins and movement down concentration gradient
__________5. refers to unequal distribution of proteins in membrane
__________6. describes cotransport of Na^+ and glucose
__________7. describes protein loosely associated with membrane
__________8. protein complexed with carbohydrate
__________9. movement of water through membrane
__________10. term describing carrier and channel proteins
__________11. indirectly regulates water flow into and out of cell
__________12. structural backbone of membrane
__________13. membrane component affecting fluidity
__________14. lipid complexed with carbohydrate charge
__________15. difference between cytoplasm and extracellular environment

II. Multiple Choice

1. Which characteristics apply to both membrane lipid and proteins?
   a) asymmetrical distribution
   b) amphipathic
   c) can form complex with carbohydrate
   d) can undergo lateral diffusion
   e) all of the above

2. Which characteristics apply to both simple and facilitated diffusion?
   a) specificity
   b) rate-limited
   c) involves intrinsic proteins
   d) have Vmax and Km values
   e) none of the above

3. Which of the following molecules would move most rapidly through the cell membrane?
   a) Na^+
   b) K^+
   c) glucose
   d) oleic acid
   e) glycerol

4. Erythrocytes are placed in a 400 mOsm saline solution. Which of the following statements is true?
   a) The erythrocytes are isoosmotic to the solution.
   b) The saline solution is hypoosmotic to the erythrocytes.
   c) Water will enter the erythrocytes
   d) The cells will actively transport water out of the cytosol
   e) The erythrocytes will lose volume but not surface area.

CHAPTER 5 CELLULAR CONTROL MECHANISMS

Chapter Outline

I. An Intracellular Control System: DNA, RNA, and Protein Synthesis

A. Overview: Protein Synthesis as Genetic Expression

1. Genetic Expression: Selective Use of the Permanent Files
   a. In a cell genes are expressed selectively according to the type and needs of the cell.
   b. Gene expression is the principal factor determining structural, functional, and behavioral characteristics of cells.
   c. Genes encode information for specifying a protein.

2. The Genetic Code. From Nucleic Acids to Amino Acids
   a. Information as to the linear sequence of amino acids in a polypeptide chain is encoded in the linear sequence of nucleotides in the DNA.
   b. Information in DNA is transcribed into RNA from which it is translated into a polypeptide.
   c. Each of the 20 amino acids is specified by a three letter base code, called a triplet, in the DNA, and a codon in the mRNA.
   d. The genetic code is consistent, universal and degenerate, i.e. more than one codon can specify the same amino acid.

B. Synthesis of Nucleic Acids

1. Synthesis of DNA: Replication of the Permanent Files
   a. DNA replication occurs during the S phase of interphase and results in the production of 2 daughter molecules of DNA identical to the parent.
   b. Replication is semiconservative in that each of the strands in the parent double helix serves as a template for the production of the daughter DNA molecules.
   c. Replication is catalyzed by DNA polymerase which reads the template and by following base pair rules incorporates the correct nucleotide in the growing DNA strand.
   d. Because the strands in the parent are antiparallel and the polymerase can only add nucleotides in the 5'→ 3' direction, one of the new strands grows as a continuous piece (the leading strand) while the other (the lagging strand) is synthesized in pieces which are later enzymatically joined together.
   e. The polymerase also proofreads the new chain as it is synthesized.

2. Synthesis of RNA: Selective Transcription of the Permanent Files
   a. Information in the DNA is transcribed into RNA
   b. Three kinds of RNA are transcribed from genes in the DNA: mRNA (messenger), tRNA (transfer) and rRNA (ribosomal).
   c. The bases in the RNA are complementary to these in the DNA.
   d. RNA differs from DNA in the type of sugar, the types of bases, its strandedness and shape in the case of tRNA.
   e. RNA polymerase reads the DNA template in the synthesis of the RNA molecule.
   f. Transcription begins and ends at promoter and terminator sites.
   g. Most RNA molecules synthesized from the DNA undergo post-transcriptional modification in which a cap and tail are

added, extraneous regions corresponding to introns in the DNA are excised, and the remaining RNA pieces corresponding to exons in the DNA, are spliced together.

C. Synthesis of Proteins: Translation of mRNA

1. RNA is the Cytoplasm: A Three-way System
   a. tRNA has two important features: an anticodon complementary to the codon in the mRNA, and an attachment site for an amino acid destined to become part of a polypeptide chain.
   b. rRNA is part of the ribosome, the site for protein synthesis
   c. mRNA carries to the ribosome the codons specifying amino acids to be used in the polypeptide chain
   d. An enzyme, amino acyl-tRNA synthetase, couples the tRNA with its correct amino acid.

2. Initiation of Protein Synthesis: Formation of the Ribosome
   a. During initiation a complex is formed between the mRNA, the ribosome and the tRNA carrying methionine, the first amino acid specified by the initiator codon, AUG.
   b. The second tRNA carrying the amino acid specified by the second codon in the mRNA joins the complex by binding to a special site in the ribosome.

3. Elongation of the Polypeptide Chain: Reading the mRNA
   a. A peptide bond forms between the methionine and the second amino acid. The second tRNA changes position in the ribosome, the first tRNA leaves and the third tRNA carrying the amino acide specified by the third codon of the mRNA enters the complex. This cycle called elongation, continues until terminator codons are exposed in the mRNA.
   b. More than one ribosome may be translating the mRNA at the same time.

D. Control of Gene Expression
   * Regulation of gene expression occurs primarily at the level of transcription, but may also occur at the levels of post-transcriptional modification, translation and post-translational modification.
   * Genetic control mechanisms can involve hormones and special regulatory proteins.

E. Repair of Damaged DNA
   * DNA is sensitive to damage by environmental factors, such as UV light, X-rays and common chemicals.

1. Photoreactivation
   a. An enzyme using the energy from visible light repairs damage caused by ultra violet light.

2. Excision Repair
   a. Enzymes may selectively excise damaged DNA and fill in the gap with the correct bases specified by the complementary strand.

3. Base Excision
   a. An enzyme recognizes the altered bases and removes them. Other enzymes fill in the correct bases and join the bases to the old DNA.

II. Cell-to-Cell Signaling: Hormones, Neurotransmitters, and other Molecules

A. Interactions Between Adjacent Cells: Gap Junctions

1. Gap Junctions
   a. They consist of a group of small pores and channels which allow for direct communication and movement of small molecules between cells.
   b. Gap junctions provide for metabolic and electrical coupling between cells.

B. Interactions Between Distant Cells: Chemical Signals

* Chemical signaling systems involve three components. (1) extracellular signals or first messengers; (2) receptors in either the membrane or cytoplasm of the target cell; and (3) intracellular signals or second messengers.

1. Extracellular Signals: First Messengers
   a. First messengers may be local chemical mediators such as neurotransmitters or hormones produced by specialized cells and transported via the blood to target tissues.
   b. Chemical signals can be classified as water soluble or lipid-soluble. The two types differ in the timing and duration of the responses they elicit.
   c. Prostaglandins and histamines are local chemical mediators.

2. Receptors: Mediating Between First and Second Messengers
   a. A receptor is a macromolecule, ususally a protein to which the first messenger can bind with high specificity and affinity.
   b. Binding of the hormone to the receptor triggers a sequence of events that leads to the changes representing cellular response to the hormone.
   c. The cellular location and mechanism of action of hormone receptors varies with the type of hormone.
   d. Receptors may be located in the cytoplasm and the plasma membrane.
   e. The number of receptors for a specific agonist in the plasma membrane may vary depending on the quantity of the agonist in the blood.

3. Intracellular Signals: Second Messengers
   a. Binding of a first messenger to the receptor usually alters its conformation. This change in the receptor generates a second messenger which initiates intra-cellular responses that modify the target cell.
   b. Cyclic AMP, calcium ions, inositol triphosphate and diacylglycerol act as second messengers. They differ in their mechanism of action in producing an intracellular response. Some activate certain enzymes that catalyze the phosphorylation of certain proteins which leads to the physiological response of the cell to the first messenger. In the absence of second messenger, the phosphorylation is readily reversed by an enzyme-mediated reaction.

Chapter Learning Objectives

1. Diagram the flow of information in a cell.
2. Describe four features of the genetic code and what the code represents.
3. Distinguish triplet, codon and anticodon as to where each occurs and how they interact with each other.
4. Diagram and describe the process of semiconservative DNA replication.
5. Discuss why one strand is synthesized as a continuous chain and the other in fragments.
6. Describe transcription and the role of signals and polymerase in this process.
7. Compare DNA and RNA regarding the types of sugars, bases, shapes, post-synthetic modifications and function.
8. Describe the roles of mRNA, tRNA, rRNA and ribosomes in protein synthesis.
9. Describe the events of the three stages of translation: initiation, elongation, termination.
10. Briefly describe the levels at which genes can be controlled.
11. Summarize the DNA repair mechanisms in the cell.
12. Describe the types of communication occurring through gap junctions.
13. Compare local chemical mediations and hormones regarding role of receptors, the duration of their response in the target cells and their mechanism of action in eliciting a response from the target cell.
14. Describe the roles of first and second messengers in generating a physiological response in the target cell.
15. List some common first and second messengers.

Key Terms

agonist
aminoacyl attachment site
antagonist
anticodon
antiparallel
codon
cyclic AMP
DNA ligase
DNA polymerase
DNA repair
down regulation
electrical coupling
elongation
first messenger
gap junction
genetic code
genome
hormone
initiation
lagging strand
leading strand
ligand
local chemical mediator
messenger RNA (mRNA)
metabolic coupling
neuro-transmitter
post-translational modification
post-transcriptional modification
promoter
receptor
replication fork
RNA polymerase
RNA splicing
ribosomal RNA (rRNA)
ribosomes
second messenger
semiconservative replication
template
termination
terminator
transcription
transfer RNA (tRNA)
translation
triplet
5'→ 3' direction

Testing Your Knowledge

I. Matching. Select the correct term from the Key Terms.

__________1. sequence of three bases in DNA specifying amino acid
__________2. sequence of three bases in tRNA
__________3. process of protein synthesis
__________4. molecule that binds to a receptor and elicits a response
__________5. enzyme for transcription
__________6. enzyme for replicating DNA
__________7. enzyme joining DNA pieces together
__________8. process of RNA synthesis
__________9. carries amino acid to growing polypeptide chain
__________10. carrier information for specifying amino acid chain to ribosomes
__________11. second messenger

_______ 12. occurs via gap junction.
_______ 13. located in cell membrane, binds to ligand
_______ 14. sequence of three bases in mRNA specifying amino acid
_______ 15. composed of Okazaki fragments

II. Fill in the Table

	Type of Sugar	Bases	# of Strands	Function
DNA				
RNA				
mRNA				
tRNA				
rRNA				

III. Complete the Table

DNA	---	---	ACA	---	---
mRNA	---	UCG	---	---	UAG
tRNA	---	---	---	CAU	---
amino acid	met	___	___	___	___

CHAPTER 6 ENERGY AND CELLULAR METABOLISM

Chapter Outline

I. Basic Principles of Energy Transformation in the Cell

A. Photosynthesis: From Radiant Energy to Organic Products in Plants
* The process of photosynthesis is summarized by the reaction: $CO_2 + H_20 + \text{radiant energy} \rightarrow (CH_20)_n + 0_2$.

B. Cellular Respiration: From Plant Products to Chemical Energy in Animals
* The process of cellular respiration is summarized by the reaction: $(CH_20)_n + 0_2 \longrightarrow CO_2 + H_2O + \text{chemical energy}$.

C. Energy Loss and the Constant Demand for ATP
* Living cells require a constant input of energy in order to survive

D. Chemical Reactions in Cells: Some Special Considerations

1. Free Energy Change in Cell Reactions
   a. Reactions with a negative ΔG are exergonic while those with a positive ΔG are endergonic.
   b. These types of reactions are coupled in the cell by the energy intermediary ATP.

2. Reversible Reactions in the Cell
   a. At equlibrium there is no net change in free energy
   b. In the cell, reactions are driven to completion by removal of the end product.
   c. Reverse reactions can occur depending on the needs of the cell because many cellular reactions take place with a very small change in free energy.

3. Oxidation - Reduction Reaction in the Cell
   a. In an oxidation reaction a hydrogen atom or electrons are given up while in a reduction reaction a hydrogen atom or electrons are gained.
   b. Generally, compounds containing many hydrogen atoms are high-energy, while compounds with few hydrogen atoms are low-energy.
   c. Photosynthesis is a reduction process and cellular respiration an oxidation process.
   d. Hydrogen atoms are transferred first to coenzymes like NAD (nicotinamide adenine dinucleotide) then to oxygen.
   e. NAD^+ has a negative redox potential and low affinity for electrons in contrast to oxygen.

4. High-Energy Phosphate Compounds

   a. ATP is a high energy phosphate compound. When one of the phosphate groups is transferred to an acceptor molecule, a large amount of free energy is released.
   b. In the cell the free energy change (ΔG) is -12 Kcal/mol. for the reaction ATP $\rightarrow$ ADP + Pi
   c. Compounds with a less negagive ΔG have a greater affinity for the phosphate group and serve as acceptors for groups donated by ATP.
   d. ATP can be produced by substrate level phosphorylation or by oxidation phosphorylation.

5. Enzymes in Cellular Metabolism
   a. Some enzymes require coenzymes, such as Coenzyme A, and NAD, for their activity.
   b. Cells can control enzyme catalyzed reactions by modification of the enzyme, by allosteric inhibition, a reversible process, or by increasing or decreasing synthesis of the enzyme protein.
   c. Oxidation of NAD^+ is expressed by the reaction:
   $NAD^+ + 2H^+ + 2e^- \longrightarrow NADH + H^+$

II. An Overview of Catabolism: Dietary Proteins, Carbohydrates, and Fats

A. Digestion in the Cytoplasm: Deamination, Glycolysis and Fatty Acid Oxidation
* In the intestine, proteins, carbohydrates and fats are broken down into amino acids, simple sugars, and fatty acids and glycerol.
* In the cell, amino acids, monosaccharides, and fatty acids are degraded further by the processes of deamination, glycolysis and fatty acid oxidation, all of which are regulated and facilitated by enzymes.

B. The Role of the Mitochondrion: The Citric Acid Cycle and the Electron Transport Chain
* The molecules resulting from the breakdown of amino acids, glucose, and fatty acids are converted to acetyl groups in the mitochondrial matrix and go on to participate in the citric acid cycle.
* In the mitochondrial matrix the acetyl groups are coupled to Coenzyme A to form acetyl CoA, which is converted to CO_2 via the Citric Acid Cycle.
* The high energy electrons released from this conversion are temporarily trapped by NAD and FAD Which feed the electrons to the respiratory chain.
* The redox reactions, which occurs as electrons pass down the chain to oxygen, release energy used to synthesize ATP in a process called oxidative phosphorylation.

III. The Metabolism of Carbohydrates: The Oxidation of Glucose.
* The metabolism of carbohydrate involves three main processes: (1) glycolysis; (2) Citric Acid Cycle; and (3) oxidative phosphorylation.

A. Glycolysis: From Glucose to Phruvic Acid
* In glycolysis glucose is degraded into two molecules of pyruvic acid with the net release of enough free energy to make two molecules of ATP by substrate level phosphorylation. Two molecules of NADH are also produced.
* Each of the ten reaction steps is enzyme-catalyzed and takes place in the cytosol.

1. The First Stage of Glycolysis
   a. The first stage consumes two ATP molecules for phosphorylating and converting glucose to a form that can be used to drive the net synthesis of ATP.

2. The Second Stage of Glycolysis
   a. In the second stage two molecules of NADH and four ATP molecules are produced from each glucose metabolized to pyruvate.
   b. Glycolysis, an anaerobic process, yields less than 3% of the maximum amount of free energy obtained from glucose.
   c. Under anaerobic conditions pyruvate is converted to lactic acid.

B. The Citric Acid Cycle: From Pyruvic Acid to Reduced Coenzymes

* Pyruvic acid enters the mitochondrial matrix where it is coupled to coenzyme A in preparation for processing via the citric acid cycle.

1. The Preparation of Acetyl Coenzyme A
   a. In the reaction of pyruvate to acetyl CoA, a molecule each of CO_2 and NADH are produced.
   b. The acetyl groups are degraded to two molecules of CO_2 via the citric acid cycle.

2. The Reduction of NAD^+ and FAD
   a. For each acetyl group entering the cycle, three molecules of NADH, one molecule of $FADH_2$ and high-energy phosphate GTP are generated.
   b. Each step in the citric acid cycle is enzyme-catalyzed and occurs in the mitochondrial matrix.

3. Allosteric Inhibition in the Citric Acid Cycle
   a. The cycle can be controlled by the concentrations of ATP and ADP, which act as allosteric inhibitors and activators, respectively, as well as other mechanisms.

C. The Electron Transport Chain: From Reduced Coenzymes to ATP.

* From the oxidation of a molecule of glucose to CO_2, 10 molecules of NADH, two molecules of $FADH_2$, and four molecules of ATP are produced. Thirty two molecules of ATP are produced by oxidation phosphorylation.

1. Cytochromes: Electron Carriers
   a. NADH and $FADH_2$ have very negative redox potentials and readily donate electrons to the electron carrier proteins in the respiratory chain.
   b. The redox potentials of the carriers increase sequentially from beginning to the end of the chain which facilitates the transfer of electrons along the cytochromes to oxygen.

2. Phosphorylation Sites
   a. At three sites in the chain sufficient energy is released to synthesize a molecule of ATP. Thus three molecules of ATP are produced for each molecule of NADH that is oxidized.
   b. For each $FADH_2$ that is oxidized, two molecules of ATP are synthesized.

3. The Flow of Protons: The Chemiosmotic Mechanism
   a. As electrons flow down the respiratory chain, protons are pumped from the matrix to the intermembrane space thus setting up an electrochemical gradient across the inner membrane.
   b. The flow of protons down the gradient occurs through special channels bearing the enzyme ATP synthetase coupled to the production of ATP.
   c. ATP synthetase transforms the energy of proton gradient into chemical energy in the form of ATP in a process known as the chemiosmotic mechanism.

D. Gluconeogenesis: The Synthesis of Glucose

* Gluconeogenesis is the pathway by which glucose can be synthesized from non-carbohydrate molecules, such as amino acids and glycerol. Many of the reactions of gluconeogenesis are the reverse of those of glycolysis.

E. The Pentose Phosphate Pathway: An Alternative Glucose Oxidation Path
   * This pathway generates pentose sugars and NADPH, which drives the oxidation-reduction reactions in various biosynthetic pathways such as the synthesis of fatty acids and steroids.

IV. Metabolism of Fats
   * Catabolism of fats occurs in the mitochondrial matrix by a series of complex reactions in which the long chain fatty acid is converted into several molecules of acetyl CoA which enter the citric acid cycle.
   * Fatty acids are synthesized from acetyl CoA by a pathway different from that used for their oxidation.

V. Metabolism of Proteins
   * Deaminated amino acids can enter the pathway of glucose oxidation at various points.

VI. Acetyl Coenzyme A: Mediating Between Catabolism and Biosynthesis
   * Most of the intermediate compounds produced by catabolism are fed into the citric acid cycle as acetyl CoA.
   * Acetyl CoA is also a precursor used in the synthesis of fatty acids and glucose.

Chapter Learning Objectives

1. Describe how the cell is able to carry out endergonic reactions and to drive reactions to completion even though there is no difference in the free energy of the reactants and products.
2. Describe the roles of electron acceptors coenzymes and oxygen in the oxidation-reduction reactions occurring in the cell.
3. Compare the processes of substrate level and oxidative phosphorylation as to where each occurs and the source of energy for ATP synthesis.
4. Describe the levels at which the cell controls enzyme-catalyzed reactions.
5. Summarize the reactions of glycolysis as to reactants, products, numbers of ATP and NADH molecules produced.
6. Summarize the reaction in which pyruvate is degraded to acetyl CoA.
7. Summarize the reactions of the citric acid cycle as to reactants, products, numbers of ATP and NAHD molecules produced.
8. Describe the driving force behind the movement of electrons down the respiratory chain and the role of cytochromes in this process.
9. Describe the chemiosmotic mechanism for the production of ATP and account for each of the 36 molecules of ATP produced from the complete oxidation of one molecule of glucose.
10. Briefly describe the reactants, products and importance of the pentose phosphate pathway.
11. Describe the oxidation of fats and proteins.

Key Terms

acetyl group
acetyl CoA
aerobic
allosteric inhibition
anaerobic
ATP synthetase
biosynthesis
catabolism
cellular respiration
chemiosmotic synthesis
citric acid cycle
coenzyme
coenzyme A
cytochrome
cytosol
deamination
electron transport chain
equilibrium
FAD, $FADH_2$
fatty acid oxidation
gluconeogenesis
glycolysis
glycogenolysis
mitochondria
mitochondrial matrix
NAD, NADH
NADP, NADPH
oxaloacetate
oxidation
oxidative phosphorylation
pentose phosphate pathway
phosphorylation
phosphorylation site
photosynthesis
pyruvic acid
redox potential
reduction
substrate level phosphorylation

Testing Your Knowledge

I. Matching. Select the correct term from the Key Terms

__________1. term analogous to end product inhibition
__________2. oxidation of glucose to pyruvic acid
__________3. reactions by which pyruvic acid degraded to CO_2
__________4. reaction in which electrons and protons are gained
__________5. reaction in which electrons and protons are lost
__________6. ATP production occurring in cytoplasm
__________7. measure of affinity of compound for electrons
__________8. location of reactions of fatty acid oxidation
__________9. electron carrier in respiratory chain
__________10. molecule regenerated in citric acid cycle
__________11. removal of amino group from amino acid
__________12. common intermediary in catabolic and biosynthetic pathways
__________13. electron and proton carrier produced by pentose phosphate pathway
__________14. channel protein through which protons flow
__________15. $C_6H_{12}O_6 + 6O_2 \rightarrow 6CO_2 + 6H_2O$ + energy

II. Fill in the Table

Reaction Series	Product(s)	Number ATP Produced	Number NADH Produced	Location
glycolysis				
pyruvic acid acetyl CoA				
oxidative phosphorylation				
fatty acid oxidation of palmitic acid				

Answers to Questions in Chapter 1 and Part I

Chapter 1

I. Matching

1. deductive reasoning
2. inductive reasoning
3. Harvey
4. Bernard
5. ventral
6. hypothesis
7. sagittal
8. ratio
9. inverse
10. proximal
11. tissue
12. connective
13. interstitial fluid
14. homeostasis
15. sensor or effector

II. Calculations

1. a. 10^{-3}g
   b. 10^{-6}g
   c. 10^{-9}g
   d. 10^{-12}g

III. Fill in the Table

Height	Weight
$1.63x10^{-3}$km	$5.45x10^{1}$kg
1.63xm	$5.45x10^{4}$g
$1.63x10^{2}$cm	$5.45x10^{7}$mg
$1.63x10^{3}$mm	$5.45x10^{10}$ug
$1.63x10^{6}$um	$5.45x10^{13}$ng
$1.63x10^{9}$nm	$5.45x10^{16}$pg

IV. Interpretation of Graphs

a) inverse
b) 25 bubbles
c) distance
d) # of bubbles
3) set up in which the light is stationary

Chapter 2

I. Matching

1. buffer
2. exergonic
3. monosaccharide
4. steroid
5. unsaturated
6. $I = (V_1 - V_2)/R$
7. $rr = RTC$
8. activation energy
9. atomic number
10. alpha helix or beta sheet
11. glycolipid
12. hydrogen
13. acid
14. covalent
15. ios-osmotic

III. Visual # 1

a) 4 b) 6 c) 6 d) 6
e) x = electron, y = nucleus f) covalent

IV. Visual # 2

a) from the bag to the beaker
b) hyperosmotic
c) hypo-osmotic
d) from the bag to the beaker
e) hyperosmotic
f) bypo-osmotic

Chapter 3

I. Matching

1. chromatin
2. nuclear envelope
3. mitochondria
4. interphase
5. ribosome
6. rough ER
7. nucleodus
8. prokaryote
9. lysosome
10. exocytosis
11. endocytosis
12. smooth ER
13. Golgi Complex
14. neoplasm
15. cytoskeleton

III. Problem

a. cytochemistry, light and electron microscopy
b. #2
c. autoradiography
d. in all pellets
e. #1
f. #3

Chapter 4

I. Matching

1. diffusion
2. active transport
3. amphipathic
4. facilitated diffusion
5. asymmetry
6. symport
7. extrinsic
8. glycoprotein
9. osmosis
10. intrinsic
11. Na^+-K^+ ATP pump
12. lipid bilayer
13. cholesterol
14. glycolipid
15. electrochemical gradient

II. Multiple Choice

1. e; 2. e; 3. d; 4. e

III. Problem Solving

a. both chambers and the epithelial cells
b. from B to the cells by diffusion; from the cells to A by active transport
c. greater

Chapter 5

I. Matching

1. triplet
2. anticoden
3. translation
4. agonist
5. RNA polymerase
6. DNA polymerase
7. DNA ligase
8. transcription
9. tRNA
10. mRNA
11. cyclic AMP
12. coupling
13. receptor
14. coden
15. lagging strand

II. Complete the Table

DNA	TAC	AGC	ACA	CAT	ATC
mRNA	AUG	UCG	UGU	GUA	UAG
tRNA	UAC	AGC	ACA	CAU	-
amino acid	met	ser	cys	val	-

Chapter 6

I. Matching

1. allosteric inhibition
2. glycolysis
3. citric acid cycle
4. reduction
5. oxidation
6. substrate level phosphorylation
7. redox potential
8. mitochondrial matrix
9. cytochrome
10. oxaloacetate
11. deamination
12. acetyl group
13. NADPH
14. ATP synthetase
15. cellular respiration

CHAPTER 7 FUNCTIONAL ORGANIZATION OF THE NERVOUS SYSTEM

Chapter Outline

I. Overview: The Central and Peripheral Nervous Systems
   * The nervous system is composed of the brain, brain stem, spinal cord, and peripheral nerves.
   * The brain is divided into parts each of which has a special function.
   * Sensory neurons transmit information about the body's external and internal environments to the central nervous system (CNS).
   * Motor neurons transmit information from the CNS to effectors to control how they operate.
   * The peripheral nervous system comprises somatic and autonomic portions.
   * The autonomic nervous system is com½osed of the sympathetic and parasympathetic systems.

II. Cells of the Nervous System
   * The nervous system is composed of neurons and glial cells. Neurons are designed to transmit information from cell to cell while glial cells help maintain the environment surrounding neurons.

   A. Glia: The Blood-Brain Barrier
      * Oligodendroglia and astroglia help form the blood-brain barrier which prevents the passage of unwanted substances from the circulatory system to cells in the brain.

   B. Neurons: Conductors of Nervous Impulses
      * Neurons have four functionally distinct regions: the soma, dendrites, axon, and axon terminal

      1. Classification of Neurons
         a. Neurons are classified structurally as bipolar, multipolar or unipolar.
         b. Neurons are classified functionally as sensory, motor, or interneurons.

      2. Cytoskeletal Structures and Axonal Transport
         a. The cytoskeleton supports neuronal form and plays a role in axonal transport.
         b. Fast axonal transport moves newly produced membranous compounds back to the cell body for recycling.
         c. Slow axonal transport moves cytoskeletal and other proteins from the soma to the terminal region.
         d. The materials moved by axonal transport play a role in the development, maintenance, and regeneration of the axon and synaptic transmission.

      3. The Ion Channels of Nerve Cell Membranes
         a. There are three basic types of ion channels: passive, chemically-activated and voltage-activated.

III. The Membrane Potential and the Action Potential
   * The movement of ions across their channels results from a difference in the electrical charge or concentration of ions across the plasma membrane.

   A. The Electrical Potential Across the Membrane of a Resting Cell
      * The electrical potential difference across the membrane, Em, is about -60mV.
      * The conductance of an ion through a channel is affected by the size of the ion relative to that of the channel, the charge of the ion and its state of hydration.

1. Concentration Gradients and Diffusion
   a. The intracellular concentration of K^+ is greater than that in the extracellular compartment while the reverse is true for Na^+.

2. The Membrane Potential of a Hypothetical Nerve Cell

B. The Action Potential: A Temporary Change in the Membrane Potential
   * The action potential is a temporary change in membrane potential from a negative resting state to a positive value.
   * The voltage changes in the action potential result from the opening and closing of voltage-sensitive ion channels that control the influx of Na^+ and efflux of K^+.

1. Ion Channels and the Action Potential

2. Initiation of the Action Potential
   a. The action potential is initiated once the threshold value of the membrane potential has been reached.
   b. The action potential is an "all or none" phenomenon.

3. Refractory Periods

4. Propagation of the Action Potential

5. The Velocity of the Action Potential
   a. The conduction velocity is proportional to the diameter of the axon.
   b. The velocity can occur rapidly by saltatory conduction in myelinated neurons.

IV. Communication Between Nerve Cells: Synaptic Transmission

A. Electrical Synapses: Communication Between Adjacent Cells
   * Electrical synapses are pathways for the direct conduction of ions from one cell to another.

B. Chemical Synapses: Communication Between Distant Cells
   * The process of synaptic transmission involves four phases: (1) synthesis of transmitter; (2) storage and release of transmitter; (3) interaction of the transmitter with postsynaptic receptor; and (4) termination of synaptic transmission.
   * Calcium ions are required for the release of neuro-transmitter from the presynaptic cell.

1. Presynaptic Mechanisms of Chemical Transmission

2. Postsynaptic Mechanisms of Chemical Transmission
   a. Excitatory postsynaptic potentials depolarize the membrane potential of postsynaptic neurons by opening Na^+ channels.
   b. Inhibitory postsynaptic potentials hyperpolarize the membrane potential of postsynaptic neurons by opening K^+ channels.
   c. Hyperpolarization and depolarization may result from the transmitter-activated closing of ion channels.

3. Termination of Synaptic Transmission

4. Recycling of Neurotransmitters

5. Diffuse and Discrete Chemical Synapses
   a. In discrete synapses the neurotransmitter is released from active zones in the presynaptic terminal into a small synaptic cleft.
   b. In diffuse synapses transmitter release is not limited to specific active zones and the cleft can be as large as 150 nm.

6. Metabotrophic Receptors

V. Neurotransmitters and Associated Receptors

A. Low Molecular-Weight Transmitters. Products of the Axon Terminal

1. Low molecular-weight transmitters like acetylcholine, biogenic amines and amino acids, are synthesized within the presynaptic terminal.

2. There are two types of acetylcholine receptors: nicotinic and muscarinic, which differ in their effect on the channel.

B. Neuropeptides: Products of the Soma

1. Neuropeptides are synthesized and packaged into vesicles in the soma, then carried to the terminal by fast axonal transport.

2. Neuropeptides are classified into one of several families of peptides based on their amino acid sequence and function.

VI. Neuronal Integration: Temporal and Spatial Summation
* The action potential discharge by a nerve cell is based upon the summation of excitatory and inhibitory postsynaptic potentials that occur in time over the space of the neuron's receptive surface.

<u>Chapter Learning Objectives</u>

1. Compare neurons and glial cells regarding function in the nervous system.
2. Describe the types of neurons as to their structure and function.
3. Compare fast and slow axonal transport systems as to the role of the cytoskeletal components in each, the material(s) moved, the direction of movement and the rate.
4. Describe the source, nature and maintenance of the electrical potential across the membrane of the resting cell and its size; include in your description the role of concentration gradients, and the ATPase pump.
5. Describe the electrical and chemical changes occurring in the neuronal membrane during the initiation and propagation of an action potential.
6. Describe how the velocity of the action potential is affected by the diameter and myelinization of the axon.
7. Compare electrical and chemical synapses as to speed, function and location.
8. Draw and label the cells and structures in a chemical synapse.
9. Describe the events occurring at the presynaptic terminal during the release of neurotransmitter.
10. Compare excitatory and inhibitory postsynaptic potentials as to the effect in the receptor, the flow of ions, the membrane potential, and the activity of the postsynaptic neuron.
11. Describe what happens to the neurotransmitter after it interacts with the receptor.
12. List and for each type describe low molecular weight transmitters as to production, interaction with the receptor, effect on the ion channels in the postsynaptic and fate after uncoupling from the receptor.

13. Compare low molecular weight and peptide neurotransmitters as to production, nature of interaction with the receptor, effect on channels in the membrane and fate after uncoupling from the receptor.
14. Compare temporal and spatial summation and the effect of each on the generation of an action potential.

Key Terms

absolute refractory period
acetylcholine
action potential
activating state
afferent (sensory) neuron
"all or none"
autoreceptor
axonal transport (fast,slow)
biogenic amine
bipolar neuron
blood-brain barrier
chemically activated ion channel (receptor)
dendrite
depolarization
diffuse synapse
discrete synapse
dopamine
efferent (motor) neuron
electrical potential
equilibrium potential
excitatory postsynaptic potential (EPSP)
feedback
gamma amino butyric acid
glia
glutamate
hyperpolarization
inactivating state
inhibitory postsynaptic potential (IPSP)
interneuron
ionic current
membrane conductance
membrane potential
multipolar neuron
muscarinic acetylcholine receptor
neuron
neuropeptide
neurotransmitter
nicotinic acetylcholine receptor
nodes of Ranvier
norepinephrine
passive ion channel
postsynaptic neuron
presynaptic neuron
regenerative process
relative refractory period
repolarization
resting state
saltatory conduction
serotonin
soma
spatial summation
synapse (chemical, electrical)
synaptic cleft
synaptic transmission
synaptic vesicle
temporal summation
threshold
unipolar neuron
voltage-activated ion channel

Testing Your Knowledge

I. Matching. Select the correct term from the Key Terms

__________1. describes state of sodium channel at -45mV
__________2. period during which exon cannot generate a second action potential
__________3. movement of action potential along nodes of Ranvier
__________4. pathway for direct conduction of ions between cells
__________5. postsynaptic potential depolarizing membrane
__________6. form blood-brain barrier
__________7. postsyaptic potential hyperpolarizing membrane
__________8. metabolic center of a neuron
__________9. transmits information about stimulus to CNS
__________10. transmitter synthesized in synaptic terminal and released in neuro-muscular synapse
__________11. contain neurotransmitter
__________12. synapse in which transmitter released from active zones
__________13. low molecular weight transmitter synthesized from tyrosine
__________14. transmitter synthesized in soma
__________15. describes situation in which two or more synaptic outputs activated together cause electrical potential to become positive.

II. Fill in the Table

Neuro-transmitter	type of channel affected	effect on channel	ion that moves	effect on postsynaptic membrane	fate of transmitter
e.g. transmitter	chemically activated ion channel	closes channel	K^+	depolarization	uptake into presynaptic cell
acetylcholine					
dopamine					
norepinephrine					
serotonin					

III. Label the Diagram

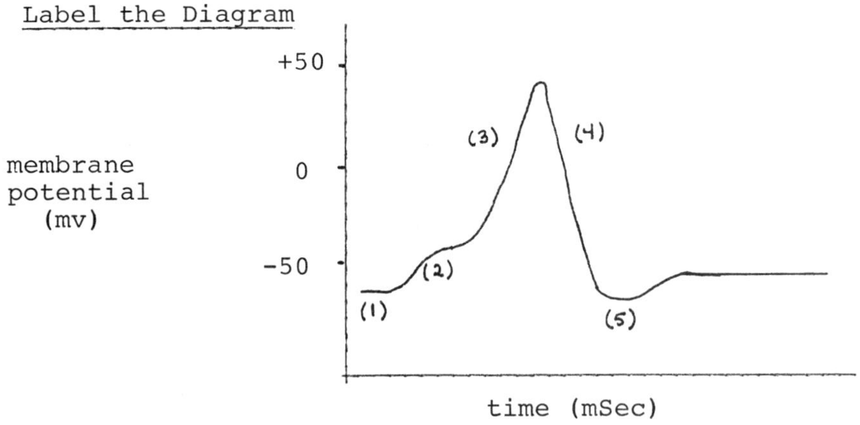

Label the diagram and describe the state of polarization of the membrane.

1. ________________
2. ________________
3. ________________
4. ________________
5. ________________

CHAPTER 8 SENSORY SYSTEMS

Chapter Outline

I. General Principles of Sensory Transduction
- * Sensory receptors are activated by a specific stimulus.
- * The transduction mechanism for all sensory systems is represented by the sequence:

Stimulus → Membrane conductance change → Generator potential → Action potential

A. The Intensity of a Stimulus: How Nerves Inform the Brain
- * Information about the intensity of a stimulus is conveyed to the brain in coded form.
- * The frequency code reflects the number of action potentials generated per unit time in a single fiber while the population code reflects the number of sensory neurons producing action potentials.

B. The Quality of a Stimulus: How Nerves Send Clear Messages
- * Information about different stimuli occurring simultaneously is transmitted along different pathways to the brain. This mechanism is referred to as the labeled line code of stimulus quality.

C. Sensory Adaptation: How Nerves Adjust to Repetitive Stimulus
- * Sensory adaptation can occur at the senory receptor or molecular level.

II. Sensory Systems and Their Processes

A. The Somatic Sensory System
- * The following principles apply to all somatic sensory systems
  - (1) Each type of somatic sensation has its own pathway
  - (2) Most somatic pathways cross over from one side of the brain to the other.
  - (3) Each pathway is made of connections between clusters of cell groups called nuclei.
  - (4) Nerve cells within each cluster are topographically organized according to the location of their sensory receptor in the surface of the body.

1. Types of Somatic Sensory Systems
   - a. Tactile receptors detect touch, pressure and vibrations applied to the skin.
   - b. Tactile receptors may be rapidly or slowly adapting.
   - c. Thermal receptors respond to temperature.
   - d. Nociceptors respond to pain and temperature.
   - e. Proprioceptors transmit information about the position of the body's limbs and changes in position.

2. The Dorsal Root Ganglion: A Cluster of Neurons
   - a. The cell bodies of sensory neurons are located in dorsal root ganglia.
   - b. The dorsal column and anterolateral pathways transmit somatic sensory information to nerve cell nuclei in the spinal cord, brain stem, thalamus and neocortex.

3. The Spinal Cord in Somatic Sensory Function
   - a. The spinal cord is subdivided into functional areas and segments.
   - b. Each of the 31 segments receives sensory information from particular areas of the skin called dermatomes.

4. The Thalamus in Somatic Sensory Function
   a. The thalamus receives all types of sensory information.

5. The Somatic Sensory Cortex
   a. The neocortex of the brain is divided into discrete areas that receive somatic, visual, auditory, and gustatory sensations.
   b. The somatic sensory cortex is topographically organized to correspond to regions of the body.
   c. The body regions with the greatest density of sensory receptors are represented by a greater proportion of the cortex.

6. Receptive Fields of Neurons in the Somatic Sensory System
   a. Stimuli detected by a sensory receptor are transmitted to various cell nuclei.
   b. The receptive fields of nerve cells in the dorsal root ganglion are different from those for the nerve cells in the dorsal column nuclei.
   c. An annular receptive field, i.e., inhibitory ring and excitatory center, is characteristic of dorsal column nerve cells and those in the thalamus.
   d. Cells with the annular receptive field are located in the primary somatosensory area while cells with a rectangular receptive field are located in the secondary somatosensory areas.
   e. Sensory receptors respond to the basic features of a complex stimulus. The different receptors break down the stimulus into its component parts. Information about each part is transmitted along different sensory pathways to the CNS where it is reassembled by nerve cells in the sensory areas of the cortex.

7. The Anterolateral Pain and Temperature Pathway
   a. Information about pain and temperature follow the pathway: receptor → sensory neuron → substantia gelatinosa → anterolateral pathway on opposite side → ventrobasal nuclei in the thalamus → primary somatosensory cortex.
   b. Inhibitory interneurons in the dorsal horn can alter the sensation of the stimlus. The interneuron can be activated by other sensory fibers or higher brain centers.

B. The Visual System

1. Anatomical Organization of the Eye
   a. The retina contains photoreceptors and other types of nerve cells organized into layers.
   b. Rods and cones are the photoreceptor cells.
   c. Photoreceptors transduce a photon of light into a more negative membrane potential which is then transformed into a series of action potentials.

2. Interactions of Cells in the Retina
   a. The order of synapses in the retina is: photoreceptor cell → bipolar cell → ganglion cell. Photoreceptor cells also form synapses with horizontal cells which inhibit ganglion cell activity.
   b. The ganglion cells have receptive fields shaped like an annulus.
   c. The spatial pattern of activated ganglion cells in the retina represents the form of the object projected onto the retina.

3. Pathways for Visual Information
   a. Axons from the ganglion cells synapse with neurons in the lateral geniculate nucleus (LGN) of the thalamus. Some of the axons cross over and form connections with the LGN on the opposite side.
   b. The LGN contains six distinct layers of neurons whose axons synapse with neurons in the primary visual cortex.
   c. The visual field is mapped onto the retina and onto the visual cortex within which the cells are organized into columns, each responding to light impinging on either the right or left eye.

4. Receptive Fields of Neurons in the Lateral Geniculate Nucleus and Visual Cortx
   a. The receptive field of the ganglion and LGN cells is annular while that of the visual cortex is rectangular.
   b. The cells in the visual cortex receive inputs from cells in the LGN that have three overlapping annular receptive fields.
   c. The columns of cells in the visual cortex are sensitive to the form and orientation of the bar of light.
   d. The cells in the visual cortex synthesize information about the form of the object being viewed.

5. Color Vision
   a. Three types of photoreceptor cones (red, blue, and green) are found in the retina. Each has a type of visual pigment capable of absorbing a particular wavelength of light.
   b. Color perception involves cones but also ganglion cells which can distinguish information about different colors. Color information is transmitted to cells in the LGN, which in turn convey it to cells in the visual cortex.

6. Disorders of Visual Sensation
   a. The fovea composed of only cones is the region of the retina with the greatest spatial resolution and the region where the lens tries to focus images of light.

C. The Auditory System

1. Sound Transduction and the Functional Organization of the Ear
   a. The pathway of sound transduction in the ear is: outer ear → eardrum → middle ear ossicles (malleus, incus, stapes) → oval window → basilar membrane in the inner ear (cochlea).
   b. The basilar membrane is designed to respond to different frequences of sound by changing its form.
   c. The deformations of the basilar membrane are transduced into generator potentials by hair cells which sit on the basilar membrane.
   d. The hair cells release transmitters which generate action potentials in auditory nerve fibers that convey information about the sound to the brain.

2. Auditory Pathways and Receptive Properties of Auditory Nerve Cells
   a. The information pathway to the primary auditory cortex is: auditory nerve → cochlea nucleus in the brain → medial geniculate nucleus of the thalamus → primary auditory cortex.

b. Auditory nerve fibers respond differently to frequencies of tones. One frequency will activate a particular fiber.
c. Neurons respond in a variety of different ways to a particular tone.
d. The fundamental features of a sound are reassembled by convergence of neurons.

3. Disorders of Auditory Sensation
   a. Hearing loss may result from destruction of hair cells, damage to ossicles, brain tumors and lesions of the auditory pathway.

D. The Gustatory System
   * Taste receptors or gustatory receptors are located in the tongue, palate and pharynx.
   * The receptors detect chemicals associated with four basic taste qualities: sweet, sour, salty and bitter.

1. Transduction of Taste Sensations
   a. Each receptor responds best to only one type of taste quality but can respond to several types of substances.
   b. The binding of the chemical to the receptor produces a generator potential in the taste bud. This in turn causes an action potential in afferent fiber associated with the receptor.
   c. One afferent fiber innervates many receptors.

2. Gustatory Pathways
   a. Taste buds are innervated by parts of different cranial nerves.
   b. The pathway of information from receptor to the brain is: receptor → afferent fiber → gustatory nucleus in the brain stem → ventral posterior medial nucleus of thalamus → gustatory area of neocortex.
   c. Alternate pathways transmit information to the limbic system and hypothalamus.

E. The Olfactory System
   * Olfactory receptors sensitive to different types of odors are located in the nasal cavity.
   * The binding of an odor molecule produces a generator potential which becomes an action potential above the threshold level.
   * The pathway of information to the brain is: receptor cell → mitral cell in olfactory bulb → olfactory tract → limbic system of cortex.

Chapter Learning Objectives

1. Describe the common characteristics of transduction mechanisms for all sensory systems.
2. Describe how information about the quality and intensity of the stimulus is transmitted to the brain.
3. List the types of somatic sensory receptors and the stimulus for each.
4. Delineate the information pathway from the receptor to the brain for a somatic sensory system.
5. Describe the concept of receptive fields in relation to the perception of a stimulus.
6. Describe the pathway by which information about a painful stimulus is transmitted to the brain, and how the pathway can be inhibited.

7. Describe the pathways by which visual information is transmitted to the brain. Identify the nerve cells and parts of the brain involved and their relationship in this pathway.
8. Describe the concept of receptive fields as it relates to perception of a visual stimulus, such as a red cube, and its visual field.
9. Distinguish rod and cone cells as to the stimulus and chemical reactions occurring within the cell.
10. Describe the trichromatic theory of color vision and how we are able to distinguish yellow and orange flowers.
11. Describe the pathway of sound transduction from the outer ear to the basilar membrane.
12. Describe the structure and function of the hair cell in hearing.
13. Describe how tones are distinguished and how information is transmitted to the brain.
14. Describe at least two disorders of visual sensation and two for auditory sensation.
15. Compare the gustatory and olfactory systems regarding location of receptors, nature of the stimulus, structure of the receptor and the pathway of information from the receptor to the brain.

Key Terms

action potential
adequate stimulus
annulus
anterolateral pathway
basal cell
basilar membrane
bipolar cells
broad-band cell
characteristic frequency
cochlea
cones (red, green, blue)
dorsal column nuclei
dorsal column pathway
dorsal horn
dorsal root ganglion
double opponent cell
fovea
frequency code of stimulus intensity
ganglion cells
generator potential
gustatory receptor
hair cell
horizontal cells
inhibitory interneuron
labeled-line code of stimulus quality
lateral geniculate nucleus
limbic system
mechanoreceptors
mitral cell
neocortex
nociceptors (mechanical, heat)
nuclei
ocular dominance column
olfactory bulb
olfactory receptor
olfactory tract
ossicles (malleus, incus, stapes)
Pacinian corpuscle
phasic discharge
photoreceptor
population code of stimulus intensity
primary somato-sensory area
proprioceptors
rapidly adapting receptor
receptive field
rods
secondary somatosensory area
sensory adaptation
single opponent cell
slowly adapting tactile mechanoreceptors
somatic sensory cortex
somatic sensory system
somatotropic organization
spinal cord
supporting cell
tactile receptor
taste bud
tectorial membrane
thalamus
thermal receptors
tonic discharge
tonotropic organization
ventral horn
visual agnosia
visual field
visual orientation column
visuotropic organization

Testing Your Knowledge

I. Matching. Select the correct word from the Key Terms.

__________1. cell bodies of sensory neurons
__________2. part of spinal cord containing nerve cells involved in processing of sensory information
__________3. change in membrane potential in a receptor
__________4. part of the brain receiving all types of sensory information
__________5. intensity of stimulus conveyed by number of action potentials per unit time
__________6. situation when continued stimulus no longer results in perception of sensation

__________ 7. detect changes in positions of limbs
__________ 8. receptors detecting painful stimuli
__________ 9. situation in which proprioceptor generates action potential only with change in direction of movement
__________ 10. most sensitive part of retina
__________ 11. cells in retina sensitive to color
__________ 12. axons of these retinal cells become the optic nerve
__________ 13. area of thalamus receiving information from the retina
__________ 14. cell which releases transmitter in response to being moved by basilar membrane
__________ 15. receptors sensitive to chemical stimulus

II. Fill in the Table. For each receptor identify the stimulus, the part(s) of the spinal cord, thalamus and brain involved in the transmission of information from the receptor to the neocortex.

receptor	stimulus	spinal cord or brain stem	thalamus	brain
1) rod				
2) cone				
3) hair cells in cochlea				
4) gustatory receptor				
5) olfactory receptor				
6) Pacinian corpuscle				
7) Nocioceptor				

CHAPTER 9 MOTOR SYSTEMS

<u>Chapter Outline</u>

I. Muscle as an Effector Organ
   * The motor system controls locomotion, posture and fine movement through muscles.
   * Muscles affect changes in the body in response to sensory stimuli and help regulate the stimuli entering the CNS.
   * The motor system is organized hierarchically according to the scheme: premotor area (highest level) → motor cortex → brain stem → spinal cord (lowest level).
   * The motor system also has a parallel organization in which information from two levels can affect a third level.

   A. Overview of the Skeletal Muscle Systems

      1. General Structure of Skeletal Muscle
         a. Muscle is composed of muscle fibers of two types: extrafusal and intrafusal.

      2. Types and Actions of Skeletal Muscle
         a. Muscles are usually arranged in antagonistic pairs.
         b. Skeletal muscles can be categorized as fast or slow and differ from each other in amount of vascularization, resistance to fatigue, and the functional properties of the motor neurons innervating these muscles.

   B. Innervation of Skeletal Muscles
      * Both sensory and motor neurons are involved in the control of skeletal muscle.

      1. Motor Neurons in Skeletal Muscle
         a. The connection between a muscle fiber and the myelinated axon of a motor neuron is called a motor end-plate, a special type of synapse.
         b. The cell bodies of motor neurons innervating skeletal muscles are located in the ventral horn of the spinal cord.
         c. A motor unit consists of an individual motor neuron and all the muscle fibers that it innervates.
         d. The motor unit size parallels the size of sensory receptive fields.
         e. The amount of contractive forces generated by a muscle is controlled by the nervous system by either a frequency or population code.

      2. Sensory Neurons in Skeletal Muscle
         a. Sensory neurons transmit to the CNS information about the state of contraction and tension in muscle fibers which has been received from the muscle spindle and Golgi tendon organs.
         b. The muscle spindle is composed of two types of intrafusal fibers that are innervated by two types of nerve fibers.
         c. Muscle spindle sensitivity is maintained by gamma motor neurons which innervate contractile elements at the poles of the spindles.
         d. Golgi tendon receptors innervate tendons and transmit information about the force exerted by the muscle.

II. The Spinal Cord in the Motor Response System

A. Organization of Motor Neurons in the Spinal Cord
   * Motor neurons are organized in the ventral horn of the spinal cord according to the position and types of skeletal muscles innervated by these neurons.
   * Motor neurons innervating a single muscle are functionally grouped in motor neuron pools.

B. Interneurons of the Spinal Cord
   * Interneurons coordinate the activity of several muscle groups through their connections with motor neurons in different regions of the spinal cord.

C. Spinal Cord Reflexes
   * Spinal cord reflexes are carried out entirely within the spinal cord and are modified by input from higher centers.

   1. The Stretch Reflex
      a. The stretch reflex occurs when a muscle spindle detects a tap on the knee and informs the spinal cord which activates motor neurons to the leg extensor and inhibits motor neurons to the flexor, causing the leg to extend.
      b. Interneurons provide for a well-coordinated motor response.

   2. The Inverse Myotatic Reflex
      a. The inverse myotatic reflex protects muscles from damage that might occur during weight lifting.
      b. The Golgi tendon organ detects excessive force and transmits this information to the spinal cord. There, the message is sent to inhibitory neurons which turn off motor neurons innervating the biceps and activate motor neurons innervating the extensors.
      c. The reflex is believed to involve the smooth onset and termination of muscular contraction in working.

   3. The Flexor Withdrawal Reflex
      a. The flexor withdrawal reflex involves cutaneous receptors and occurs in response to a painful stimulus.

D. Control of Locomotion
   * Interneurons and their interconnections comprise the locomotor generators which coordinate the flexor and extension of leg muscles in walking.
   * The locomotor generators are under the control of a "locomotor command center" in the brain stem.

III. The Brain in the Motor Response System

A. The Brain Stem: Control of Posture and the Spinal Cord
   * Three pathways from the brain stem provide input to the motor neurons of the spinal cord.

   1. The Ventromedial Pathway
      a. Axons in the ventromedial pathway affect motor neurons controlling axial muscles.

   2. The Lateral Reticulospinal Tract
      a. Fibers in the lateral reticulospinal tract innervate flexors in the control of posture.

3. The Rubrospinal Tracts
    a. Fibers in the rubrospinal tract innervate motor neurons controlling distal flexor muscles.

B. The Motor Cortex and Fine Voluntary Movement
* The fine control of voluntary movement is due to instructions from the motor cortex.
* Cells in the motor cortex are organized in a somatotropic manner.
* The amount of cortical space devoted to different parts of the body is in proportion to the degree of fine motor control.

1. Organization of the Motor Cortex
    a. The cells of the cortex are organized in functional columns called cortical efferent zones.
    b. Neurons in the motor cortex are organized horizontally into six different layers.

2. Descending Pathways from the Motor Cortex
    a. Fibers in the corticospinal pathway control distal limb muscles.
    b. Fibers in the corticobulbar pathway control axial muscles near the midline.
    c. Nerve fibers existing from the lateral corticospinal tract innervate motor neuron pools controlling distal limb muscles.
    d. Fibers in the ventral corticospinal tract innervate motor neurons associated with axial muscles.

3. Sensory Feedback to the Motor Cortex
    a. Sensory feedback to the motor cortex is by way of the somatic sensory cortex.
    b. The nerve cells in the sensory cortex are connected to those in the motor cortex in a topographic manner.

4. Cortical Coding of Contractile Force
    a. Coding of contractile force is carried out by two types of neurons: dynamic neurons and neurons coding for steady-state force.
    b. Dynamic neurons change their activity when there is an increase in the level of applied force.
    c. Neurons coding for steady-state force discharge action potentials throughout the entire period during which force is maintained.

C. The Supplemental and Premotor Areas: Programming Movement
* The supplemental and premotor cortex, as well as the posterior parietal cortex, cerebellum, and basal ganglia are involved in planning and programming of movements.
* The motivational areas of the brain, responding to the need to accomplish a particular task, transmit this information to the supplemental and premotor cortex.

D. The Posterior Parietal Cortex: Sensory Stimuli and Purposeful Movement.
* The posterior parietal cortex is necessary for the processing of sensory stimuli leading to purposeful movement.
* Three types of neurons (arm projection, hand-eye-coordination, and hand manipulation) in the posterior parietal cortex become active only with very specific behavioral motor responses.

E. The Cerebellum and Basal Ganglia

* The cerebellum and basal ganglia both receive inputs from the neocortex and transmit information back to the cortex by way of the thalamus.

1. The Cerebellum: Planning, Coordination and Posture
   a. The cerebellum has three major functions each associated with a specific location.
   b. Planning of a movement is the responsibility of the lateral region of the anterior and posterior lobes.
   c. The control of posture and equilibrium is centered in the flocculonodular lobe.
   d. The control of limb movement involves the midline and intermediate regions of the anterior and posterior lobes.
   e. Purkinje cells, the most prominent type of neuron, in the cerebellum, are packed tightly into a single cellular layer.
   f. Axons of Purkinje cells located in different regions of the cerebellum form synapses with neurons in one of three deep cerebellar nuclei, the dendate nucleus, the interpositus nucleus or the fastigial nucleus. The type of information transmitted between the Purkinje cells and cells of the deep cerebellar nuclei depends on the location of the Purkinje cells.
   g. Outflow of information from the cerebellum is via the deep cerebellar nuclei but is modulated first by inhibitory actions of the Purkinje cells.
   h. The inputs to the Purkinje cells occur by two routes: climbing fibers and parallel fiber pathways. Climbing fibers are thought to modulate the responsiveness of Purkinje cells to parallel fiber inputs.

2. The Basal Ganglia: Planning of Movements
   a. The caudate and putamen receive inputs to the basal ganglia from the neocortex, thalamus and substantia nigra of the brain stem.
   b. The globus pallidus of the basal ganglia provides the output to the perfrontal and premotor cortices via the thalamus.
   c. The basal ganglia are involved in the programming of motor patterns.

IV. Vestibular Control of Equilibrium and Balance

* The vestibular system aids in maintaining the body's balance by detecting the position and motion of the head in space.
* The vestibular apparatus consists of three semicircular canals, which detect angular acceleration in one of three planes in space, and the utricle and saccule which detect linear acceleration.
* When stimulated by the movement of fluid, hair cells in the semicircular canals and otolithic organs, excite or inhibit vestibular nerve fibers that innervate them.
* The information from vestibular nerves is transmitted to the vestibular nucleus located in the brain stem from which it is sent down to neurons regulating movement and up to the cerebellum and somatosensory cortex.
* The cerebellum and somatosensory cortex use the information to coordinate muscular activity in order to maintain balance.

IV. Disorders of the Motor System

A. Lesions of the Corticospinal Tract

* The type of lesion and the symptoms depend on the area of the tract damaged.

B. Lesions of the Cerebellum

* Cerebellar lesions are characterized by a lack of coordination and equilibrium.

Chapter Learning Objectives

1. Describe what is meant by the hierarchical and parallel organizations of the motor system.
2. List the types of and describe the actions of skeletal muscle.
3. Describe the general characteristics of a motor unit.
4. Describe the structure, mechanism of action, and type of information transmitted by muscle spindles and Golgi tendon organs.
5. Describe the organization of motor neurons in the spinal cord.
6. Compare the stretch, flexor withdrawal, and inverse myotatic reflexes as to function, and mechanism of action, and diagram a reflex.
7. Describe the role of locomotor generators in walking.
8. List the three pathways from the brain stem to the spinal cord and the role of each in control of posture.
9. Describe the organization of the motor cortex especially regarding the relationship between size of the cortical area and degree of fine motor control.
10. Describe how information is transmitted from the motor cortex to the brain stem and to motor neurons exiting from the spinal end.
11. Describe sensory feedback pathways to the motor cortex and the necessity for such feedback pathways.
12. Describe the roles of the supplemental and premotor cortex, posterior parietal cortex, cerebellum and basal ganglia in programming movement.
13. List the three functions of the cerebellum and correlate each with the part of the cerebellum responsible for the function.
14. Describe the locations of the Purkinje cells in the cerebellum, the nature of their interactions with cells of the deep cerebellar nuclei, and their role in modulating cerebellar output.
15. Describe the effects of input via the climbing and parallel fibers in the activity of Purkinje cells.
16. Describe the structure and role of the vestibular apparatus in maintaining equilibrium and balance.

Key Terms

anterior lobe of cerebellum
antagonistic pair
basal ganglia
brain stem
caudate
cerebellum
climbing fiber
cortical efferent zones
corticobulbar pathway
corticospinal pathway
dendate nucleus
dynamic neuron
extensor
extrafusal fiber
hair cell
insertion
interpositus nucleus
intrafusal fiber
inverse myotatic reflex
lateral corticospinal tract
lateral reticulospinal tract
lesion
locomotor generators
mossy fiber
motor cortex
motor neuron (alpha, gamma)
motor neuron pool
posterior parietal
premotor area
Purkinje cell
putamen
pyramidal tract
reflex action
rubrospinal tract
saccule
semicircular canal
slow skeletal muscle
stretch receptor
stretch reflex
supplemental area
utricle
ventral corticospinal tract

fast skeletal muscle
fastigial nucleus
flexor
flexor withdrawal reflex
flacculonodular node
frequency code
globus pallidus
Golgi tendon organ
granual cells
motor unit
muscle spindle
myoneural junction
origin
otolith
population code
posterior lobe of cerebellum
ventral norm
ventromedial pathway
vestibular apparatus
vestibular nerve fiber

Testing Your Knowledge

I. Matching. Select the correct word from the Key Terms.

__________1. neurons that directly innervate muscle cells
__________2. strongest and most common muscle fiber
__________3. poorly vascularized, rapidly contracting muscle
__________4. synonymous with motor end plate
__________5. neuron synapsing with extrafusal fiber
__________6. functional unit of neuromuscular system
__________7. detects length of muscle and its velocity of contraction
__________8. detects tension in muscle
__________9. exemplified by knee jerk
_________10. reflex regulating muscle tension
_________11. coordinate felxion and extension of leg muscles in walking
_________12. location of motor neurons in spinal cord
_________13. most prominent cell in the cerebellum
_________14. detects angular acceleration
_________15. detects linear acceleration

II. Complete the Table. For each structure in the brain describe its location and function in the neuromuscular system.

Structure	Location	Function
supplemental cortex		
premotor cortex		
posterior parietal cortex		
anterior lobe		
posterior lobe		
flocculonodular lobe		
dendate nucleus		
interpositus nucleus		
fastigial nucleus		
inferior olivary nucleus		
mossy fibers		
caudate		
putamen		
globus pallidus		

II. Fill in the Table. For each tract or pathway list the origin of the axons, its location, the type of information carried and the role in controlling movement, posture, coordination, etc.

Tract/Pathway	Origin	Location	Type of Information	Role
ventromedial pathway				
lateral reticulo-spinal tract				
rubrospinal tract				
corticospinal pathway				
corticobulbar pathway				
pyramidal tract				
lateral cortico-spinal tract				

CHAPTER 10 THE AUTCNOMIC NERVOUS SYSTEM

Chapter Outline

I. Organization of the Autonomic Nervous System
   * The autonomic nervous system (ANS) coordinates and regulates bodily functions that are needed for survival.
   * The actions of the ANS are not under direct voluntary control.

   A. The Peripheral Autonomic Nervous System
      * The peripheral ANS is composed of the sympathetic and parasympathetic nervous system. These systems differ in function, the types of neurotransmitters released, origin of nerves from the spinal cord, and their effects on target organs which they innervate.

   B. The Central Autonomic Nervous System

   C. Neurotransmitters in the Autonomic Nervous System
      * Acetylcholine and norepinephrine and the two major transmitters.
      * Cholinergic receptors are classified as either nicotinic or muscarinic.
      * Adrenergic receptors are classified as alpha or beta.

II. Control of Bodily organs by the Sympathetic and Parasympathetic Systems
   * The actions of the sympathetic and parasympathetic inputs to the target organ have opposite effects.
   * Receptors for norepinephrine and acetylcholine are found in the membranes of cholinergic and adrenergic fibers, respectively. These receptors provide for local control at the site of the target organ.
   * Organs that have a vegetative function are activated by inputs from the parasympathetic system but inactivated by the sympathetic nervous system.
   * Organs involved in stress responses are activated by inputs from the sympathetic system but inactivated by the parasympathetic system.

III. Reflexes Governed by the Autonomic Nervous System

   A. The Spinal Autcnomic Reflex Arc
      * Information, conveyed by sensory neurons from the target organ to the spinal cord is transmitted up to the brain and to preganglionic neurons in the interomedial lateral (IML) column. This loop forms the spinal autonomic reflex arc:

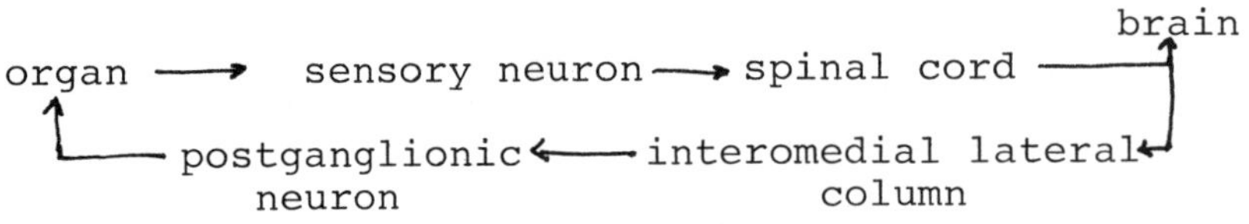

   B. The Urinary Bladder Reflex
      * The reflex involves the actions of two groups of muscles (smooth and skeletal), sensory receptors and nerves, somatic motor neurons, a higher brain center and the ANS.

   C. The Defecation Reflex
      * The defecation reflex involves the actions of smooth and skeletal muscles innervated by parasympathetic and somatic motor neurons, respectively, sensory stretch receptors and neurons, and higher brain centers.

D. Referred Pain and Segmental Spinal Reflexes

* Referred pain results from the convergence of nerve fibers from pain receptors in internal organs and on the surface of the body.

IV. Regulatory Systems of the Autonomic Nervous System

* Autonomic regulatory systems maintain a constant internal environment for optimal functioning of various organs and their cells.
* These systems, which involve the brain stem and hypothalamus, operate by a negative feedback mechanism.

A. Regulation of Thirst, Osmolarity, and Water Volume

* Osmoreceptors in the hypothalamus and water-volume sensors in large veins detect changes in osmolarity and volume of the blood.
* The hypothalamus releases a hormone, vasopressin, which acts on the kidneys and causes them to reabsorb more water.
* Information from peripheral sensors is conveyed to centers in the brain stem which then activate sympathetic nerves to the kidneys. The kidneys release an enzyme which activates a hormone that causes the hypothalamus to release vasopressin.

B. Regulation of Breathing

* Chemoreceptors in the ANS called carotid bodies and aortic bodies, monitor the amounts of O_2 available to cells and CO_2 produced by cells.
* Chemoreceptors located in the medulla monitor the amounts of CO_2 and H^+.
* The peripheral and central chemoreceptors act together to coordinate the intake of oxygen and removal of CO_2 by regulating breathing according to the metabolic demands of the body.

C. Regulation of Blood Pressure

* Regulation of blood pressure involves baroreceptors which detect changes in blood pressure and three brain stem centers, the depressor center, the nucleus of the vagus, and the pressor center.
* The hypothalamus affects the regulation of blood pressure by its excitatory inputs to the pressor center and preganglionic sympathetic neurons.

V. Autonomic Functions of the Hypothalamus

* Activation of the dorsal hypothalamus enhances responses associated with feeding behaviors such as increasing intestinal mobility and blood pressure.
* Activation of the ventral hypothalamus enhances responses associated with defense behaviors or the "fight or flight responses" such as increasing blood supply to the skeletal muscles and decreasing blood supply to the intestines.

VI. Autonomic Functions of the Adrenal Medulla

* The cells of the adrenal medulla are innervated by preganglionic sympathetic nerve fibers and are homologous to postganglionic neurons.
* The cells, when activated, release catecholamines, norepinephrine and epinephrine.
* The adrenal medulla coordinates the body's response to stress.

Chapter Learning Objectives

1. Compare the parasympathetic and sympathetic nervous systems as to general effect and the nature of the target organs, the relative lengths of the pre- and post-ganglionic neurons, the location of preganglionic cell bodies in the spinal cord and the types of neurotransmitters released by each neuron.
2. Distinguish cholingergic and adrenergic fibers and describe the receptors for each type of fiber.
3. Describe in general how the parasympathetic and sympathetic systems control bodily organs. Be able to provide specific examples.
4. Diagram the three autonomic reflexes described in the text, and compare them.
5. Diagram and describe the regulation of thirst, osmolarity and water volume, the regulation of breathing and blood pressure. Compare these three types of regulatory mechanisms.
6. Describe how the hypothalamus coordinates the functions of different organs and its involvement in activating the "fight or flight" responses.
7. Describe how the adrenal medulla activates the "fight or flight" responses.

Key Terms

acetylcholine
adrenal medulla
adrenergic
alpha receptor
angiotensin
aortic bodies
autonomic nervous system
autonomic regulatory system
baroreceptors
beta receptor
carotid bodies
catecholamine
cerebiospinal fluid (CSF)
chemoreceptor
cholinergic
continence
defecation
defecation reflex
depressor center
fight or flight response
effector system
expiration
ganglia
hyperalgesic zone
hypothalamus (dorsal, ventral)
inspiration
interomedial lateral nuclei
medulla
micturition
muscarinic receptor
negative feedback system
nicotinic receptor
norepinephrine
nucleus of the vagus
osmorereceptor
pacemaker cells
parasympathetic nervous system
paraventricular nucleus
postganglionic neuron
preganglionic neuron
pressor center
referred pain
renin
sensor system
sphincter (internal, external)
spinal autonomic reflex arc
supraoptic nucleus
sympathetic nervous system
urinary bladder reflex
vasopressin (ADH, antidiuretic hormone)
water-volume sensor

Testing Your Knowledge

I. Matching. Select the correct term from the Key Terms.

__________ 1. transmitter released from postganglionic parasympathetic neurons
__________ 2. location of cell bodies of preganglionic sympathetic neurons
__________ 3. receptors associated with cholinergic fibers
__________ 4. receptors associated with adrenergic fibers
__________ 5. ability to retain urine in the bladder
__________ 6. detect changes in water-volume and located in hypothalamus
__________ 7. acts on kidney to increase reabsorption of water
__________ 8. chemoreceptors sensitive to CO_2 and O_2
__________ 9. location of central chemoreceptors sensitive to CO_2 and H^+
__________ 10. detect changes in blood pressure
__________ 11. regulatory center causing decrease in blood pressure
__________ 12. regulatory center causing increase in blood pressure

_________13. cells are homologous to postganglionic sympathetic neurons
_________14. bathes brain and provides extracellular environment for brain cells
_________15. transmitter secreted by postganglionic sympathetic fibers

II. Fill in the Table for the autonomic nervous system

Component	General Role	Type of Neuro-Transmitter	Level of origin from spinal cord	Length of pre-ganglionic neuron	Post-ganglionic neuron
parasympathetic nervous system					
sympathetic nervous system					

CHAPTER 11 CENTRAL INTEGRATIVE SKILLS

Chapter Outline

I. Bodily Rhythms, Cyclic Systems, and the Hypothalamus
   A. Circadian Rhythms and the "Master Clock"
      * Many bodily functions and biochemical processes vary in accordance with a 24-hour schedule.
      * The suprachiasmatic nucleus of the hypothalamus is thought to be the "master clock" that is responsible for coordinating various biological rhythms.

   B. Sleep and Wakefulness

      1. The Stages of Sleep
         a. The brain displays several different stages of electrical activity during one night of sleep.
         b. Based on changes of frequency and amplitude of the brain's electrical activity, four distinct stages of sleep have been distinguished. In Stage 1 the lowest amplitude and highest frequency of electrical activity is seen while the reverse is seen in Stage 4.
         c. REM sleep, characterized by rapid eye movements, is the period of visual dreaming.
         c. The amount of sleep and the proportion of REM and non-REM sleep vary with age.

      2. Neural Mechanisms of Sleep
         a. The hypothalamus and brain stem are the brain areas responsible for the sleep-wake cycle.
         b. Electrical stimulation of the preoptic area of the hypothalamus induces non-REM sleep. The suprachiasmatic nucleus receives input from the retina and provides input to the preoptic area to entrain sleep-wake cycle.
         c. The raphe nucleus of the brain stem is believed responsible for REM sleep.

      3. Sleep Disorders
         a. Insomnia is the general term for inability to sleep.
         b. Narcolepsy, a sleep disorder in which an individual suddenly lapses into sleep at unexpected times, is thought to result from activation of the REM-sleep generator.

II. Motivational Systems: Maintaining an Internal Balance and Ensuring Survival
   * Motivational systems initiate behaviors that satisfy bodily needs to ensure survival of the individual or species.
   * Motivational systems are activated by internal and/or external signals.

   A. Hunger: Maintaining Levels of Glucose and Triglycerides
      * The long term regulation of food intake appears to involve the maintenance of body weight as reflected in the amount of adipose tissue, particularly the volume of individual fat cells.
      * Insulin plays a role in the long term regulation of body fat and in the short term regulation of hunger.

   B. Thirst: Maintaining Osmoloarity of the Blood
      * Thirst is a drive to maintain a constant level of osmolarity in the body's internal environment.

C. The Sexual Drive: Perpetuating the Species

* Mating is a basic drive common to all mammals and involves the anterior hypothalamus in both sexes. Mating posture is similar among animals though sexual behaviors are quite different.
* Pheromones activate sexual behavior in many species.
* The development of a particular pattern of sexual behavior results from the pressure or absence of androgens during critical periods of development.
* Androgens are thought to exert their effect on sexual behavior through the nerve cells in the preoptic area of the hypothalamus. These cells, when exposed to androgens, release LH, leuteinizing hormone at constant levels as adults. Nonandrogenized brains develop a cyclical pattern of LH release.

D. The Reward System of the Brain

* The reward areas of the brain comprise a powerful motivational system able to override drives such as hunger, sex, and even the avoidance of pain and punishment.
* Several areas of the brain are involved: the substantia nigra, hypothalamus, nucleus accumbens, caudate nucleus and frontal cortex. These areas are linked together by the dopamine nerve fiber pathway originating in the substantia nigra.
* The release of dopamine at synaptic connections is critical to the reward process.
* The reward system may play a role in learning and memory through the dopamine nerve fiber pathway.

III. Learning and Memory

* Learning is the acquisition of knowledge while memory is the retention of knowledge.

A. Associative and Nonassociative Learning

* In nonassociative learning adaptation to a stimulus depends on its relevance to our survival.
* In classical conditioning, a type of associative learning, an animal acquires an understanding about the relationship between two stimuli.
* In operant conditioning, a second type of associative learning, an animal acquires an understanding of the relationship between its own behavior and a subsequent reward (cr punishment).
* The critical factor in both types is the time interval between the appearance of the two stimuli or of a behavior and its reward.
* The most effective types of stimuli are those relevant to survival of the animal.

B. Short-and Long-term Memory

* Memory has different components and progresses through different stages. Short-term and long-term memory differ in stability and length of time information is retained.

C. Memory Circuits: Neuronal Pathways for Learning

* Learning and memory systems involve neuronal memory circuits in several areas of the brain.
* The hippocampus plays a role in the transformation of short- to long-term memory.

D. Learning and the "Split Brain"

* Through "split-brain studies" it has been determined that different mammalian species store information in different ways in the cerebral hemispheres.

E. Cellular Mechanisms of Learning

* The cellular mechanisms of learning involve alterations of synaptic function.

1. Habituation: A Decrese in Synaptic Transmission
   a. Habituation can be explained in terms of a decrease in synaptic transmission as a result of inactivation of Ca^{2+} channels in the presynaptic terminal.

2. Sensitization: An Increase in Synaptic Transmission
   a. The underlying mechanism is called presynaptic facilitation and involves interneurons that form synapses with axons of other neurons. The facilitating interneurons enhance the release of neurotransmitter.

3. Classical Conditioning: A Sensitization Process

F. The Effects of Use and Nonuse of Neural Pathways

* The use and nonuse of neural pathways can strengthen or weaken the connections between nerve cells, as well as alter topographical maps in the cortex.

IV. Language Systems

A. The Dominant Hemisphere: Comprehension and the Motor Aspects of Language

* The language centers are located in the dominant hemisphere in regions of the brain called Wernicke's area and Broca's area.
* Wernicke's area is responsible for comprehension of language and Broca's area is responsible for motor aspects of speech and language.
* The pathway for information transfer of written language is:

written word → retina → primary and secondary visual cortices →

association cortex called angular gyrus → Wernicke's area (where it is recognized or comprehended) →

Broca's area (where motor programs for speech reside).

B. The Nondominant Hemisphere: Intonation and the Emotional Aspects of Language

* The regions in the nondominant hemisphere residing in the same location as Wernicke's and Broca's areas in the dominant hemisphere are responsible for the affective aspects of language.

C. Disorders of Speech and Language

1. Aphasia: Damage to the Language Centers

2. Dyslexia: A Congenital Reading Disability

V. Laterality of Brain Function

A. Laterality of Spatial Abilities
   * Spatial abilities appear to reside in the right hemisphere.

B. Differences of Laterality in Male and Female Brains

Chapter Learning Objectives

1. Describe the role of the hypothalamus in the sleep-wake cycles.
2. Describe the characteristics of sleep stages 1, 4, and REM sleep.
3. Describe the role of the hypothalamus and brain stem in inducing REM and non-REM sleep.
4. Compare short-term and long-term regulation of food intake as to the role of insulin in each.
5. Describe the interrelationship between the regulation of thirst, water, volume, and osmolarity.
6. Describe the effects of androgen on the development of sexual behavior in the male and female.
7. Compare habituation and sensitization as to the neuronal pathways and cellular mechanisms responsible for each.
8. Compare operant and classical conditioning as to the neuronal pathways and cellular mechanisms responsible for each.
9. Describe neuronal pathways involved in learning and memory.
10. Describe the aspects of language centered in the dominant and nondominant hemisphere.
11. Define the concept of laterality of brain function and provide an example.

Key Terms

adipose tissue
androgen
angular gyrus
anterior hypothalamus
aphasia
aprosodias
associative learning
Broca's area
circadian rhythm
conditioned response
conditioned stimulus
conditioning (operant, classical)
critical period
dominant hemisphere
dopamine nerve fiber pathway
dyslexia
electroencephalogram (EEG)
habituation
insomnia
language
learning
luteinizing hormone
long-term memory
lordosis
"master clock"
memory
memory circuits
motivational system
mounting
narcolepsy
nonassociative learning
nondominant hemisphere
non-REM sleep
pheromone
planum temporate
preoptic area
presynaptic facilitation
raphe nucleus
REM sleep
sensitization
short-term memory
sleep
split-brain studies
substantia nigra
suprachiasmatic nucleus
supraoptic nucleus
Wernicke's area

Testing Your Knowledge

I. Matching. Select the correct word from the Key Terms.

_________1. coordinates various biological rhythms
_________2. measures brain activity
_________3. stage of sleep during which visual dreaming occurs
_________4. electrical stimulation of this area induces non-REM sleep
_________5. believed responsible for generation of REM sleep
_________6. one of brain centers for sexual drive
_________7. location of osmoreceptors
_________8. hormone affecting development of sexual behavior
_________9. area of brain associated with reward system

________10. inability to sleep
________11. decrease of response to repeated stimulus
________12. learning resulting in understanding of relationship between two stimulus
________13. area responsible for comprehension of language
________14. area responsible for motor aspects of speech and language
________15. language disorder resulting from damage to brain

Fill in the Table. List the function and location for each structure or region.

Structure/Region	Function	Location
Suprachiasmatic nucleus		
preoptic area		
raphe nucleus		
supraoptic nucleus		
anterior hypothalamus		
substantia nigra		
hippocampus		
Wernicke's area		
Broca's area		
angular gyrus		
corpus callosum		

CHAPTER 12 ENDOCRINE CONTROL MECHANISMS

Chapter Outline

I. General Concepts of Endocrine Control

A. The Nature of a Hormone
* Hormones are generally considered to be substances usually secreted into the blood by specialized cells or glands in very small amounts, which are then carried to other parts of the body to interact with specific receptors in target tissues, where they produce a biological response.
* Some hormones diffuse to their site of action, which may be the cell producing the hormone (autocrine mechanism) or to adjacent cells (paracrine mechanism).

B. The Relationship between the Nervous System and the Endocrine System
* Neuroendocrine cells function as an interface between the nervous and endocrine systems. They convert electrical signals from nerve cells into hormonal signals.

C. Principles of Feedback Regulation in the Endocrine System
* Hormone production by endocrine cells is regulated, in most instances, by a negative feedback mechanism. The rate of hormone secretion is regulated to maintain homeostasis.

D. The Major Endocrine and Neuroendocrine Glands and the Hormones They Produce
* The specific effect of individual hormones can be categorized as being related to the regulation of one of four physiological processes: (1) energy production, use, and storage; (2) salt and water metabolism; (3) growth and development; (4) reproductive function.

II. The Chemistry of Hormones

A. Structures and Synthesis of Hormones

1. Hormones Derived from Amino Acids
   a. Epinephrine and melatonin, derived from tyrosine and tryptophan,respectively, are known as amines. Amine production and secretion are triggered by the same stimulus.
   b. Thyroxine is composed of four iodide molecules joined to a pair of tyrosines and is stored as larger precursor protein, known as thyroglobulin.

2. Hormones that are Peptides or Proteins
   a. Most hormones are either peptides or proteins, some of which contain a significant amount of carbohydrate.
   b. Many peptide hormones are first synthesized as larger precursor molecules.

3. Hormones Derived from Cholesterol Steroids
   a. Cholesterol is the precursor for all steroid hormones and vitamin D.
   b. Steroid hormones are grouped into five categories according to the type of biological process they regulate:
      (1) glucocorticoids
      (2) mineralocorticoids
      (3) androgens
      (4) estrogens
      (5) progestins

c. There are several common steps in the formation of each of the five classes of steroids.
d. The type of steroid synthesized depends on the relative amounts of the specific enzymes needed to produce the particular type of steroid.
e. Genetic defects leading to deficiences in single enzymes of steroid synthetic pathways can cause endocrine abnormalities.
f. In contrast to the situation with other hormones, steroids are synthesized and secreted only on demand and their production depends on the availability of cholesterol.

B. Transport of Hormones in the Blood

* Mechanisms are needed to transport hormones because of their limited solubility in aqueous solutions or the possibility of urinary loss due to small size.

1. Specific Transport Proteins
   a. Thyroxine and steroids bind to two types of transport proteins:
      (1) those with high specificity and high affinity for one hormone; and,
      (2) those without high specificity or affinity, such as albumin and prealbumin.

2. Albumin and Prealbumin
   a. Albumin and prealbumin are synthesized in the liver and play an important role in the transport of some steroid hormones.

3. Free and Bound Hormones: A Dynamic Equilibrium
   a. The free hormone is the physiologically active form and is able to move from the blood to target cell receptors.
   b. Carrier proteins release hormone to maintain a relatively constant concentration of the free hormone in the blood.

C. Peripheral Transformation, Degradation, and Excretion of Hormones

* For most hormones the form that is secreted is the active one.
* The kidneys and liver are the major pathways for removal or degradation for most hormones.

D. Measurement of Hormone Concentrations in the Blood

* The technique, radioimmunoassay, is used to measure the concentration of hormones in the plasma.

III. Mechanisms of Hormone Action

* Hormones produce their effects by one of two mechanisms of action involving either intracellular or membrane receptors.

A. Properties of Hormone Receptors

* Hormones and their receptors have complementary shapes.
* Binding between receptor and hormone involves weak chemical forces and is usually readily reversible.
* For any particular hormone there is a finite number of receptors in its target tissue and a maximal response produced.
* The receptor serves as a signal transducer converting a specific extracellular hormonal signal into an intracellular signal that will redirect or alter cell function.

B. The "Second Messenger" Model of Hormone Action

* Peptide hormones utilize intracellular signals or second messengers to produce their effects. The binding of peptide hormone to its membrane-bound receptor results in the generation of the second messenger.
* Three intracellular second messenger systems have been described:
  (1) the adenylate cyclase/cyclic AMP system;
  (2) the phosphatidyl inositol and diacylglycerol system; and,
  (3) receptor-linked ion channels.

1. Cyclic AMP as a Second Messenger
   a. The activity of adenylate cyclase is coupled to membrane receptors by G-proteins, integral membrane proteins.
   b. Binding of hormone to G_s protein stimulates adenylate cyclase and increases intracellular cAMP, while binding of hormone to G_i protein inhibits adenylate cyclase and results in a reduction of cAMP.

2. Inositol Trisphosphate and Diacylglycerol as Second Messengers
   a. Binding of hormone to another type of G protein stimulates phospholipase C resulting in the hydrolysis of PIP_2 to IP_3 and DG which function as second messengers.
   b. IP_3 causes an increase in the intracellular concentration of calcium which plays an important role as a mediator in a variety of different processes.
   c. DG activates, C-kinase, a membrane-bound protein, which catalyzes the phosphorylation of proteins that produce specific changes in cell function.

3. Ions as Second Messengers
   a. Binding of hormone to its receptor results in the opening of specific, gated, ion channels, which generates a signal in one of two ways depending on cell type.
      (1) A transient flux of ions alters membrane potential in electrically active cells.
      (2) A major influx of ions initiates a cellular reponse in cells that are not electrically active.

C. The Gene Expression Model of Hormone Action

* Steroids and thyroxine bind to intracellular receptors in contrast to peptide hormones.
* Receptors for steroids and thyroid hormones are located in the nuclear envelope within the nucleus.
* The hormone-receptor simplex interacts with specific "acceptor sites" in nuclear DNA, thus affecting differential transcription and the production of specific hormones.
* Responses to steroid or thyroid hormones last longer than responses to peptide hormones.

D. Amplification of Hormone Signals

* Signal amplification of hormone action can occur at various steps.

<u>Chapter Learning Objectives</u>

1. Define the term "hormone."
2. Compare the nervous and endocrine systems as to speed and nature of the response, mechanism of effecting the response, and the role of receptors.
3. Describe the concept of negative and positive feedback regulation and provide an example.

4. For each of the major endocrine glands, list the hormone(s), the target cell(s), and primary biological effect.
5. Compare amine, peptide, and steroid hormones as to synthesis, storage and secretion.
6. Describe how hormones are transported in the blood and factors affecting the dynamic equilibrium between free and bound hormones.
7. Describe the three types of second messengers and how each act.
8. Compare peptide and steroids hormones as to their mechanism of action, particularly with regard to the nature and location of receptors, and the involvement and types of second messengers.

Key Terms

adenylate cyclase
albumin
amine
androgen
autocrine
cholesterol
conjugation
cyclic AMP
cAMP-dependent protein kinases
diacylglycerol (DG)
dynamic equilibrium
epinephrine
estrogen
feedback (negative, positive)
G-protein
glucocorticoid
hormone
inositol triphosphate (IP_3)
mineralocorticoid
neuroendocrine
paracrine
peptide hormone
phospholipase C
phosphatidylinositol 4,5-bisphosphate (PIP_2)
prealbumin
progestin
radioimmunoassay
receptor mediated endocytosis
second messenger
signal transducer
steroid
testosterone
thyroglobulin
thyroxine
TRH

Testing Your Knowledge

I. Matching. Select the correct word from the Key Terms.

__________1. lipid hormone, composed of four interlocking rings
__________2. transports steroid and thyroxine in plasma
__________3. hormones like epinephrine which have a free amino group
__________4. contains iodide and derived from tyrosine
__________5. describes hormones composed of amino acids
__________6. describes relationship between free and bound hormones
__________7. internalization of hormone-receptor complex
__________8. second messenger whose production depends on G_s and G_i proteins
__________9. activation of phospholipase C results in production of these second messengers
__________10. second messenger which increases intracellular concentration of calcium ions
__________11. hormone with intracellular receptor
__________12. hormone regulating salt and water content
__________13. hormone regulating concentration of plasma glucose
__________14. chemical molecules from which steroids derived
__________15. describes functional aspect of receptor

II. Fill in the Table

Hormone	Gland or Source	Chemical Nature	Type of Receptor	Type of Second Messenger	Target Tissue	Primary Biological Effect
growth hormone						
insulin						
glucagon						
aldosterone						
thyroid hormones						
parathyroid hormone						
androgens						

CHAPTER 13 THE PITUITARY GLAND

Chapter Outline

I. Anatomy of the Pituitary and its Relation to the Hypothalamus

A. Gross Anatomy of the Pituitary and its Relation to the Hypothalamus

1. Gross Anatomy of the Pituitary Gland
   a. The pituitary gland is composed of three lobes:
      (1) anterior lobe (a true endocrine gland)
      (2) pituitary lobe (an extension of the nervous system)
      (3) intermediate lobe (little or no endocrine function in humans)
   b. The pituitary is connected to the hypothalamus by a stalk.

2. Functional Anatomy of the Pituitary Gland
   a. The posterior pituitary contains axons and terminals of neurons whose cell bodies are located in the hypothalamus.
   b. The anterior pituitary receives messages from the hypothalamus via the hypothalamic-pituitary portal system in the median eminence.
   c. The short portal system connects the anterior and posterior lobes.

II. Regulation of Pituitary Hormone Secretion by the Hypothalamus

A. The Posterior Pituitary: A Neuroendocrine System
   * The posterior pituitary secretes oxytocin and antidiuretic hormone (ADH or vasopressin) which are synthesized in the cell bodies of the neurons in the hypothalamus. Synthesis of these hormones depends on neural inputs to the hypothalamus from other areas of the hypothalamus and the brain.

B. The Anterior Pituitary: An Endocrine System
   * The anterior pituitary synthesizes six different hormones whose secretion is under the control of different releasing/inhibiting hormones produced in the hypothalamus.
   * The hypothalamic inhibitory/releasing factors travel via the hypothalamic-pituitary portal systems to the anterior pituitary.

III. Actions and Effects of the Pituitary Hormones

A. Hormones of the Posterior Pituitary

1. Antidiuretic Hormone (ADH): An Increase in Water Retention
   a. The primary effect of ADH, a small peptide, is to increase water retention by the kidney.
   b. ADH secretion is affected primarily by changes in
      (1) osmolality of the blood or extracellular fluid; and,
      (2) blood volume.
   c. Other factors such as certain drugs and alcohol affect ADH release.

2. Oxytocin: Regulation of Breast Milk Release
   a. Oxytocin, a small peptide secreted by the hypothalamus, stimulates the release of milk from the alveoli, the sites of milk production, into the larger ducts of the breast. It also stimulates contraction of the smooth muscle during labor.

B. Hormones of the Anterior Pituitary

* Within the anterior pituitary there are five different hormone-secreting cell types:
  (1) somatotrophs - produce growth hormone
  (2) corticotrophs - produce ACTH
  (3) lactotrophs - produce prolactin
  (4) thyrotrophs - produce TSH
  (5) gonadotrophs - produce both FSH and LH.

* The size and activity of these cells vary under different physiological conditions.

1. Luteinizing Hormone (LH) and Follicle Stimulating Hormone (FSH): Regulation of Reproductive Function
   a. The primary effects of FSH and LH, the gonadotropins, are:
      (1) to promote maturation and development of the sperm and egg; and,
      (2) to stimulate production of sex steroid hormones by the gonads.

2. Prolactin: Regulation of Milk Synthesis
   a. Secretion of prolactin is under dual control of
      (1) prolactin-releasing hormone (PRH); and,
      (2) prolactin-inhibiting hormone (PIH).

3. Adrenocorticotropic Hormone (ACTH): Regulation of Cortisol
   a. ACTH regulates the synthesis and secretion of control from the adrenal cortex
   b. The secretion of ACTH is regulated by corticotropin-releasing hormone (CRH) produced in the hypothalamus.

4. Growth Hormone (GH): Body Growth and Metabolism
   a. Growth hormone is structurally similar to prolactin and human chorionic somatomammotropin secreted by the placenta.
   b. Secretion of growth hormone is regulated by growth-hormone-releasing hormone and somatostatin both of which are produced in the hypothalamus.
   c. Several factors or physiological conditions affect secretion of growth hormone through their effects on the brain and hypothalamus.
   d. Some of the effects of growth hormone are similar to those of insulin (insulin-like effects) while some antagonize or impair the actions of insulin (anti-insulin effects). Insulin-like effects include:
      (1) uptake of amino acids and stimulation of protein synthesis in muscle cells,
      (2) stimulation of protein synthesis in the liver.
   e. Anti-insulin effects include:
      (1) decrease of glucose into adipose tissue and muscle,
      (2) increase of gluconeogenesis in the liver.
   f. Growth hormone stimulates the production of somatomedins produced predominantly by the liver. The two most abundant ones are:
      (1) insulin-like growth factor I (I G F I); and,
      (2) insulin-like growth factor II (I G F II).
   g. The production of somatomedins is affected by the concentration of GH, insulin, and thyroid hormones.
   h. IGFS have two types of effects:
      (1) stimulation of events leading to an increase in linear growth of the skeleton,
      (2) stimulation of processes such as protein and RNA syntheses needed for tissue growth and repair.
   i. The particular clinical symptoms associated with deficiency or excess of growth hormone depend on the age of the individual when the deficiency or excess occurs.

5. The Thyroid Gland and Thyroid-Stimulating Hormone (TSH)
   a. The thyroid gland consists of cells arranged in closely packed follicles.
   b. Large amounts of thyroglobulin, the thyroid hormone precursor, are stored in the follicles to ensure sustained thyroid hormone secretion in the absence of dietary iodine.
   c. Iodide is trapped in follicle cells where it undergoes oxidation and joins with tyrosine residues to form iodinated tyrosines within the thyroglobulin protein. Coupling of DIT and MIT residues in different combinations produces T3 and T4 which are released when the thyroglobulin molecules is enzymatically degraded.
   d. TSH is the primary regulator of thyroid follicle cell activity and thyroid hormone secretion.
   e. The relationship between the hypothalamus, anterior pituitary, and thyroid gland is known as the hypothalamic-pituitary-thyroid axis.
   f. The secretion of TSH is regulated primarily by TRH whose secretion from the hypothalamus can be influenced by a variety of factors.
   g. Thyroid hormones exert negative feedback effects on the thyroid gland, thus limiting their own production.
   h. Thyroid hormones are transported in the plasma by carrier proteins like thyroxine-binding globulin and albumin.
   i. T_3 is more active than T_4 within the target cell.
   j. Thyroid hormones affect many tissues and metabolic processes. These are listed in Table 13-6.

Chapter Learning Objectives

1. Compare the anterior and posterior pituitary as to embryonic formation, types of hormones secreted and functional relationship to the hypothalamus.
2. List the hormones synthesized and secretion by the anterior pituitary, and their primary effect on target cells.
3. List the hormones secreted by the posterior pituitary and their primary effect on target cells.
4. Describe the relationship between the hypothalamus and anterior pituitary regarding production and secretion of growth hormone.
5. Describe insulin-like and diabetogenic effects of growth hormone.
6. Describe the relationship between growth hormone and somatomedins and the effects of IGFs on growth.
7. Describe the effects of excess or deficiency of growth hormone.
8. Describe the anatomy of the thyroid and the production of thyroid hormones from iodide and tyrosine.
9. Describe the effects of thyroid stimulating hormones on thyroid hormone production.
10. Diagram the hypothalamic-pituitary-thyroid axis, using arrows to indicate negative feedback of thyroid hormone production.
11. List factors affecting the production and secretion of thyroid hormones and describe the level at which and how the factor might exert its effect.
12. Summarize the effects of thyroid hormones on metabolic processes.
13. Compare hyperthyroidism and hypothyroidism as to clinical symptoms and causes.

Key Terms

acromegaly
adrenocorticotropic hormone (ACTH)
albumin
anabolic hormone
anterior pituitary
antidiuretic hormone (ADH)
anti-insulin effect
calorigenesis
catabolic hormone
chrondrocytes
corticotrophs
corticotropin-releasing hormone (CRH)
cretinism
deiodinases
diiodotyrosine (DIT)
dwarfism
epiphyseal plates
follicle stimulating hormone (FSH)
gigantism
goiter
gonadotrophs
gonadotropin-releasing hormone (GHRH)
growth hormone (GH)
growth hormone-releasing hormone (GHRH)
hyperthyroidism
hypothalamic-pituitary portal system
hypothalamic-pituitary-thyroid axis
hypothalamus
hypothyroidism
inhibiting hormone
insulin-like effect
insulin-like growth factors I, II (IGF-I,-II)
iodide trip
luteinizing hormone (LH)
median eminence
monoiodotyrosine (MIT)
myxedema
negative feedback
osmoreceptors
oxytocin
paraventricular nucleus
pituitary stalk
posterior pituitary
proinsulin
prolactin
prolactin-releasing hormone (PRH)
prolactin-inhibitory hormone (PIH)
Rathke's pouch
releasing hormone
short portal system
somatomedin
somatostatin
somatotrophs
somatomammotropic hormone
supraoptic nucleus
thyroglobulin
thyroid follicle
thyroid-stimulating hormone (TSH)
thyrotrophs
thyrotropin-releasing hormone (TRH)
thyroxine (T_4)
thyroxine-binding globulin (TBG)
triiodothyrosine (T_3)

Testing Your Knowledge

I. Matching. Select the correct word from the Key Terms

__________1. forms from Rathke's pouch, produces growth hormone
__________2. forms as outpocketing from hypothalamus
__________3. location of cell bodies of neurons secreting oxytocin
__________4. composed of two capillary networks and through which TRH moves
__________5. inhibits release of growth hormone
__________6. secretion is increased when osmolality increases
__________7. stimulates contraction of smooth muscle in breast and uterus
__________8. destruction of gonadotrophs would result in deficiency of which hormone(s)
__________9. inhibited by REM sleep and high blood glucose concentration,
__________10. stimulated by low blood glucose concentration and deep sleep
__________10. production stimulated by growth hormone
__________11. stimulates skeletal growth by increasing formation of cartilage
__________12. results from deficiency of growth hormone or somatomedin
__________13. precursor of thyroid hormones
__________14. deficiency results in no production of T_3
__________15. results from hypothyroidism

II. Complete the Table

stimulates

Hypothalamic hormone → stimulates → Cell type in anterior pituitary → releases → hormone → stimulates → gland → releases → hormone or product

Hypothalamic hormone	Cell type in anterior pituitary	hormone	gland	hormone or product
	CORTICOTROPHS			
TRH				
		prolactin		
			ovaries	
			testis	

III. For each of the situations, indicate whether growth hormone increases, decreases, or is unaffected.

_________1) absence of somatotrophs
_________2) low blood glucose concentration
_________3) excess of somatostatin
_________4) destruction of posterior pituitary
_________5) high blood glucose concentration
_________6) cut through median eminence

IV. For each situation, indicate the effect (increase, decrease, none) on the secretion of thyroid hormones.

_________1) dietary deficiency of iodide
_________2) cut through median eminence
_________3) destruction of posterior pituitary
_________4) destruction of gonadotrophs
_________5) lack of TSH
_________6) excess of TRH
_________7) excess of thyroid hormones in plasma
_________8) dietary deficiency of protein
_________9) decrease in body temperature

CHAPTER 14 THE ADRENAL GLANDS

Chapter Outline

I. Gross Anatomy of the Adrenal Glands
 * The endocrine components of each adrenal gland are the cortex, which produces and secretes several different steroid hormones, and the medulla which secretes catecholamines.

II. The Adrenal Cortex

A. Cell Structure of the Adrenal Cortex
 * The adrenal cortex can be divided into three different zones:
 (1) zona glomerulosa which produces mineralocorticoids;
 (2) zona fasciculata which produces glucocorticoids; and,
 (3) zona reticularis which produces and secretes primarily androgens.

B. Regulation of the Functions of the Adrenal Cortex by ACTH
 * The activity of the adrenal cortex is under control of ACTH which is regulated by CRH. The relationship between CRH, ACTH and the adrenal cortex is the hypothalamo-pituitary-adrenal axis.
 * ACTH promotes growth and function of all three zones and regulates glucocorticoid secretion by the cells of the zona fasciculata.

C. Biosynthesis of Steroid Hormones by the Adrenal Cortex
 * The first step in steroid synthesis is the conversion of cholesterol to pregnenolone. Steroid synthesis occurs on demand and is regulated by the availability of the enzyme catalyzing the first step.
 * Each zone in the cortex contains the enzymes for synthesizing its specific steroid hormone.

D. Secretion and Actions of Glucocorticoids

1. Regulation of Glucocorticoid Secretion
 a. Secretion of glucocorticoid is regulated by a sequence of steps beginning with the release of CRH by the hypothalamus.
 b. The release of CRH is determined by inputs from higher brain centers to the hypothalamus.
 c. Glucocorticoid secretion is responsive to circadian variations in CRH and ACTH secretion which are related to the individual's sleep-wake patterns.
 d. Glucocorticoid synthesis and secretion are responsive to physically or physiologically stressful stimuli such as hypoglycemia, physical trauma and strenuous exercise, and by emotionally stressful stimuli such as acute anxiety.
 e. Glucocorticoid secretion is regulated by a series of negative feedback loops.
 f. Cortisol is transported in the blood by carrier proteins.
 g. Glucocorticoids complex with intracellular receptors and exert their effect on DNA.
 h. Cortisol exerts its primary effects on the liver, skeletal muscle, and adipose tissue. The overall effect is catabolic. The effects are summarized in Table 14.2.
 i. Cortisol has an amplifying effect on the action of other hormones and enhances the responsiveness of blood vessels.

2. The Pharmacological Effects of Glucocorticoids
   a. The two most important pharmacological effects of glucocorticoids are their
      (1) anti-inflammatory effects; and
      (2) immunosuppressive effects.

E. Secretion and Actions of Mineralocorticoids

1. Regulation of Mineralocorticoid Secretion
   a. The two primary regulators of aldosterone secretion are:
      (1) potassium ions; and,
      (2) angiotensin II, a peptide hormone.
   b. Angotensin II is formed by a sequence of steps that begins in the kidney and is collectively known as the renin-angiotensin system.
   c. Renin, produced by the kidney, acts on angiotensinogen to form angiotensin I. In the lungs this molecule is converted to angiotensin II which then travels to the adrenal cortex. The amount of aldosterone is related to the amount of renin released from the kidney.
   d. An increase in plasma potassium concentration stimulates aldosterone secretion. Aldosterone promotes potassium excretion by the kidneys. Aldosterone and the kidneys comprise two components of a feedback loop regulating plasma potassium concentration.

2. The Effects of Mineralocorticoids
   a. Aldosterone plays an important role in regulating fluid balance in the body and acts primarily on the kidneys.

F. Abnormalities of Adrenal Cortex Function

1. Excess Secretion of Glucocorticoids
   a. Cushing's Syndrome results from excess cortisol secretion.

2. Insufficient Secretion of Adrenal Cortex Steroids
   a. Addison's disease results from an overall deficiency in steroid production by the adrenal cortex.

III. The Adrenal Medulla
   * The adrenal medulla is an important component of the sympathetic nervous system and secretes catecholamines.

A. Anatomy of the Adrenal Medulla
   * The functional unit of the adrenal medulla is the chromaffin cell which is innervated directly by preganglionic fibers of the sympathetic nervous systems.
   * Chromaffin cells secrete epinephrine which is carried via the blood to various effector organs in the body.

B. Synthesis and Secretion of Epinephrine
   * The pathway for synthesis of epinephrine is: tyrosine $\longrightarrow$ DOPA $\longrightarrow$ norepinephrine $\longrightarrow$ epinephrine. The rate limiting step is the conversion of tyrosine to DOPA. Epinephrine is packaged and concentrated in vesicles known as chromaffin granules which are released when the sympathetic neuron discharges.

C. The Actions of Epinephrine
   * The adrenal medulla triggers a sequence of events appropriate to "fight-or-flight" situations.
   * Many effects serve to increase and redistribute blood flow between various tissues.

* Epinephrine increases the ability of the blood to transport oxygen and affects metabolic processes in several tissues such as the liver, skeletal muscle, and adipose tissue. It increases the breakdown of stored fuels into metabolizable substrates. A summary of the metabolic effects of epinephrine is presented in Table 14-4.

IV. Summary of Effects of Adrenal Hormones
  * The hormones of the adrenal glands produce effects which promote survival and enable the body to adapt to potentially harmful situations.

Chapter Objectives

1. Identify the hormones produced by each of the three zones in the adrenal cortex.
2. Describe the hypothalamo-pituitary adrenal axis regarding regulation of the functions of the cortex by ACTH.
3. Describe the biosynthesis of steroid hormones from cholesterol and factors affecting it.
4. Describe two types of stimuli affecting secretion of glucocorticoids.
5. Diagram negative feedback mechanisms in glucocorticoid secretion.
6. Describe the general physiological effects of glucocorticoids and specific effects on the liver, skeletal muscle, adipose tissue, and blood vessels.
7. Describe two pharmacological effects of glucocorticoids.
8. Describe the steps in the renin-angiotensin system and discuss the roles of the kidney, liver and lungs and this system in the regulation of mineralocorticoid secretion.
9. Describe the feedback loop involving the kidney, potassium ions, sodium and aldosterone in the regulation of mineralocorticoid secretion.
10. Summarize the physiological effects of hyposecretion and hypersecretion of glucocorticoids.
11. Describe the relationship between the adrenal medulla and sympathetic nervous system and then compare their effects on the body.
12. Outline the synthetic pathway for epinephrine.
13. Summarize the effects of epinephrine on the cardiovascular system, muscle, the liver, and adipose tissue.
14. Summarize the effects of adrenal hormones.

Key Terms

Addison's disease
adrenal cortex
adrenal medulla
adrenocorticotropic hormone (ACTH)
aldosterone
androgen
angiotensin I, II
angiotensin-converting enzyme
angiotensinogen
anti-inflammatory
catabolic
chromaffin cell
chromaffin granule
circadian rhythm
corticosteroid-binding globulin
cortisol
Cushing's syndrome
dihydroxyphenylalanine (DOPA)
epinephrine
fight-or-flight
glucocorticoid
gluconeogenesis
granular cells
hypothalamo-pituitary adrenal axis
immunosuppressive
lipolysis
mineralocorticoid
negative feedback
norepinephrine
permissive action
renin
renin-angiotensin system
steroidogenic effect
sympathodrenal system
trophic effect
tyrosine hydroxylase
vascular reactivity
zona fasciculata
zona glomerulosa
zona reticularis

Testing Your Knowledge

I. Matching. Select the correct word from the Key Terms

_________1. cells produce glucocorticoids
_________2. cells produce mineralocorticoids
_________3. cells produce androgens
_________4. site of production of epinephrine
_________5. caused by hypersecretion of glucocorticoids
_________6. caused by hyposecretion of glucocorticoids and mineralocorticoids
_________7. production affected by sleep-wake pattern and circadian variation
_________8. pharmacological effect of high concentration of cortisol
_________9. immunosuppressive hormone produced from cholesterol
_________10. role in regulation of mineralocorticoid secretion, produced by kidney
_________11. end product of renin-angiotensin system that binds to receptors in cortex
_________12. increase in plasma potassium ion concentration causes increase of this hormone
_________13. hormone synthesized from tyrosine
_________14. stimulates lipolysis in adipose tissue
_________15. transports cortisol in blood

II. For each situation indicate the effect (increase, decrease, none) on the production of a glucocorticoid like cortisol.

_________1) cut through median eminence
_________2) destruction of posterior pituitary
_________3) destruction of zona glomerulosa
_________4) hypoglycemia
_________5) increased plasma concentration of cortisol
_________6) decrease in level of ACTH
_________7) increase in CRH

III. For each situation indicate the effect (increase, decrease, none) on the production of aldosterone.

_________1) destruction of anterior pituitary
_________2) destruction of zona reticularis
_________3) lack of ACTH
_________4) deficiency of renin
_________5) deficiency of receptors to angiotensin II
_________6) increase in blood flow to kidney
_________7) decrease in plasma potassium ion concentration

IV. For each situation indicate the effect (increase, decrease, none) on the production of epinephrine by the adrenal medulla.

_________1) deficiency of tyrosine hydrexylase
_________2) stimulation of sympathetic nervous system
_________3) being chased by an angry dog
_________4) destruction of the posterior pituitary
_________5) cut in the hypothalamic-pituitary portal system

CHAPTER 15 THE ENDOCRINE PANCREAS

Chapter Outline

I. The Islets of Langerhans: Functional Units of the Endocrine Pancreas
   * The islets of Langerhans that comprise the endocrine pancreas, consist of four major cell types:
     (1) alpha cells which produce glucagon,
     (2) beta cells which produce insulin,
     (3) delta cells which produce somatostatin,
     (4) F cells which produce pancreatic polypeptide.
   * Each islet shows an orderly arrangement of the different types of cells.
   * Islets are innervated by the sympathetic and parasympathetic divisions of the autonomic nervous system.

II. The Synthesis and Secretion of Pancreatic Hormones

   A. Insulin: A Response to Increased Glucose in the Blood

      1. Synthesis of Insulin by Beta Cells of the Pancreas
         a. Insulin is derived from the precursor, proinsulin which consists of a single peptide chain containing the insulin subunits A and B linked together by a third peptide.
         b. As the hormone is packaged into secretory vesicles, enzymes cleave proinsulin into the A and B chains and the C-peptide whose only function appears to be its role in insulin synthesis.

      2. Secretion of Insulin in Response to Various Stimuli
         a. Several factors stimulate the release of insulin which is stored in secretory vesicles in the beta cells. These include:
            (1) increase in blood glucose concentration,
            (2) ingestion of high-protein meat and amino acids like arginine,
            (3) presence of fatty acids,
            (4) gastrointestinal hormones such as gastrin and secretin,
            (5) acetylcholine from postgangliance fibers of the parasympathetic nervous system,
            (6) drugs like sulfonylureas,
            (7) other hormones like glucagen.
         b. Inhibitors of insulin secretion include:
            (1) somatostatin,
            (2) epinephrine,
            (3) norepinephrine.

   B. Glucagon: A Response to Decreased Glucose in the Blood

      1. Synthesis of Glucagon by Alpha Cells of the Pancreas
         a. Glucagon is derived from a precursor, proglucagon, which is converted to the active hormone.

      2. Secretion of Glucagon in Response to Various Stimuli
         a. Several factors stimulate glucagon secretion from the alpha cells. These include
            (1) decrease in blood glucose concentration,
            (2) amino acids like arginine,
            (3) acetylcholine and epinephrine and norepinephrine from the parasympathetic and sympathetic divisions of the ANS.

b. Inhibitors of glucagon secretion include:
   (1) increase in circulatory fatty acids,
   (2) insulin,
   (3) somatostatin.

C. Somatostatin: A Response to Increased Glucose and Glucagon in the Blood
   * Somatostatin is derived from the precursor, prosomatostatin.
   * Factors stimulating secretion of somatostatin from delta cells include:
     (1) increased blood glucose,
     (2) increased plasma glucagon,
     (3) amino acids.
   * Secretion of insulin, glucagon, and somatostatin is interrelated.

III. The Metabolic Effects of Pancreatic Hormones
   * Glucagon and insulin serve as key components in feedback loops which regulate full homeostasis.
   * Tight regulation of blood glucose concentration is necessary to ensure that the central nervous system, which relies almost solely on glucose for its metabolic needs, has an adequate supply.

A. The Effects of Insulin on Metabolism
   * The major target tissues of insulin are skeletal muscle, adipose tissue (fat), and liver.

1. The Effects of Insulin on Carbohydrate Metabolism
   a. Brain and liver cells are readily permeable to glucose even in the absence of insulin
   b. Glucose enters other tissues like muscle and adipose by both simple and facilitated diffusion. Insulin promotes the movement of glucose transporters from their intracellular location to the plasma membrane.
   c. Insulin
      (1) stimulates glycogenesis in liver and muscle,
      (2) stimulates enzymes of the glycolytic pathway,
      (3) decreases glucose output by the liver.

2. The Effects of Insulin on Lipid Metabolism
   a. Insulin:
      (1) promotes the storage of excess fuel as triglycerides,
      (2) promotes the synthesis of both fatty acid and glycerolphosphate components of triglycerides,
      (3) inhibits lipolysis or triglyceride breakdown.

3. The Effects of Insulin on Protein Metabolism
   a. Insulin:
      (1) promotes protein accumulation in muscle, liver and adipose tissue by increasing protein synthesis and decreasing protein degradation,
      (2) produces a "positive nitrogen balance."

B. The Effects of Glucagon in Metabolism
   * The effects of glucagon are exactly opposite to those of insulin and are mediated through second messengers.
   * Glucagon acts principally on the liver and its overall effect on metabolism is catabolic.

1. The Effects of Glucagon in Carbohydrate Metabolism
   a. Glucagon increases blood glucose concentration by stimulating glycogenolysis and gluconeogenesis.

2. The Effects of Glucagon on Lipid Metabolism
   a. Glucagon stimulates lipolysis and ketogenesis in the liver.

3. The Effects of Glucagon on Protein Metabolism
   a. Glucagon:
      (1) stimulates protein degradation in the liver,
      (2) stimulates the transport of amino acids from the blood to the liver for gluconeogenesis,
      (3) stimulates urea synthesis.

C. The Importance of the Insulin/Glucagon Ratio
   * The insulin-to-glucagon (I/G) ratio is probably more important in determining the overall metabolic state than is the absolute concentration of either hormone.
   * When the I/G ratio is high, the effects of insulin predominate and an anabolic state exists.
   * When the I/G ratio is low, the effects of glucagon predominate and a catabolic state exists.

IV. Overview of the Metabolic Regulation by Hormones: The Fed State Versus the Fasted State

A. Fuel Storage Forms
   * Most calories in the body are stored as triglycerides in adipose tissue. Muscle protein represents about 15% of total stored fuels. Few calories are stored in glycogen in the muscle and liver.

B. The Flow of Nutrients in the Fed State
   * In the fed state the combination of high insulin and low glucagon promotes fuel storage in liver, adipose, and muscle. Glycogen storage is increased in liver and muscle, tryglyceride storage is increased in adipose tissue and protein synthesis is promoted in all three tissues.

C. The Flow of Nutrients in the Fasted State
   * In the fasted state glycogen stores are depleted, muscle protein is degraded and amino acids are used for gluconeogenesis in the liver. The triglyceride stores in adipose tissue are broken down.

V. Diabetes Mellitus
   * Diabetes mellitus is a heterogeneous disease characterized by high blood glucose concentration which results from a deficiency, either relative or absolute, in insulin action. Two forms of diabetes make up 98% of all cases. In both forms there is a genetic component.

A. Type I Diabetes: Insulin-Dependent Diabetes Mellitus
   * Type I Diabetes (IDDM) is characterized either by very low levels of insulin or by an absolute lack of insulin secretion by the pancreas and results from a loss of beta cell function.

B. Type II Diabetes: Non-Insulin-Dependent Diabetes Mellitus
   * Type II diabetes (NIDDM) results when target tissues of insulin lose their responsiveness to the hormone.

C. Complications of Diabetes

1. Acute Complication of Diabetes
   a. Complications resulting from the absence of either insulin or insulin action, include:
      (1) hyperglycemia,
      (2) polyurea and dehydration,
      (3) ketoacidosis and electrolyte imbalances in type I.

2. Chronic Secondary Complications of Diabetes
   a. Secondary complications may include:
      (1) reduced circulation to the brain, heart and lower extremeties resulting in stroke, heart attack or loss of limb;
      (2) lesions in microvasculature in the kidney and retina which may lead to kidney disease and diabetic retinopathy;
      (3) diabetic neuropathy involving fibers of the ANS and peripheral sensory nerves.

Chapter Learning Objectives

1. List the major cell types of the islets and the function of each.
2. Describe the synthesis of insulin.
3. List several factors stimulating insulin secretion and two factors inhibiting it.
4. List several factors stimulating glucagon secretion and three factors inhibiting it.
5. Describe the general effects of insulin on carbohydrate, lipid, and protein metabolism.
6. Describe the general effects of glucagon in carbohydrate, lipid and protein metabolism.
7. Relate the concept of insulin/glucagon (I/G) ratio to the metabolic activities.
8. List the fuel storage forms according to amount of energy stored.
9. Compare the fed and fasted states as to flow of nutrients like glycogen, glucose, amino acids, triglycerides and proteins.
10. Compare type I and type II forms of diabetes as to cause of elevated blood glucose, characteristics and treatment.
11. Describe acute and chronic secondary complications of diabetes.
12. Discuss the physiological reasons for the tight regulation of blood glucose concentrations and feedback loops operating to maintain homeostasis for glucose.

Key Concepts

alpha cells
anabolic effect
beta cells
C-peptide
calorie density
catabolic effect
dehydration
delta cells
diabetic neuropathy
diabetic retinopathy
electrolyte imbalance
endocrine pancreas
exocrine pancreas
F cells
gestational diabetes
glucagon
glucosuria
gluconeogenesis
glycogenolysis
hormone-sensitive lipase
hyperglycemia
insulin
insulin-dependent diabetes mellitus (IDDM, Type I)
insulin-to-glucagon ratio (I/G)
insulin resistance
islets of Langerhans
ketoacidosis
ketogenesis
ketone
ketone bodies
lipoprotein lipase
nitrogen balance (positive, negative)
non-insulin-dependnet diabetes mellitus (NIDDM, Type II)
pancreatic polypeptide
polyuria
proglucagon
proinsulin
prosomatostatin
somatostatin
sulfonytureas
triglyceride
urea synthesis

Testing Your Knowledge

I. Matching. Select the correct word from the Key Terms

________1. pancreatic cells producing glucagon
________2. pancreatic cells producing insulin
________3. groups of cells comprising endocrine pancreas
________4. precursor of insulin and C-peptide
________5. secreted in response to low blood glucose
________6. secreted in response to high blood glucose
________7. general effect of insulin
________8. conversion of glycogen to glucose
________9. conversion of nonglucose substrates into glucose
________10. disease condition caused by loss of beta cell function
________11. disease condition cause of relative lack of insulin action on its target tissues
________12. describe elevated blood glucose level
________13. secondary effect resulting from urinary loss of ketones
________14. results in loss of feeling in lower limbs
________15. pancreatic cells producing somatostatin

II. Complete the Table

Hormone	Source	Stimulators	Inhibitors	Effect of hormone on: carbohydrate Metabolism	lipid metabolism	protein metabolism
insulin						
glucagon						

III. For each situation, indicate the effect (increase, decrease, no direct effect) on insulin secretion.

________1) decrease in blood glucose level
________2) ingestion of meal high in proteins
________3) increased secretion of somatostatin
________4) destruction of anterior pituitary
________5) activation of sympathetic nervous system
________6) destruction of alpha cells.

IV. For each situation, indicate the effect (increase, decrease, none) on glucagon secretion

________1) increase in blood glucose level
________2) ingestion of high-protein meal
________3) decrease in fatty acid concentration
________4) activation of parasympathetic nervous system
________5) destruction of beta cells
________6) destruction of anterior pituitary

Answers to Questions in Part II

Chapter 7

I. Matching

1. activating state
2. absolute refractory period
3. saltatory conduction
4. electrical synapse potential
5. excitatory postsynaptic
6. glia
7. IPSP
8. soma
9. sensory neuron
10. acetylcholine
11. synaptic vesicle
12. discrete synapse
13. dopamine
14. neuropeptide
15. spatial summation

III. Label the Diagram

1. resting stage
2. threshold, depolarization
3. rising phase, depolarization
4. repolarizing phase, hyperpolarization
5. absolute refractory period, hyperpolarization

Chapter 8

I. Matching

1. dorsal root ganglion
2. dorsal horn
3. generator potential
4. thalamus
5. frequency code of stimulus intensity
6. sensory adaptation
7. proprioceptors
8. nocioceptors
9. phasic discharge
10. fovea
11. cones
12. gnaglion cell
13. lateral geniculate nucleus
14. hair cell
15. gustatory or olfactory

Chapter 9

I. Matching

1. motor neurons
2. extrafusal fiber
3. fast skeletal muscle
4. myoneuronal junction
5. alpha motor neuron
6. motor unit
7. spindle fiber
8. Golgi tendon organ
9. stretch reflex
10. inverse myotatic reflex
11. locomotor generator
12. ventral horn
13. Purkinje
14. semicircular canals
15. saccule, utricle

Chapter 10

I. Matching

1. acetylcholine
2. interomedial lateral nuclei
3. muscarinic, nocotinic
4. alpha, beta
5. continence
6. osmoreceptors
7. ADH, vasopressin
8. carotid, aortic bodies
9. medulla
10. baroreceptors
11. depressor center
12. pressor center
13. adrenal medulla
14. CSF
15. norepinephrine

Chapter 11

I. Matching
1. superchiasmatic nucleus
2. electroencephalogram
3. REM
4. preoptic area
5. raphe nucleus
6. anterior hypothalamus
7. supraoptic nucleus
8. androgen
9. substantia nigra, hypothalamus
10. insomnia
11. habituation
12. classical conditioning
13. Wernicke's area
14. Broca's area
15. aphasia

Chapter 12

I. Matching
1. steroid
2. albumin, prealbumin
3. amine
4. thyroxine
5. peptide hormones
6. dynamic equilibrium
7. receptor-mediated endocytosis
8. tAMP
9. IP_3, DG
10. IP_3
11. steroid
12. mineralocorticoid
13. insulin, glucagon
14. cholesterol
15. signal transducer

Chapter 13

I. Matching
1. anterior pituitary
2. posterior pituitary
3. supraoptic paraventricular nuclei system
4. hypothalamus-pituitary portal
5. somatostatin
6. ADH
7. oxytocin
8. FSH, LH
9. growth hormone
10. somatomedins, IGF-I,-II
11. IGF-I
12. dwarfism
13. thyroglobulin
14. TSH, TRH
15. myxedema

II. 1, 3, 5, 6 decrease
2 increase
4 no effect

IV. 1, 2, 5, 7, 8 decrease
3, 4 no effect
6, 9 increase

Chapter 14

I. Matching
1. zona fasciculata
2. zona glomerulosa
3. zona reticularis
4. chromaffin cell, adrenal medulla
5. Cushing's syndrome
6. Addison's disease
7. ACTH, cortisol
8. anti-inflammatory, immunosuppressive
9. cortisol, glucocorticoid
10. renin
11. angiotensin II
12. aldosterone
13. epinephrine, norepinephrine
14. epinephrine
15. corticosteroid-binding globulin

II. 1, 5, 6, decrease
2, 3 no effect
4, 7 increase

III. 1, 4, 5, 6, 7 decrease
2, 3 no effect

IV. 1 decrease
2, 3 increase
3, 4 no effect

Chapter 15

I. Matching
1. alpha
2. beta
3. islets of Langerhans
4. proinsulin
5. glucagon
6. insulin, somatostatin
7. anabolic
8. glycogenolysis
9. gluconeogenesis
10. Type I IDDM
11. Type II NIDDM
12. hyperglycemia
13. electrolyte imbalance
14. diabetic neuropathy
15. delta

III. 1, 3, 5 decrease
2, 6 increase
4 no direct effect

IV. 1 decrease
2, 3, 4, 5 increase
6 no direct effect

CHAPTER 16 MUSCLE

Chapter Outline

I. Overview: The Roles and Types of Muscle

A. Muscle is an Effector
* Muscle effects changes prescribed by the nervous system.

B. Muscle as a Motor
* Muscle acts as a biological motor. They consume fuel, do useful work and produce heat.

C. Muscle as a Regulator
* Muscle helps regulate many body functions.

D. Classification of Muscle Types.
* Muscles may be categorized by location and function, microscopic structure or mode of control and action.

1. Classification of Muscles by Location and Function.
   a. Skeletal muscles are used for locomotion and maintaining body posture.
   b. Visceral muscles line the walls of internal organs but are also located in blood vessels and sensory organs.
   c. Cardiac muscle is found only in the heart.

2. Classification of Muscles by Structure
   a. Skeletal and cardiac muscles appear striated upon viewing with a microscope while smooth muscle is not.

3. Classification of Muscles by Mode of Action and Control
   a. Skeletal muscle must receive a specific signal from the CNS in order to function.
   b. Most movements of skeletal muscle are voluntary.
   c. The actions of most smooth muscle are involuntary and initiated by the ANS.
   d. Smooth muscle may be classified as multiunit or unitary smooth muscle depending on its mode of control.

II. The Structure of Muscle
A. The Structure of Skeletal Muscle
a. Gross Structure of Skeletal Muscle
(1) The gross structure of skeletal muscle reflects its major function, contraction.
(2) The skeleton works with the muscles as a lever system.
(3) Muscles are arranged in antagonistic pairs.
(4) A muscle is composed of muscle fibers (cells) that are covered by a connective tissue sheet.
b. Cellular and Molecular Structure of Skeletal Muscle
(1) The striations seen in muscle fibers are composed of myofilaments, which differ from each other in their size and molecular composition.
(2) Myofilaments are organized into a sarcomere, the basic unit of contraction in the skeletal muscle.
(3) The thick myofilaments which overlap the thin filaments are composed of myosin, while the thin myofilaments are composed of action.
(4) Extensions of the sarcolemma extend inward as t-tubules.

B. The Structure of Cardiac Muscles
   * There is a strong mechanical and electrical connection among cardiac muscle cells.

C. The Structure of Smooth Muscle

   1. The Ultrastructure of Smooth Muscle
      a. The cells form gap junctions which allow for coordination of smooth muscle activity.

   2. Mechanical Arrangements of Smooth Muscle
      a. Smooth muscle is organized into layers.
      b. Coordinated movement often involves the alternate contraction and relaxation of two muscle layers.

III. The Function of Muscle

A. The Nature of Skeletal Muscle Contraction

   1. Isometric Contractions in the Laboratory
      a. The sliding filament hypothesis describes muscle cell contraction.
      b. The length of a muscle before contraction has an important effect on the amount of force the muscle can exert when it is stimulated.
      c. The isometric length-tension curve describes the relationship in which the force capability of the muscle is greatest at some intermediate length.

   2. Isotonic Contractions in the Laboratory
      a. The weight of the afterload affects the length of the isometric portion of the mixed contraction.
      b. The weight of the afterload affects the speed at which a muscle shortens. This relationship is described by the force-velocity curve.
      c. The power output of the muscle varies with the afterload.

B. The Nature of Contraction in Cardiac Muscle and Smooth Muscle
   * The contraction of cardiac and smooth muscle can be described by force velocity curves.

IV. The Control of Muscle

A. Control of Muscle by Cellular Membrane Systems

   1. Action Potentials in the Plasma Membrane
      a. Stimulation of the muscle membrane generates an action potential.

   2. Action Potentials in the Transverse Tubular System
      a. The action potential is also conducted into the depths of the muscle fiber through the transverse tubular system (t-system).

   3. Calcium Ions in the Sarcoplasmic Reticulum
      a. The t-tubules come in close contact with membranes of the sarcoplasmic reticulum (SR) that stores and releases ionized calcium, the substance controlling contractile activity of muscle proteins.

B. Control of Muscle by Calcium Ions

1. The Molecular Mechanisms of Muscle Contraction
   a. The sequence of events during msucle contraction is:
      (1) generation of action potential through t-tubules.
      (2) release of calcium ions from SR.
      (3) binding of calcium ions to troponin complex attached to tropomyosin on action.
      (4) interaction of actin with myosin crossbridge.
      (5) movement of actin filaments toward center of sarcomere by myosin head.
      (6) repetition of cycle of formation of crossbridges between actin and myosin, power stroke, and detachment of myosin from actin.
   b. ATP provides energy for power stroke of myosin head and for detachment of myosin head from actin.
   c. The cycle is repeated as long as ATP and calcium ions are present.
   d. When stimulation of the muscle ceases, calcium ions are pumped back into the SR.

2. Actin-Linked Regulation of Muscle Contraction
   a. Skeletal and cardiac muscle contraction is regulated through some action on the thin filaments.

3. Myosin-Linked Regulation of Muscle Contraction
   a. Smooth muscle contraction is regulated through myosin filaments.
   b. Attachment of phosphate ion to the myosin light chain is mediated by an enzyme controlled by a calmodulin molecule.
   c. Calcium ions activate calmodulin and the series of reactions leading to muscle contraction.

C. Types of Stimuli that Activate Muscle Contraction

1. Summation of Action Potentials: Producing a Sustained Contraction in Skeletal Muscle.
   a. Stimulation of a muscle before relaxation is complete can result in a contraction that lasts longer and produces more than a single twitch. This process is called summation.

2. Distancing of Action Potentials: Producing Discrete Twitches in Cardiac Muscle
   a. Cardiac muscle is a twitch-only type. In contrast to skeletal muscle, the action potential lasts as long as the contraction itself.
   b. Contractions can be adjusted by the amount of calcium made available for each contraction, and by changes in muscle length.

3. Phasic and Tonic Contractions: A Variety of Responses in Smooth Muscle
   a. Some smooth muscles give twitchlike or phasic contracting in response to a single stimulus or brief bursts of stimuli.
   b. Tonic contractions are long and sustained and develop in response to single or continued stimulation by nerve, drugs or hormones.

D. Control of Muscle by the Central Nervous System

1. Nervous Control of Skeletal Muscle
   a. Skeletal muscle contraction depends on nervous innervation from the somatic division of the CNS.
   b. Acetylcholine is released from the motor neuron into the myoneuronal junction.
   c. All muscle fibers innervated by axons from the same motor neuron are activated together.

2. Nervous Control of Smooth and Cardiac Muscle
   a. Multiunit smooth muscles are very diversely innervated by autonomic nerve fibers and each cell has a rudimentary motor end plate.
   b. In unitary smooth muscles most cells are not innervated, and instead receive their stimulus via local current flow. The muscle acts as a functional syncytium.

V. The Metabolism of Muscle Contraction

A. Energy Pathways in Muscle Contraction
   * The muscle cell uses ATP for contraction and must have an adequate and constant supply for this process.
   * Creative phosphate, a high energy compound, transfers its phosphate to ADP to form ATP.

1. Glycolysis: An Anaerobic Pathway
   a. Glycolysis yields a small amount of ATP.

2. The Citric Acid Cycle: Aerobic Metabolism
   a. Through an aerobic reaction pathway 36 molecules of ATP are produced from a glucose molecule.

3. The Need for an Anaerobic Pathway
   a. Under ordinary activity aerobic metabolism can supply sufficient ATP.
   b. When the level of activity reaches about 70% of the maximum possible, anaerobic metabolism takes over.

4. The Oxygen Debt
   a. After strenuous exercise the muscle is deficient in its stores of creatine phosphate and glycogen but has an excess of lactic acid, the so-called oxygen debt.
   b. The metabolic imbalances are corrected by aerobic metabolism. The lactic acid is oxidized and glycogen resynthesized. Both processes are responsible for the high oxygen consumption of the resting muscle.

5. Muscle Efficiency and Heat Production
   a. Eighty percent of the energy used in muscle metabolism is converted to heat.

B. Types of Muscle Fiber
   * In muscle there are specialized types of fibers that are adapted structurally and biochemically to particular tasks.

1. Red Muscle Fibers and Aerobic Metabolism
   a. Red muscle fibers which contain much myoglobin are categorized as fast twitch or slow twitch.
   b. Their speeds of contraction and resistance to fatigue differ.

2. White Muscle Fibers and Anaerobic Metabolism
   a. In contrast to red fibers, white muscle fibers are adapted for fast and powerful contractions, but fatigue quickly.

3. Patterns of Innervation and Muscle Growth
   a. Most muscles contain a mixture of the different fiber types.
   b. Patterns of innervation and usage during early development play an important role in deciding the ultimate distribution of fiber types.
   c. The Development of Muscle in Response to Use
      * Muscle responds to increased or decreased use.

<u>Chapter Learning Objectives</u>

1. Describe three different ways that muscle could be categorized.
2. Describe the gross structure of a skeletal muscle and the arrangement of muscles in the body.
3. Describe the cellular and molecular structure of skeletal muscles, particularly a sarcomere.
4. Describe the interrelationship among the sarcolemma, the t-tubules, and sarcoplasmic reticulum.
5. Describe the cellular structure of cardiac muscle.
6. Describe the cellular structure of smooth muscle.
7. Compare the three types of muscle as to gross and cellular structure.
8. Compare isometric and isotonic contractions.
9. Compare length-tension curve and force velocity curve as to the relationship represented by each curve.
10. Compare the three types of muscle regarding the mechanics of contraction.
11. Describe the sequence of events that occurs when an action potential reaches the synaptic terminal of a motor neuron.
12. Describe the sequence of events by which the action potential in the muscle fiber results in sliding of the myofilaments and shortening of the sarcomere.
13. Describe how calcium ions control muscle contraction.
14. Describe how a sustained contraction in skeletal muscle is generated and how contractions in cardiac muscle can be adjusted.
15. List some factors blocking myoneuronal transmission.
16. Compare skeletal, smooth and cardiac muscles as to the nature and amount of innervation.
16. Compare a resting muscle, a muscle being used normally and a muscle being strenuously exercised regarding type of energy metabolism occurring and source of energy.
17. Compare white, slow red and fast red muscle fibers as to contraction speed, ability to resist fatigue, ATPase activity, myoglobin content, glycogen content, number of mitochondria, vascularity and role in the body.
18. Describe what happens in a muscle that is exercised isometrically, isotonically or not at all.

Key Terms

A-band
acetylcholine
acetylcholinesterase
actin
actin-linked regulation
afterload
antagonistic pairs
calcium ions
calmodulin
cardiac muscle
contraction
isometric
isotonic
phasic
tonic
creative phosphate
crossbridge
disuse atrophy
end-plate potential
fatigue
force
force-velocity curve
functional syncytium
gap junction
hypertrophy
I-band
inotropic agents
insertion
intercalated disc
involuntary
isometric length-tension curve
lactic acid
lever system
M-line
motorend plate
motor neuron
motor unit
multiunit smooth muscle
muscle fiber
myofibril
myofilament
myoglobin
myoneuronal junction
myosin
myosin-linked regulation
origin
oxygen debt
power output
power stroke
red fibers (fast, slow)
resting force
rigor mortis
sarcolemma
sarcomere
sarcoplasmic reticulum
skeletal muscle
sliding-filament hypothesis
smooth muscle
striated muscle
summation
t-tubules
tendon
tension
tetanus
thick filament
thin filament
tonus
triad
tropomyosin
troponin
twitch (fast, slow)
unitary smooth muscle
voluntary
white fibers
work
Z-line

Testing Your Knowledge

I. Matching. Select the correct word from the Key Terms

__________1. connective tissue attaching muscle to bone
__________2. term describing flexor/extensor combination
__________3. basic unit of contraction in myofiber
__________4. comprise thin filament
__________5. comprise thick filament
__________6. composed of muscle cell plasma membrane and thin layer of connective fibers
__________7. storage sites for calcium ions
__________8. specialized area between cardiac cells providing electrical connection
__________9. contraction in which muscle develops force but does not shorten
__________10. contraction in which force remains constant while muscle shortens
__________11. rate of doing work
__________12. carries action potential to interior cell
__________13. contraction resulting from summation
__________14. produced during oxygen debt
__________15. fiber with fast contraction speed, low myoglobin content and low number of mitochondria

II. Name the structure in the diagram and match with its definitions.

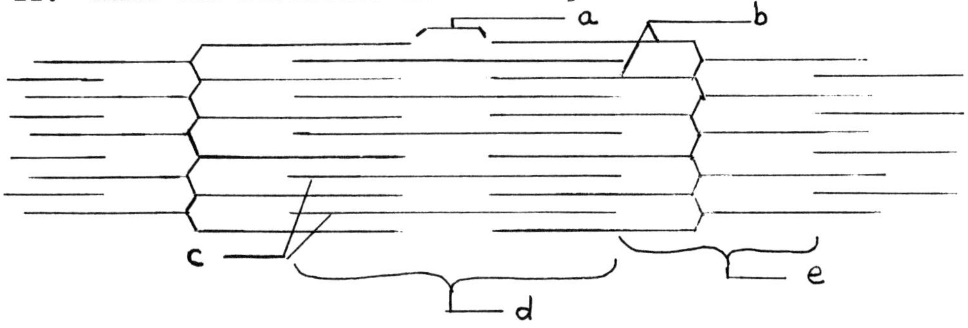

letter			structure
______	1.	composed of myosin	______
______	2.	composed of actin	______
______	3.	location of tropomyosin	______
______	4.	site of Z band	______
______	5.	decreases in size in contracted sarcomere	______
______	6.	stays the same during contraction	______

III. For the given conditions describe what happens to the ability of the skeletal muscle to contract.

______________ 1. deficiency of ADP

______________ 2. high quantity of lactic acid

______________ 3. nonfunctional calcium pump in SR membrane

______________ 4. deficiency of acetylcholinesterase

______________ 5. no t-system

CHAPTER 17 HEMATOLOGY AND IMMUNOLOGY

Chapter Outline

I. Overview: The Nature and Properties of Blood

A. Hematopoiesis: The Generation of Blood Cells
* Whole blood consists of plasma in which erythrocytes, leukocytes and thrombocytes are suspended.
* All blood cells derive from pluripotent uncommitted stem cells located mainly in the bone marrow.

B. The Properties of Whole Blood

1. Volume, Specific Gravity, and Viscosity of Blood
a. Blood volume varies with age and sex.
b. The specific gravity is usually greater than 1.000 and depends on the number of cells and concentration of chemicals dissolved in the plasma.
c. Blood viscosity is much greater than that of water and is determined by the number of cells present and mutual attraction of molecules in the plasma.

II. Erythrocytes: Red Blood Cells

A. Characteristics of Erythrocytes
* Erythrocytes transport oxygen and carbon dioxide in the blood. They have a shape suited to their function.

B. Hemoglobin and the Oxygen-Carrying Capacity of Erythrocytes
* Hemoglobin is composed of a globin molecule and four attached heme groups each of which carries an oxygen.
* About 98% of oxygen is carried in the blood as oxyhemoglobin.

C. Variations and Abnormalities in Hemoglobin Structure
* Several forms of hemoglobin have been found in human blood. The heme part is the same but the globin part varies depending on the composition of its subunit peptide chains.
* The type of hemoglobin varies with developmental stages.

D. Erythropoiesis: The Generation of Red Blood Cells
* Erythopoiesis involves a series of steps during which an uncommitted stem cell differentiates into a reticulocyte which matures into an erythrocyte. During this process the cell loses its nucleus and acquires hemoglobin.
* Erythropoiesis requires iron, amino acids, copper, vitamins B_2, pyridoxine, and folic acid. A stable supply of iron is maintained through a feedback mechanism.
* Erythropoiesis is hormonally controlled by erythropoietin.

E. Hemolysis: Destruction of Erythrocytes
* After about four months erythrocytes are destroyed by macrophages.
* Important components of the cell are recycled within the body.

F. Red Blood Cell Indices and Anemia
* Anemia is characterized by an abnormally low oxygen-carrying capacity of the blood that can result from a low number of erythrocytes and/or hemoglobin.
* Anemia may result from a failure of erythrocyte production or an excessive rate of destruction.
* Red cell indices are used to detect abnormalites in erythrocyte size, shape and color.

G. Polycythemia: An Increase in Red Blood Cells
   * Polycythemia is a relative or absolute increase in the number of circulating red cells above 6 million per cubic millimeter.

III. Leukocytes: White Blood Cells

A. Types of Leukocytes
   * Leukocytes are classified according to the shapes of their nuclei and the presence or absence of cytoplasmic granules.
   * Granular leukocytes include basophils, nuetrophils and iosinophils. Agranular leukocytes include monocytes and lymphocytes.
   * Each type of leukocyte plays a different role in body defense.

1. Granulocytes: Granular Leukocytes
   a. Neutrophils actively phagocytize microorganisms, particulate matter and fibrin. They are the first cells to arrive at the site of a bacterial invasion.
   b. Eosinophils detoxify foreign proteins and other substances.
   c. Basophils release histamine in areas of tissue damage to increase blood flow and attract leukocytes to the damaged area.

2. Agranulocytes: Agranular Leukocytes
   a. T-lymphocytes originate from stem cells in the bone marrow but complete their development in the thymus where they acquire receptors enabling them to recognize antigens.
   b. Upon the presence of a foreign antigen preconditional T-lymphocytes may
      (1) attach directly,
      (2) release lymphokenes or toxins that neutralize the antigen or activate complement,
      (3) stimulate B-lymphocytes, or
      (4) produce a clone of lymphocytes responsive to the antigen, i.e., confer cell-mediated immunity.
   c. B-lymphocytes originate in the bone marrow from which they migrate to lymphoid tissues in the spleen, tonsils, lymph nodes and walls of the small intestine.
   d. When stimulated by a foreign antigen B-lymphocytes become specialized to produce antibodies against the antigen and as memory cells.
   e. Monocytes originate in bone marrow and develop into macrophages, large phagocytic cells.

B. Leukopoiesis: The Generation of White Blood Cells
   * The life span of a leukocyte depends on the role it plays in defense.

C. Leukocytosis: An Increase in White Blood Cells
   * Leukocytosis is an abnormal increase in the total number of circulating leukocytes and may have physiological or pathological causes.

D. Leukopenia: A Reduction in White Blood Cells

IV. Thrombocytes (Platelets)
* Platelets which break off megakaryocytes play a role in maintaining hemostasis.

V. Plasma

A. The Composition of Plasma
* Plasma contains inorganic substances, proteins, nonprotein organic substances and varying amounts of hormones, enzymes, pigments, dissolved gases, etc.

B. Plasma Proteins
* Plasma proteins play roles in maintaining fluid balance and pH.

1. Albumin plays a role in transport and maintenance of fluid balance.

2. Globulin
   a. Alpha and beta globulins transport metals, lipids, vitamins, hormones, and other substances in addition to maintaining fluid balance.
   b. Gamma globulin functions in immunological defense.

3. Fibrinogen plays a role in the formation of blood clots.

VI. Hemostasis: Mechanisms to Prevent Blood Loss

A. Vasoconstriction: An Autonomic Nervous System Response
* Vasoconstriction results from local muscle spasm in the wall of the injured blood vessels and is maintained by vascostrictor chemicals released from platelets accumulating at the damaged site.

B. Platelet Aggregation: The Framework for Coagulation
* At the damaged site platelets release stored chemicals and form an aggregate or plug.

C. Coagulation: The Production of Fibrin
* Blood clot production occurs in three stages.

1. Stage I: Formation of a Prothrombin Converting Factor
   a. The sequence of steps in the extrinsic pathway is:
      (1) release of tissue lipoprotein thromboplastin (Factor III);
      (2) interaction of Factor III with Factor VII and calcium ions to form Factor X;
      (3) Factor X plus calcium ions complexes with Factor V to form prothrombin converting factor.
   b. The sequence of steps in intrinsic coagulation is:
      (1) activation of Factor XII which then activates Factor XI,
      (2) Factor XI plus calcium ions activate Factor IX which interacts with Factor VIII in the presence of calcium ions to form a complex activating Factor X.

2. Stage II: Conversion of Prothrombin to Thrombin
   a. Prothrombin is converted to thrombin in the presence of calcium ions and prothrombin-converting factor.

3. Stage III: Conversion of Fibrinogen to Fibrin
   a. Thrombin converts fibrinogen to fibrin monomer which spontaneously polymerize to form the clot.

D. The Retraction of a Clot
  * Retraction is caused by platelet factor thrombosthenin.

E. Fibrinolysis. The Dissolution of a Clot
  * The dissolution of a clot may occur enzymatically or by neutrophils and macrophages.

F. Anticoagulants
  * Antithromboplastin, antithrombin and heparin are physiological anticoagulants.
  * Therapeutic coagulants are classified on the bans of action into three groups.

G. Disorders of Hemostasis
  * Abnormalities of hemostasis occur as a result of platelet defects, coagulation defects, excessive production of anticoagulants, or a combination of these.

VII. Immunology: The Body's Defense System

A. The Recognition of "Self" and "Nonself"

B. Nonspecific Defense Processes

1. Physical and Chemical Barriers
   a. Nonspecific defense processes include
      (1) the skin,
      (2) mucous membranes and mucus,
      (3) antimicrobial chemicals in body secretions like sweat, tears, saliva.

2. Interferons
   a. Interferons, secreted by cells infected by a virus, stimulate production of antiviral proteins in adjacent cells and activate natural killer cells.

3. Complement
   a. Complement proteins interact in a defined sequence to promote lysis of certain microbes and the release of chemical signals. The sequence is initiated when an antibody reacts with an antigen.

4. Inflammation
   a. The clinical signs of inflammation are redness, heat, edema, and pain.

5. Phagocytosis
   a. Phagocytes are divided into two groups:
      (1) neutrophils,
      (2) monocyte/macrophages.
   b. Some macrophages are fixed while others wander.
   c. Macrophages need to be activated by complement proteins, etc. to become highly phagocytic.

C. Specific Defense Processes
  * There are two types of specific defense responses: cell-mediated immune responses and antibody-mediated immune responses.

1. Cell-Mediated Immune Responses
   a. This type of response involves macrophages and T-lymphocytes which collaborate in the direct destruction of viruses and foreign cells.

b. The macrophage presents the foreign antigen to a competent T-lymphocyte which has an antigen-MHC receptor.
c. T-lymphocytes are divided into two major groups depending on the class of MHC proteins they recognize.
d. Cell-mediated immune response involves several types of cells and occurs in a sequence of steps:
   (1) macrophage presents antigen-MHCII protein to a competent T_4 cell which becomes activated.
   (2) macrophage secretes interleukin-1 that stimulates T_4 cell to differentiate and form a clone of inducer T and helper T cells.
   (3) inducer T cells secrete lymphokine which induces T_8 cells to differentiate and form a clone of cytotoxic and suppressor T cells.
   (4) cytotoxic T cells kill infected cells
   (5) some of the helper and cytotoxic T's remain as memory cells.

2. Antibodies
   a. Antibodies are composed of two identical light and two identical heavy chains, each of which has a constant portion and variable portion.
   b. The variable portion contains the antigen-specific binding site.
   c. The structure of the heavy chain defines the class and role of immunoglobulin, IgG; IgA; IgD; IgM; IgE.
   d. The antibody-antigen complex may stimulate phagocytosis activate complement, etc.

3. Antibody-Mediated Immune Response
   a. The B-lymphocytes with assistance from the T_4 helper cells are responsible for antibody-mediated immunity.
   b. The reaction between antigen and antibody is specific.
   c. B-lymphocytes develop competency in the bone marrow.
   d. An activated B-lymphocyte displays an antigen-MHC complex which is recognized by a helper T cell. The T cell secretes interleukines which stimulate the B-lymphocyte to divide and differentiate into clones of plasma cells and memory cells.
   e. Plasma cells secrete antibodies which travel via the lymph and blood to the invasion site.
   f. Memory cells permit rapid mobilization of immune response upon subsequent exposure to the same antigen.

VII. Blood Types
   * Incompatibilities of blood are due to the presence of agglutinogens within red blood cell membranes and specific antibodies called agglutinins in the blood plasma.

   A. The ABO Blood Group

   B. The Rh Blood Group

<u>Chapter Learning Objectives</u>

1. List and describe the various cellular components as to function, production, and distinguishing characteristics.
2. Compare erythropoiesis and hemolysis of erythrocytes.
3. Describe the three red cell indices and how they would vary in the following disease states: hemolytic anemia, pernicious anemia, aplastic anemia and polycythemia.
4. Describe the physiological role of plasma proteins.

5. List and discuss the main points of the four interrelated events constituting hemostasis.
6. Describe five nonspecific defense mechanisms.
7. For cell-mediated immune responses identify the four types of T cells and their function.
8. Describe how a T-lymphocyte becomes competent.
9. Describe the structure of an antibody molecule and the function of each part.
10. List the five classes of immunoglobulins and the general function of each.
11. Outline the steps in antibody-mediated immune response.
12. Compare cell-mediated and antibody-mediated immune responses as to cells involved, development of competence, activation, mechanism by which antigen is destroyed, and the production of memory cells.
13. Compare the A, B, AB and O blood types as to the type of agglutinogen and agglutinin that are present on cells and in the plasma, respectively.
14. Describe the molecular basis of the Rh blood group system and the consequences of incompatibility between mother and fetus.

Key Terms

agglutinin
agglutinogen
agranulocyte
albumin
amoeboid movement
anemia
antibody
antibody-mediated immune response
anticoagulant
antigen
antithrombin
aplastic anemia
basophil
bilirubin
bone marrow
cell-mediated immunity
chemotaxis
coagulation
competence
complement
cytotoxic T cell
differential white blood cell count
erythrocyte
erythropoiesis
erythropoietin
extramedullary erythropoiesis
fibrin
fibrinogen
fibrinolysin
fibrinolysis
globin
granulocytes
granulopoiesis
helper T cell
hemophilia
hematocrit
heme group
hemoglobin (types A1, A2, F)
hemolysis
hemolytic anemia
hemostasis
heparin
hypoxia
immunoglobulin (IgA, E,D,G,M)
inducer T cell
inflammation
Kupffer cells
leukemia (acute, chronic)
leukocyte
leukocyte-inducing factor
leukopenia
leukopoiesis
lymphocyte (B,T4,T8)
lymphokines
lysozyme
macrophage
major histocompatibility complex
mean corpuscular hemoglobin (MCH)
mean corpuscular hemoglobin concentration (MCHC)
mean corpuscular volume index (MCV)
megakaryocyte memory cell
monocyte
natural biller cell
opsonization
oxygen-carrying capacity
oxyhemoglobin
pathogen
phagocytosis
plasma
plasma cell
platelet (thrombocyte)
pluripotent uncommitted stem cell
polycythemia
prothrombin-converting factor
reticulocyte
sedimentation rate
serum
specific gravity
suppressor T cell
thrombin
thymus
titer
transferrin
variable portion
vicosity

Testing Your Understanding

I. Matching. Select the correct word from the Key Terms.

__________ 1. red blood cells
__________ 2. development of red blood cells from stem cells
__________ 3. measure of blood's resistance to flow

__________ 4. oxygen carrying molecule
__________ 5. term defining destruction of erythrocytes
__________ 6. blood condition characterized by low oxygen carrying capacity
__________ 7. most numerous type of granulocyte
__________ 8. granulocyte which increase in number in allergic and autoimmune reactions
__________ 9. type of immunity involving T-lymphocytes
__________ 10. cells producing antibodies
__________ 11. disease characterized by proliferation of hematopoietic cells that are immature
__________ 12. anucleate, membrane bodies that play a role in clot formation
__________ 13. converts fibrinogen to fibrin
__________ 14. set of proteins which promote types of microbes
__________ 15. T cells that attack and kill infected cells displaying antigen

II. <u>Complete the Table.</u>

Type of Cell	Origin	Characteristics # nuclei, shape, granules	Function
erythrocyte			
neutrophil			
basophil			
eosinophil			
T-lymphocyte			
B-lymphocyte			
thrombocyte			
monocyte			

CHAPTER 18 THE HEART

Chapter Outline

I. Overview of the Cardiovascular System
  * The systemic circulation consists of many separate pathways called vascular beds which are arranged in parallel with one another.
  * Blood flow to vascular beds is controlled according to the needs of different body parts.

  A. The Systemic Circulation
    * The pathway to blood flow through the systemic circulation is: aorta → arteries → arterioles → capillaries → venules → veins → inferior and superior vena cavae.

  B. The Pulmonary Circulation
    * The pathway of blood flow through the pulmonary circulation is: pulmonary trunk → pulmonary arteries → capillaries → pulmonary veins.

  C. Blood Flow and Blood Pressure: Physical Principles
    * Blood flow occurs in response to the pressure gradient between two points and is proportional to the difference in blood pressure between the two points.
    * Resistance measures opposition to blood flow.
    * The relationship between blood flow (F), driving pressure (P_1-P_2) and resistance (R) is:

$$F = \frac{P_1 - P_2}{R}$$

II. The Heart: A Muscular Pump

  A. Chambers of the Heart
    * The right and left atria receive blood from the systemic and pulmonary circulations, respectively.
    * The right and left ventricles pump blood into the pulmonary and systemic circulations, respectively.

    1. Valves in the Heart
      a. The unidirectional flow of blood through the heart is: right atrium → tricuspid valve → right ventricle → pulmonary valve → pulmonary circulation → left atrium mitral valve → left ventricle → aortic valve → systemic circulation.
      b. Valves ensure unidirectional blood flow

    2. The Walls of the Heart
      a. The walls of the heart are composed of three distinct layers:
        (1) endocardium (the inner lining);
        (2) myocardium (cardiac muscle); and,
        (3) epicardium (outer surface).

  B. Electrical Activation of the Heart: The Cardiac Action Potential

    1. Phases of the Cardiac Action Potential
      a. The action potential can be broken down into the following phases, depending on changes occurring in the membrane:
        (1) Phase 0 - rapid depolarization due to influx of sodium ions
        (2) Phase 1 - repolarization when sodium permeability declines
        (3) Phase 2 - plateau - influx of calcium ions, efflux of potassium ions leads

(4) Phase 3 - repolarization
(5) Phase 4 - steady membrane potential at original value until next beat

2. The Cardiac Action Potential and Contraction of Heart Muscle
   a. During the absolute refractory period, the muscle cannot be stimulated.
   b. Cardiac muscle cells communicate directly with one another as a functional syncytium. The heart is stimulated at one point and the message is relayed to the rest of the heart muscle.

3. Initiation of the Action Potential by Pacemaker Cells
   a. The pacemaker region is the sinoatrial node in the right atrium.
   b. There are several pacemakers, but only one is active at one time.

4. The Sequence of Cardiac Activation
   a. The sequence of cardiac activation is:
      (1) SA node pacemaker → right atrial muscle → left atrial muscle
      (2) right atrial muscle → atrioventricular node in the right atrium → Bundle of His → right and left bundle branches to each ventricle
      (3) Bundle branches → array of Purkinje fibers on endocardial surfaces → muscle of ventricular wall.
   b. As the wave of depolarization passes from the base to the apex, a wave of repolarization passes in the opposite direction.
   c. The electrical activity of the heart can be detected at the body surface by electrocardiography.

C. The Ventricular Pump and the Cardiac Cycle

1. The Ventricular Pump
   a. The pumping process consists of four steps:
      (1) ventricular filling
      (2) ventricular contraction
      (3) ventricular ejection
      (4) ventricular relaxation

2. The Cardiac Cycle
   a. Diastole and systole refer to periods of the cardiac cycle during which ventricles are filling with blood and actively contracting and pumping blood out of the heart. The end of ventricular filling corresponds to the end of diastole.

3. Heart Sounds
   a. The first distinct heart sound occurs at the time of closure of the AV valves at the beginning of systole.
   b. The second distinct heart sound occurs at the time of closure of the semilunar valves and defines the end of systole.

D. Cardiac Output
   * Cardiac output (CO) equals the amount of blood pumped out of the left ventricle and into the aorta in one minute.
   * Stroke volume (SV) is the volume of blood ejected in a single beat
   * Cardiac output = heart rate (HR) times stroke volume:
     CO = HR x SV

1. Regulation of Heart Rate
   a. Heart rate is determined by the rate of depolarization of the SA node.
   b. The rate of depolarization can be altered by:
      (1) stimulation of parasympathetic and sympathetic nerve fibers to the heart;
      (2) presence of hormones like epinephrine;
      (3) plasma electrolyte concentrations; and
      (4) body temperature.

2. Regulation of Stroke Volume
   a. Stroke volume is regulated by intrinsic mechanisms and extrinsic factors such as neural stimulation and circulating hormones
   b. The Frank-Starling law states that the heart adjusts its output in response to changes in input. It describes how changes in end-diastolic volume result in changes in stroke volume.
   c. Changes in contractility result from changes in intracellular calcium and do not require a change in end-diastolic volume.

3. Energy Consumption by the Heart
   a. Cardiac muscle relies upon continuous oxidative metabolism of circulating glucose and fatty acids to produce ATP.
   b. The ability of the heart to contract depends on the availability of oxygen.

Chapter Learning Objectives

1. Diagram the flow of blood through the system circulation.
2. Diagram the flow of blood through the pulmonary circuit.
3. Describe the relationship between blood flow, driving pressure and resistance.
4. Diagram blood flow through the heart.
5. Describe the membrane activities of each of phases (0-4) of the action potential.
6. Describe the sequence of cardiac activation from the SA node through to spicardial surface.
7. Draw and label a normal ECG recording and relate each feature to cardiac activity.
8. Describe the sequence of events in a cardiac cycle.
9. Describe the relationship between cardiac output, heart rate and resistance.
10. Discuss factors affecting the regulation of heart rate and stroke volume.
11. State Frank-Starling Law and discuss its implications on the regulation of stroke volume.

Key Terms

absolute refractory period
aortic valve
atria
atrioventricular node
atrioventricular valve
bicuspid valve (mitral)
blood pressure
bundle brances
Bundle of His
cardiac output (CO)
CO = HR X SV
coronary vessels
diastole
diastolic potential
electrocardiogram (ECG)
end-diastolic volume
endocardium
epicardium
$F = \frac{P1 - P_2}{R}$
Frank-Starling Law
heart block
heart rate (HR)
myocardial infarction
myocardium
P-wave
pacemaker
pressure gradient
pulmonary circulation
pulmonary valve
Purkinje fibers
QRS complex
resistance
semilunar valve
sinoactrial node (SA node)
systemic circulation
stroke volume (SV)
systole
T-wave
tachycardia
vascular bed
ventricle
ventricular fibrillation

Testing Your Knowledge

I. Matching. Select the correct word from the Key Terms

_______ 1. receiving heart chamber
_______ 2. pumping heart chamber
_______ 3. located between atrium and ventricle
_______ 4. located between right ventricle and artery to lungs
_______ 5. muscular wall of heart
_______ 6. supply blood-to heart muscle
_______ 7. pacemaker of heart
_______ 8. specialized muscle fibers which spread impulse over endocardial surface of ventricles
_______ 9. recording of heart beat
_______ 10. period when ventricles filling
_______ 11. period when ventricles pumping
_______ 12. period when aortic pressure $>$ left ventricular
_______ 13. amount of blood ejected in a single beat
_______ 14. very rapid heart rate
_______ 15. equals number of beats/minute times amount of blood ejected in a single beat

CHAPTER 19 THE CIRCULATION

<u>Chapter Outline</u>

I. Overview of the Vascular System

II. The Arterial System: Carrying Blood away from the Heart

A. Blood Pressure in the Arteries
  * The equation for blood flow, $F = \frac{P_1 - P_2}{R}$, can be modified to $F = \frac{\text{arterial pressure}}{R}$ if P_2, the pressure in the vena cava is 0, and arterial pressure is equivalent to aortic pressure.

  1. Pulse Pressure
     a. Energy stored in the elastic wallas of the arteries during systole is dissipated during diastole.
     b. Pulse pressure is the difference between systolic and diastolic pressures.
     c. The magnitude of pulse pressure is determined by
        (1) the stroke volume,
        (2) the distensibility of the arteries.

  2. Measurement of Arterial Pressure

  3. Mean Arterial Pressure
     a. The mean arterial pressure (MAP) is calculated by the equation: MAP = 1/3 pulse pressure and diastolic pressure.
     b. Because MAP is related to blood flow, the equation for flow can be modified as: F = arterial pressure/R=MAP/R.

B. Resistance in the Arterioles

  1. The Diameter of Arterioles
     a. Blood flow through different organs and tissues can be adjusted by altering blood flow through arterioles.
     b. The resistance to flow through a blood vessel is inversely proportional to the radius raised to the fourth power:

$$R = \frac{1}{\text{radius}^4}$$

  2. The Water System Analogy for the Regulation of Blood Flow

  3. Regulation of Blood Flow by Local Factors
     a. In its normal resting state the arteriolar smooth muscle is contracted.
     b. Vascular beds can maintain a constant blood flow through an autoregulatory mechanism involving arteriolar smooth muscle cells.
     c. Increased blood flow to an organ or tissue through vasodilation can be caused by
        (1) increased carbon dioxide or decreased oxygen.
        (2) increased adenosine.
        (3) increased hydrogen ion and potassium ion concentration.
        (4) histamine.

4. Regulation of Blood Flow by Nerves and Hormones
   * Redistribution of blood flow requires communication between the various users.
   a. Arteriolar smooth muscle is innervated by sympathetic nerve fibers which, when stimulated, cause vasoconstriction.
   b. The effect of epinephrine on myogenic activity depends on the presence and number of alpha and beta receptors on smooth muscle cells.
   c. The sympathetic transmitter norepinephrine binds to alpha receptors to cause vasoconstriction.
   d. The hormone epinephrine binds to beta receptors to cause vasodilation.

III. The Capillary System: The Exchange of Molecules

A. The Function of Capillaries
   * Capillaries are the sites of molecular exchange between the blood and interstitial fluid.

B. The Microcirculation
   * The metarterioles directly connect arterioles and venules.
   * Blood flow through the capillary network is regulated by precapillary sphincters and arteriolar diameter.

C. The Capillary Wall and Endothelial Pores
   * The capillary wall is one call thick and contains no smooth muscle.
   * Endothelial pores, whose size and number vary greatly among different tissues, allow for the passage of molecules.

D. Movement of Substances Across the Capillary Wall
   * Substances can cross the capillary wall by diffusion, pinocytosis, and bulk flow.

   1. Pinocytosis

   2. Diffusion
      a. Molecules diffuse across capillary walls either through water-filled pores or directly through endothelial cells. The path a molecule takes is determined by its relative solubility in water and lipids.
      b. Several factors contribute to the rapid diffusional exchange of substances across the capillary wall. These include
         (1) short diffusion distances.
         (2) extensive surface area of capillaries.
         (3) slow rate of blood flow through the capillaries.

   3. Bulk Flow and Oncotic Pressure
      a. Exchange of water and dissolved solutes occurs through endothelial pores by bulk flow that results from a hydrostatic pressure differential across the capillary wall.
      b. Osmotic pressure of plasma proteins prevents loss of vascular volume.

   4. Filtration and Absorption: Starling's Hypothesis
      a. Starling's hypothesis describes the balance of hydrostatic and oncotic pressures across the capillary endothelium.
      b. Vasoconstriction promotes absorption of fluid while vasodilation promotes filtration across the capillary endothelium.

IV. The Venous System: Returning Blood to the Heart
* Venules also contain endothelial clefts and together with capillaries are often referred to as exchange vessels.

A. Venous Capacitance
* Veins function as a low-pressure reservoir for blood and are often referred to as capacitance vessels.
* Through contraction of their smooth muscle veins can alter their capacity and redistribute blood.

B. Venous Return
* Venous return is assisted by one way valves and by changes in intrathoracic pressure during breathing.

V. The Lymphatic System

* The lymphatic system returns to the circulatory system the fluid and plasma protein that leaked from the capillary into the interstitial space.

A. The Structure of Lymphatic Vessels
* Lymphatic capillaries which are composed of a single layer of epithelial cells drain into larger vessels eventually draining into the subclavian veins.

B. The Flow of Lymph
* The flow of lymph is assisted by (1) one-way valves; (2) contractions of smooth muscles in lymphatic vessel wall; and (3) compression of lymphatic vessels by skeletal muscle activity.

C. The Filtration of Lymph
* Other functions of the lymphatic system include: (1) transporting fat from the gastrointestinal tract to blood; and (2) filtering microorganisms and other foreign material from the lymph.

D. Failure of the Lymphatic System

VI. Regulation of Systemic Arterial Pressure
* The relationship between cardiac output (CO), mean arterial pressure (MAP), and total peripheral resistance (TPR) is described by the equation:

$$CO = MAP/TPR \text{ or } MAP = CO \times TPR$$

* Total peripheral resistance is the total resistance to the flow of blood from the aorta back to the right atrium.
* Changes in peripheral resistance are entirely due to changes in the diameter of the arterioles.

A. Cardiac Output, Venous Return, and End-Diastolic Volume
* Cardiac output is sensitive to changes in end diastolic volume, which in turn depends on the total blood volume and the distribution of blood within the vascular system.

B. Arterial Baroreceptors: Sensory Receptors for Blood Pressure

1. Location of Baroreceptors
   a. Baroreceptors are located in the wall of the aortic arch and in the carotid senses.

2. Activation of Baroreceptors
   a. An increase in arterial pressure causes the baroreceptor to stretch. This initiates a transmission along the sensory neuron to the cardiovascular control center in the brain.

3. Patterns of Baroreceptor Activation by Changes in Blood Pressure
   a. The pattern of action potential firing of stretch receptors reflects changes in both mean and pulsatile arterial pressures.

C. The Cardiovascular Control Centers of the Brain
   * The cardiovascular control center for the baroreceptor reflex is located in the medulla.

D. Cardiovascular Response to Blood Pressure Changes
   * Changes in baroreceptor activity cause reciprocal changes in parasympathetic and sympathetic activity to heart and blood vessels.

1. Cardiac Output and Total Peripheral Resistance
   a. The overall response of the system to a change in blood pressure can be represented:
      (1) ↑ arterial pressure causes ↑ firing in baroreceptor which causes ↓ sympathetic nerve activity and ↑ parasympathetic nerve activity to heart and ↓ cardiac output
      (2) ↓ sympathetic activity to arterioles leads to ↑ diameter in highly innervated vascular beds (skin, muscle) causing ↓ in peripheral resistance.
      (3) MBP = CO x TPR ↓ TPR and ↓ CO → ↑ MBP

2. Venomotor Tone
   a. Increased arterial pressure and baroreceptor activity lead to a decrease in sympathetic activity to the veins and venodilation. This leads to a ↓ in end-diastolic volume and cardiac output.

3. Long-Term Regulation of Blood Pressure
   a. Decreased cardiac output can be increased by
      (1) increases in total circulatory blood volume.
      (2) shifting of blood volume from peripheral vascular blood to the heart by increasing venomotor tone.
      (3) increases in reabsorption of interstitial fluid by capillaries.

E. Disturbances of Cardiovascular Homeostasis: Hemorrhage, Hypotension, and Exercise

1. Hemorrhage
   a. Hemorrhage causes a drop in arterial blood pressure which triggers the baroreceptor reflex. This results in increases in CO, TPR and MBP.
   b. The vascular resistance to the heart and brain does not increase because of sparse sympathetic innervation.

* Selective innervation of different vascular beds provides a means for channeling blood to vital organs and away from nonvital organs to maintain homeostasis.

c. With hemorrhage stroke volume is reduced.
d. To compensate for hemorrhage and increase blood volume the following mechanisms operate:
   (1) increase in venoconstriction.
   (2) increase in absorption in capillary beds of interstitial fluid because of reduction of MBP and venous pressure.

2. Hypotension: Low Blood Pressure
   a. Hypotension results from inadequate filling of the heart. This leads to decrease CO and inadequate flow of blood to the brain.
   b. The compensatory mechanisms include
      (1) a slight increase in sympathetic nerve activity.
      (2) an increase in venomotor tone.
      (3) an increase in CO.

3. Exercise and Cardiovascular Homeostasis
   a. During exercise cardiac output and blood flow to skeletal muscles increase.
   b. Compensatory responses to exercise include
      (1) increase in vascular resistance to skin, kidney and gastrointestinal tract.
      (2) release of vasodilator substances in precapillary resistance vessels.
      (3) reflexive vasodilation of subcutaneous vessels.

VII. Cardiovascular Disease

A. Congestive Heart Failure

1. Cardiovascular Effects of Heart Rate

2. Compensation for Heart Failure

3. Left Heart Failure Versus Right Heart Failure

4. Treatment of Heart Failure

<u>Chapter Learning Objectives</u>

1. Define arterial pressure and pulse pressure and relate each to activities of the cardiac cycle.
2. Define mean arterial pressure and describe how it is determined and affected by changes in blood flow.
3. Describe how the arterioles can regulate blood flow.
4. Describe local chemical factors that affect blood flow through a vascular bed.
5. Describe control of blood flow by neural activity and hormones.
6. Describe the three different mechanisms by which materials cross the capillary wall.
7. Describe the physical processes involved in filtration and absorption of fluids across the capillary wall and factors affecting each process.
8. Describe the mechanisms which provide for venous return of blood to the heart.
9. Describe the anatomy of the lymphatic system and its roles in the body.
10. Describe the role of baroreceptors and the cardiovascular control center in regulating arterial pressure.
11. Describe cardiovascular responses to an increase or decrease in blood pressure.
12. Describe cardiovascular responses to hemorrhage, hypotension and exercise.
13. Describe cardiovascular effects of heart failure.

Key Terms

absorption
acetylcholine
alpha receptors
angiotensin II
arterial pressure
arteriole athero-sclerosis
atrial natriuretic peptide
autoregulation
baroreceptor
beta receptors
bulk flow
capacitance vessel
capillary
cardiac output (CO)
cardiovascular control center
circulatory shock
congestive heart failure
diastolic pressure
diffusion
end-diastolic volume
endothelial pores
epinephrine
filtration
hemorrhage
hydrostatic pressure
hypertensicn
hypotension
lymph
lymphatic system
MAP = CO x TPR
mean arterial pressure
metarteriole
microcirculation
myogenic activity
norepinephrine
oncotic pressure
osmotic pressure
pinocytosis
precapillary sphincter
pulse pressure
resistance
Starling's hypothesis
systolic pressure
thrombus
total peripheral resistance (TPR)
vasoactive center
vasoconstriction
vasodilation
vasomotion
vein
venomotor tone
venous return
venule

Testing Your Knowledge

I. Matching. Select the correct word from the Key Terms

__________ 1. difference between systolic and diastolic pressures
__________ 2. arterial pressure occurring during contraction of the ventricle
__________ 3. increase in contractile activity in response to stretch
__________ 4. ability of individual vascular beds to maintain constant blood flow
__________ 5. effect of increased carbon dioxide and decreased oxygen on arteriolar smooth muscle
__________ 6. effect of norepinephrine binding to alpha receptors or vascular smooth muscle
__________ 7. effect of epinephrine binding to beta receptors on smooth muscle
__________ 8. pressure of blood due to presence of plasma proteins
__________ 9. describes balance of hydrostatic and oncotic pressures across capillary endothelium
__________ 10. process favored when hydrostatic pressure much greater than oncotic pressure
__________ 11. process favored when precapillary sphincters contracted
__________ 12. function as low pressure reservoir for blood
__________ 13. structures sensitive to stretch
__________ 14. functions to return fluid in interstitial space to the heart
__________ 15. elevated arteriol pressure

II. Complete the Table. In the table indicate the effect of the factor on vascular smooth muscle

Factor	Effect
1. increased carbon dioxide	
2. decreased oxygen	
3. increased hydrogen ion concentration	
4. decrease in arterial pressure	

5. norepinephrine binding to alpha receptors	
6. epinephrine binding to beta receptors	
7. angiotensin II	
8. atrial natriuretic peptide	

III. Complete the Table. In the table indicate the effect of the condition on arterial pressure and cardiac output.

Condition	arterial pressure	cardiac output
1. increase in venomotor tone		
2. increase in neural activity of baro-receptor		
3. decrease in neural activity of baro-receptor		
4. increase in end-diastolic volume		
5. hemorrhage		
6. hypertension		
7. decrease in sympathetic activity in heart		
8. increase in parasympathetic activity in heart		

CHAPTER 20 RESPIRATION

Chapter Outline

I. The Structure of the Lung
   * Movement of gases in and out of cells occurs by simple diffusion.
   * All respiratory organs have three features in common:
     (1) very thin walls.
     (2) moist surfaces.
     (3) high vascularity.

   A. The Internal Surface Area of the Lung
      * The surface area of lungs is increased by the formation of septa whose walls are highly vascularized.

   B. Alveoli Microscopic Air Sacs
      * In the mammalian lung, septa evolved into microscopic air sacs called alveoli, each of which is surrounded by a capillary network.

   C. Airways
      * Each lung is composed of two treelike structures, the vascular and airway trees, which are embedded in elastic tissue.
      * The flow of air through the airway tree is: trachea → two bronchi (one to each lung) → bronchiles → alveoli, the exchange units.
      * The conducting units (trachea, bronchi, and bronchioles) have three important functions.
        (1) to warm and humidify air
        (2) to distribute air to alveoli
        (3) to serve as part of the body defense system

II. Lung Volumes and Ventilation

   A. Air Flow
      * Ventilation is the process of moving air in and out of the lungs.

      1. Turbulent Air Flow
         a. Turbulent air flow occurs at high flow rates and consists of disorganized patterns of air flow.
         b. Turbulent flow increases resistance to breathing and is greatly affected by gas density.

      2. Laminar Air Flow
         a. Laminar air flow is characterized by streamlined flow that is parallel to the side of the airways
         b. Laminar flow is silent in contrast to turbulent flow and is directly related to the radius raised to the fourth power (Flow $\propto$ radius^4).

   B. Spirometry and Lung Volumes
      * A spirogram measures the rate of air flow in and out of the lungs and the volume of air moved.

      1. Forced Vital Capacity
         a. Forced vital capacity, the maximum amount of air forcefully and rapidly exhaled after a deep breath, is determined primarily by three factors:
            (1) strength of chest and abdominal muscles,
            (2) airway resistance, and
            (3) lung volume

      2. Residual Volume and Functional Residual Capacity

a. Residual volume and functional residual capacity are measured indirectly by a dilution technique based on the relationship: $C_1 \times V_1 = C_2 \times V_2$ where C is concentration and V is volume.

C. Ventilation

1. Dead Space Volume
   a. Dead space volume is wasted air located in the conducting airways.
   b. Thirty percent of tidal volume is wasted air.

2. Alveolar Ventilation
   a. Alveolar ventilation, the volume of fresh air available for gas exchange, is equal to the (tidal volume minus the the dead space volume) times the breathing frequency.
   b. Alveolar ventilation is affected by depth and rate of breathing.

III. The Mechanics of Lung Action

A. The Muscle of Breathing

1. Muscle Movements during Inspiration
   a. During inspiration the lungs play a passive role.
   b. Contraction of the diaphragm and external costal movements occurs during normal inspiration.

2. Muscle Movements during Expiration
   a. Relaxation of the diaphragm occurs during normal expiration.
   b. With exercise or forced expiration the expiratory muscles, the abdominal and internal costal muscles contract.

B. Lung Pressures During the Breathing Cycle
   * Three important relative pressures are associated with lung inflation and air flow:
     (1) pleural pressure,
     (2) alveolar pressure, and
     (3) transpulmonic pressure, the gradient across the lung wall.
   * Transpulmonic pressure (P_{tp}) is equal to alveolar pressure (Pa) minus plural pressure (P_{pe}) and keeps the lungs from collapsing.

1. Lung Pressures during Inspiration
   a. The sequence of events in inspiration is:
      (1) contraction of inspiratory muscles,
      (2) expansion of thoracic cavity,
      (3) decrease in pleural pressure,
      (4) increase in transpulmonic pressure,
      (5) inflation of lungs,
      (6) decrease in alveolar pressure,
      (7) flow of air into lungs.

2. Lung Pressures during Expiration
   a. The sequence of events during expiration is:
      (1) relaxation of respiratory muscles,
      (2) decrease in volume of thoracic cavity,
      (3) increase in pleural pressure,
      (4) decrease in transpulmonic pressure,
      (5) decrease in lung size,
      (6) increase in alveolar pressure,
      (7) flow of air out of lungs.

C. Elastic Properties of the Lung: Compliance

* The elasticity of the lungs affects how well they inflate and deflate with a change in transpulmonic pressure.
* The elastic properties of a lung are determined by measuring changes in lung volume that occur with changes in pressure, plotted on a pressure-volume curve. The slope of the line is compliance which provides a measure of distensibility.
* Lungs with abnormally low compliance are difficult to inflate while lungs with abnormally high compliance have poor elastic recoil.

D. Surface Properties of the Lung: Surface Tension

* Compliance is affected by surface tension occurring within the inner alveolar surface at the gas-liquid interface and producing a force that pulls inwardly.
* Pulmonary surfactant lowers surface tension making the lung more compliant.

E. The Work of Breathing

* The amount of work involved in ventilating the lungs is affected by the degree of
  (1) elasticity of the lung.
  (2) surface tension in the alveoli.
  (3) airway resistance.

IV. The Control of Breathing

* The basic automatic rhythm of breathing can be modified by both neural and chemical stimuli.

A. The Rhythm of Breathing

1. Inspiratory Neurons in the Medulla
   a. Inspiratory neurons are responsible for the basic rhythm and activate the inspiratory muscles.
   b. Neuronal inputs from the pons modulate the inspiratory center and act as a "cut off" signal to inhibit inspiration in automatic breathing.

2. Pulmonary Stretch Receptors
   a. Pulmonary stretch receptors in the smooth muscles of the airways send messages to the inspiratory neurons to inhibit inspiration and prevent overinflation.

3. Expiratory Neurons in the Medulla
   a. Expiratory neurons activate expiratory muscles during forceful breathing.

4. Failure of the Respiratory Center
   a. The respiratory center can be disrupted by cerebral concussions and pressures in addition to drugs like barbiturates.

B. Chemical Control of Ventilation

* The rate and depth of breathing vary depending on metabolic demands.
* Oxygen, carbon dioxide and hydrogen ions affect both the rate and depth of breathing.

1. Central and Peripheral Chemoreceptors
   a. Central chemoreceptors in the medulla monitor changes in cerebral arterial carbon dioxide levels.
   b. Peripheral chemoreceptors in the aortic arch and at the bifurcation of the common carotid artery monitor levels of O_2, CO_2 and (H^+) in arterial blood. Sensory neurons

from these receptors extend to the respiratory center in the medulla.

c. Arterial carbon dioxide has the greatest effect on ventilation.

2. Hyperventilation and Hypoventilation: Control of Arterial CO_2
   a. An increase in CO_2 causes increased alveolar ventilation while a decrease in CO_2 causes hypoventilation.
   b. The control of ventilation by CO_2 is mediated by central and peripheral chemoreceptors.
   c. The control of ventilation by (H^+) occurs exclusively through peripheral chemoreceptors.
   d. A change in arterial (H^+) is caused by altered blood CO_2, and other factors.

3. Oxygen and Control of Ventilation
   a. Oxygen has the smallest effect on ventilation.

C. Abnormal Patterns of Breathing

1. Sleep Apnea
   a. Sleep apnea involves obstruction of the upper airways during sleep.

2. Shallow-Water Blackout

3. The Diving Reflex

4. The Pickwickian Syndrome

Chapter Learning Objectives

1. Describe the structure of the respiratory system.
2. List three functions of the conducting units and describe how these units serve as part of the body defense system.
3. Compare turbulent and laminar air flows as to production of noise, effect of siameter and location in respiratory system.
4. Describe factors affecting forced vital capacity.
5. Distinguish residual volume and functional residual capacity and describe how each is measured.
6. Describe factors affecting alveolar ventilation.
7. Compare inspiration and expiration as to the role of muscles, changes in alveoli, pleural, and transpulmonic pressures, and in the size of the thoracic cavity, alveoli, and lungs.
8. Describe how compliance is measured, what it represents, the effect of surface tension, and the medical significance of abnormally high and low values.
9. Describe factors affecting the amount of work involved in ventilating the lungs.
10. Describe the control of breathing by inspiratory and expiratory neurons and the role of pulmonary stretch receptors in regulation.
11. Describe the effects on ventilation of high and low levels of oxygen, carbon dioxide and hydrogen ions, and how changes in the concentration of these chemicals are detected.
12. List and describe the four abnormal patterns of breathing: sleep apnea, shallow-water blackout, driving reflex, and the Pickwickian syndrome.

Key Terms

airway tree
alveolar pressure
alveolar ventilation
alveolus
aortic bodies
asthma
bronchitis
bronchiole
bronchus
carotid bodies
cellular respiration
chemoreceptor (central, peripheral)
compliance
conducting unit
dead space volume
diaphragm
diving reflex
elastic property
elastic recoil
emphysema
exchange unit
expiration
expiratory neurons
forced vital capacity
functional residual capacity
hyperventilation
hypoventilation
hypoxemia
inspiration
inspiratory neurons
intercostal muscles (internal, external)
laminar flow
medulla
minute ventilation
mucociliary transport system
Pickwickian Syndrome
pleural pressure
pleural space
pneumothorax
pressure-volume curve
pulmonary stretch receptors
pulmonary surfactant
relative pressure
residual pressure
residual volume
respiration
respiratory distress syndrome
shallow-water blackout
sleep apnea
spirometry
surface tension
thoracic cavity
tidal volume
trachea
transitional flow
transpulmonic pressure
turbulent flow
vascular tree
ventilation

Testing Your Understanding

I. Matching. Select the correct word from the Key Terms.

__________1. gas exchange area of lung
__________2. process of moving air into and out of lung
__________3. type of air flow in trachea and bronchi
__________4. amount of air entering or leaving lungs during a single breath
__________5. maximum amount of air forcefully and rapidly exhaled after maximal inspiration
__________6. air remaining in lungs after forced expiration
__________7. volume of air remaining in lungs after normal expiration
__________8. amount of air in conducting units
__________9. dome-shaped muscle contracts during inspiration
__________10. pressure gradient across lung wall
__________11. condition caused by lung collapse
__________12. pressure became subatmospheric during inspiration
__________13. size or capacity increases during this process
__________14. determined by slope of pressure-volume curve
__________15. reduces surface tension.

II. Complete the Table. Indicate what happens to the pressure or structure during inspiration (A) and expiration (B).

	diaphragm	thoracic cavity	pleural pressure	alveolar pressure	transpulmonic pressure	lung capacity
A.						
B.						

III. Fill in the Table. For each condition indicate the effect on ventilation.

Condition	Ventilation
1. increase in arterial CO_2	
2. decrease in arterial O_2	
3. increase in (H^+)	
4. decrease in arterial CO_2	
5. decreased blood pH	
6. vomiting	

CHAPTER 21 THE PULMONARY CIRCULATION AND GAS UPTAKE

Chapter Outline

I. Structure of the Pulmonary Circulation

A. Pulmonary Arteries
   * The branching of the vascular tree parallels that of the airway tree.

B. Pulmonary Capillaries and Veins
   * Capillaries are embedded in alveolar walls.

C. Pulmonary Lymphatic Vessels
   * Lymph vessels drain excess fluid from the interstitial spaces and return it to systemic veins.

D. Metabolic Functions in the Pulmonary Circulation
   * Other functions of endothelial cells in the capillary wall include:
     (1) conversion of angiotensin I to active angiotensin II, a vasoconstrictor;
     (2) release and inactivation of other vasoactive substances like histamine, serotonin, and prostaglandins.

II. Vascular Pressure and Blood Flow in the Pulmonary Circulation

A. Cardiac Catherization
   * Cardiac catherization provides a way to measure blood pressure in all four chambers of the heart.

B. Blood Pressures in the Pulmonary Circulation
   * Mean pulmonary arterial pressure for a normal resting adult is 15 mm Hg.
   * Most of the blood flows through the lower lung.

C. Ventilation-Perfusion Balance
   * Uneven distribution of inspired air to the alveoli results in regimal hypoxia.
   * Through a mechanism called hypoxic vasoconstriction the lung balances the flow in perfusion of blood with the availability of regional alveolar oxygen. Blood flow to hypoxic areas is restricted.

D. Whole Lung Hypoxia
   * Whole lung hypoxia leads to a rise in pulmonary arterial pressure which forces blood to the upper regions of the lungs where oxygen is relatively abundant.

E. Exercise and Pulmonary Blood Pressure

1. Capillary Recruitment during Exercise
   a. As cardiac output and pulmonary arterial pressure increase, more blood flows to the upper lung where reserve capillaries are recruited.

2. Capillary Transit Time During Exercise
   a. As cardiac output increases, transit time through pulmonary capillaries decreases which allows more blood to be oxygenated every second during exercise.

III. Diffusion of Gases in the Alveoli

A. Partial Pressures in the Alveoli

* The partial pressure of oxygen (PO_2) in air is 160mmHg.

B. The Alveolar-Capillary Membrane

* The oxygen gradient favors movement of oxygen from alveolar gas into capillary blood while the reverse is true for carbon dioxide.
* Oxygen dissolves in the capillary membrane into the plasma, and then passes through the erythrocyte membrane to hemoglobin.

IV. Uptake and Transport of Gases by the Blood

A. Transport of Oxygen by the Blood

1. Oxygen Uptake during Rest and Exercise
   a. At rest 250ml/min of oxygen are taken up through pulmonary capillaries and transported to tissue capillaries.
   b. During heavy exercise 3750 ml/min of oxygen are taken up through pulmonary capillaries.

2. Hemoglobin in Oxygen Exchange
   a. Each hemoglobin molecule combines reversibly with four oxygen molecules to form oxyhemoglobin. In tissues hemoglobin releases oxygen.
   b. The capacity of hemoglobin for oxygen is much higher than that of plasma.

3. The Oxyhemoglobin Dissociation Curve
   a. The oxyhemoglobin dissociation curve shows the way in which oxygen binds to hemoglobin in the lung and unloads oxygen in the tissues.
   b. Under normal conditions the partial pressure of oxygen in arterial and venous bloods is 100 mmHg and 40 mmHg, respectively.

4. Oxygen Delivery during Rest
   a. Under normal conditions arterial blood saturation is 97% and venous blood is 75%.

5. Oxygen Delivery during Exercise
   a. Heavy exercise enlarges the oxygen gradient which favors the movement of oxygen from capillary blood to the tissue.
   b. Hemoglobin unloads oxygen more readily under conditions of acid pH and increased temperature. The oxyhemoglobin dissociation curve shifts to the right.
   c. A leftward shift of the oxyhemoglobin dissociation curve enhances oxygen loading and occurs when the pH is more basic or the temperature drops.

B. Transport of Carbon Dioxide by the Blood

1. Bicarbonate Ions in CO_2 Transport
   a. The largest fraction (60-70%) of CO_2 is transported as bicarbonate ions which are formed inside erythrocytes by the following reaction series:

(1) $CO_2 + H_2O \xrightarrow{\text{carbonic anhydrase}} H_2CO_3$

(2) $H_2CO_3 \longrightarrow HCO_3^- + H^+$

(3) $H^+ + Hb^- \longrightarrow HHb$

b. The bicarbonate ion (HCO_3^-) moves into the plasma.
c. The H^+ combines with hemoglobin.

2. Carbaminohemoglobin in CO_2 Transport
   a. CO_2 can combine loosely with hemoglobin at a different binding than oxygen to form carbaminohemoglobin.
   b. Between 15-30% of CO_2 is transported in this way.
   c. Hemoglobin has a higher affinity for CO_2 when it is oxygen-desaturated.

3. Dissolved Carbon Dioxide in CO_2 Transport
   a. Between 7-10% of CO_2 is transported in a dissolved state in the plasma and erythrocytes.

V. Disorders of the Pulmonary Circulation

A. Pulmonary Edema
* Pulmonary edema results from the accumulation of fluid in interstitial spaces. It increases the thickness of fluid through which oxygen must diffuse.
* Pulmonary edema is caused by failure of the left ventricle and increased permeability of the capillaries.

VI. Fetal and Neonatal Circulatory Physiology

A. Fetal Circulation
* In the fetus blood is shunted away from the lungs by two passages:
  (1) the foramen ovale between the right and left atria, and
  (2) the ductus arteriosus between the pulmonary artery and aorta.

B. Circulatory Changes at Birth
* At birth the formen ovale and ductus arteriosus close so blood passes from the right atrium to the right ventricle and through the pulmonary artery to the lungs.

C. Congenital Heart Diseases
* Failure of the closure of the ductus arteriosus can lead to pulmonary hypertension and right ventricular failure.
* Atrial and ventricular septal defects result from incomplete formation of the septa between the atria and between the ventricle.

Chapter Learning Objectives

1. Describe the vascular tree and the structure and function of the lymphatic system in the lungs.
2. List two metabolic functions of pulmonary endothelial cells.
3. Describe how the flow or perfusion of blood in pulmonary capillaries is balanced with the availability of regional alveolar oxygen.
4. Describe two ways which improve oxygen uptake from alveolar gas during exercise.
5. Describe the physical process by which oxygen moves between the alveolar air and blood and the tissues.
6. Describe the role of hemoglobin in the transport of oxygen.
7. Draw an oxyhemoglobin dissociation curve and describe what it represents.
8. Describe factors which shift the curve to the right and left and relate these factors to a tissue's need for oxygen.
9. Describe three ways CO_2 is transported in blood and the amount of CO_2 transported by each.
10. Define pulmonary edema and list its causes and adverse effects.
11. Describe fetal circulation and changes occurring at birth.
12. Describe three congenital heart diseases.

Key Terms

alveolar-capillary membrane
angiotensin I, II
atrial septal defect
bicarbonate ion
capillaries
carbaminohemoglobin
carbonic anhydrase
cardiac catherization
desaturated
diffusion
ductus arteriosus
embolus
foramen ovale
hemoglobin
hypoxemia
hypoxia
hypoxic vasoconstriction
oxygenated
oxyhemoglobin
oxyhemoglobin dissociation curve
partial pressure
patent ductus arteriosus
pulmonary artery
pulmonary edema
pulmonary hypertension
pulmonary venous tree
pulmonary vein
ventricular septal defect

Testing Your Understanding

I. Matching. Select the correct word from the Key Terms.

__________1. carries blood from the right ventricle to the lungs
__________2. accumulation of fluid in the lung
__________3. vasoconstrictor converted to active form by endothelial cells
__________4. describes low oxygen concentration in the lung
__________5. condition of low blood oxygen
__________6. condition of elevated arterial pressure in the lungs
__________7. form in which most CO_2 transported in blood
__________8. molecule formed from binding of CO_2 to hemoglobin
__________9. blood clot
__________10. opening between right and left atria

II. Fill in the Table. For each condition indicate which direction (right or left) an oxyhemoglobin dissociation curve would shift and whether loading or unloading of oxygen is facilitated.

Condition	Shift (right, left)	Loading/Unloading
1. presence of high (H^+)		
2. low P_{O2}		
3. elevated temperature		
4. more basic pH		
5. high (CO_2)		

CHAPTER 22 RESPIRATION IN UNUSUAL ENVIRONMENTS

Chapter Outline

I. Respiration in Low Oxygen Environments

A. Immediate Effects of Low Oxygen

* The partial pressure of oxygen depends on the barometric pressure. The partial pressure of oxygen drops at higher altitudes.
* One of the body's chief responses to altitude is hyperventilation which is triggered by the increased firing of peripheral chemoreceptors, the carotid bodies.
* Hyperventilation eliminates alveolar carbon dioxide and decreases arterial and cerebrospinal fluid pH which decreases the firing of central and peripheral chemoreceptors ventilation decreases.

B. Long-Term Effects of Low Oxygen

* Long-term effects include
  (1) increased erythrocyte production.
  (2) increased ventilation, cardiac output and circulating hemoglobin.
  (3) increased number of mitochondria.

II. Respiration in Deep Sea Diving

A. Gas Pressures Under Water

* Pressure increases with depth because of the weight of the water.

B. Effects of High Pressures on Respiration

* Air enters the lungs at higher than normal pressure which causes problems as the diver ascends.
* As the diver surfaces, nitrogen is released from tissues. If ascent is rapid, bubbles can form both in the blood and in tissues, causing pain or the "bends."

C. Marine Mammals: Champion Divers

* Marine mammals have developed numerous diving reflexes that assist in conserving oxygen. These include:
  (1) decreasing the blood supply to nonessential organs by vasoconstriction,
  (2) decreasing heart rate and cardiac output,
  (3) collapsing of alveoli.

D. Respiration in Submarines

E. "Homo Aquaticus"

* Two methods in the research stage offer promise for underwater use. These are:
  (1) breathing a hyperoxygenated saline solution, and
  (2) development of artificial gills which would extract oxygen from water and secrete CO_2.

III. Respiration in High-Oxygen Environments

A. Atelectasis: Collapse of Alveoli

* Atelectasis can occur when small airways become plugged with mucus. Oxygen in the plugged alveoli gets absorbed and the alveoli collapse.

B. Toxicity Associated with Breathing High Oxygen

1. Free-Radical-Induced Toxic Effects
   a. The primary target for oxygen toxicity is the lungs.
   b. Oxidizing free radicals formed from molecular oxygen cause destructive and lethal cellular effects by
      (1) oxidizing membrane lipids,
      (2) oxidizing cellular proteins, and DNA, and
      (3) oxidizing enzymes in cellular respiration.
   c. Breathing ozone or nitrogen dioxide from polluted air also causes free radical injury to the lung.

2. Retrolental Fibrosis
   a. Retrolental fibrosis occurs in the eye behind the lens and causes blindness.

3. Toxic Effects of High-Pressure Oxygen
   a. When oxygen is breathed at 2 to 4 atm, it stimulates the CNS leading to convulsions.

IV. Respiration in Unusual Gaseous Environments

A. High Concentrations of Carbon Dioxide and Respiration
   * Breathing of high carbon dioxide concentration leads to severe acidose and respiratory failure.

B. Carbon Monoxide and Respiration
   * Carbon monoxide does not stimulate respiration and instead competes with oxygen for the same binding site on hemoglobin.
   * The formation of carboxyhemoglobin (CO+Hb) interferes with the transport of oxygen to the cells.
   * The binding affinity of hemoglobin for CO is about 210 times that for 0_2.

C. Anesthetic Gases and Respiration
   * The three stages of anesthesia with inhaled anesthetics are:
     (1) analgesia - loss of response to pain,
     (2) loss of consciousness,
     (3) surgical anesthesia-loss of all sensations, and inhibition of motor functions.

V. Respiration in Space Travel

A. High G-Forces and the Human Body
   * When a positive G force is exerted in a head to foot direction, blood is pulled toward the lower parts of the body. The effects depend on the number of G forces, and the length of time and elevated G force.
   * With a negative G force (foot to head) the motion of blood is toward the head.

B. Weightlessness and Respiration
   * The physiological problems associated with weightlessness include:
     (1) lack of hydrostatic pressure resulting in decreased blood volume, red cell mass and cardiac output;
     (2) diminished physical activity which leads to a decrease in work capacity and a loss of calcium from bones.

C. Artificial Atmosphere in Spacecraft
   * All U.S. space flights use air as a gas mixture.

D. Radiation Hazards in Space

Chapter Learning Objectives

1. Describe immediate physiological responses to low oxygen environments.
2. Describe long-term physiological responses to low oxygen environments.
3. Describe symptoms of altitude illness.
4. Discuss problems which arise when a diver ascends too rapidly and how the probelms could be alleviated.
5. Describe physiological changes which occur in a seal when it dives and stays submerged.
6. Discuss problems and toxic effects resulting from breathing high oxygen.
7. Discuss respiratory problems which arise from breathing high concentrations of carbon dioxide and carbon monoxide.
8. Describe the effects of high G forces and weightlessness on the cardiovascular and respiratory systems.

Key Terms

acclimatization
acute mountain sickness
analgesia
anesthetic
anoxic
atelectasis
bends
carboxyhemoglobin
free radicals
gravitational attraction (G-force)
high-altitude cerebral edema
high-altitude pulmonary edema
hyperventilation
hypoxia
nitrous oxide
polycythemia
redout
retrolental fibrosis
Van Allen radiation belt

Testing Your Understanding

I. Matching. Select the correct word from the Key Terms

__________1. loss of sensation of pain
__________2. formed from binding of CO and Hb
__________3. condition of collapsed alveoli
__________4. condition caused by exposure to high oxygen
__________5. effect of negative G-forces
__________6. deprived of oxygen
__________7. cause tissue damage under high oxygen conditions
__________8. triggered by decreased alveolar oxygen tension
__________9. possible long-term effect of living at high altitude
__________10. condition of accumulation of nitrogen bubbles in blood and tissues

CHAPTER 23 THE GASTROINTESTINAL SYSTEM

Chapter Outline

I. Overview of the Gastrointestinal System
   * Four processes essential for the nutritive function of the gastrointestinal system are:
     (1) motility (movement of food through digestive system),
     (2) secretion (production and release of digestive juice by endocrine glands),
     (3) digestion (conversion of large organic molecules to smaller ones),
     (4) absorption (movement of smaller molecules across wall of small intestine to blood or lymph).

   A. Anatomy of the Gastrointestinal System
      * The digestive tract consists of the mouth, pharynx, esophagus, stomach, and small and large intestines.
      * Accessory structures include salivary glands, pancreas, liver and gallbladder.

      1. Cellular Arrangements in the Gastrointestinal System
         a. The wall of the digestive tract is composed of four coats:
            (1) mucosa (consisting of the epithelial lining, lamina propria and muscularis mucosa),
            (2) submucosa (consisting of a layer of connective tissue with lymph and blood vessels, exocrine glands, and a plexus of nerve cells),
            (3) muscularis externa (consisting of circular and logitudinal muscle layers and a network of nerve cells), and,
            (4) serosa (consisting of a layer of connective tissue.

      2. Gastrointestinal Circulation
         a. The circulation of the stomach, small and large intestines, pancreas, and liver is called the splanchnic circulation.
         b. The portal circulation brings blood from the stomach, intestines and the pancreas to the liver where digestive products are metabolically processed.

   B. Processes of the Gastrointestinal System

      1. Motility: Mixing Movements and Propulsive Movements
         a. The motor functions of most of the digestive tract are performed by smooth muscle layers.
         b. The two basic types of motor activity involved in the digestive and absorptive functions are
            (1) mixing movements, and,
            (2) propulsive movements.
         c. The rate of propulsive movement depends on the function served by the organ.

      2. Secretion: Inorganic Ions, Digestive Enzymes, Liver Products, and Mucin.
         a. Important inorganic ions are hydrogen ions and bicarbonate ions secreted by the stomach and pancreas, respectively.
         b. Important organic components include digestive enzymes of the salivary glands, stomach and pancreas, bile salts, pigments and cholesterol secreted by the liver and mucin produced by all regions of the

digestive tract.

c. Water and solutes are transferred across secretory cell membranes by a variety of active and passive transport processes.

3. Digestion: Breakdown of Food into Small Molecules
   a. By the process of enzyme digestion large organic molecules are broken down into smaller molecules that can be absorbed.
   b. Digestion begins in the mouth and ends in the small intestine.

4. Absorption: Transfer of Nutrients to the Blood and Lymph
   a. Various transport systems are used to move digestive products from the lumen to the blood and lymph.

C. The Regulation of Gastrointestinal Function

* Motility and secretion are regulated by neural and hormonal mechanisms while digestion and absorption are not.
* Many of the stimuli that initiate the regulatory events are present in the lumen of the digestive system.
* Chemoreceptors and mechanoreceptors respond to the stimuli.

1. Neural Control of Gastrointestinal Processes
   a. Two types of neural pathways are involved in the regulation of gastrointestinal motor and secretory activity:
      (1) short reflexes mediated by nerves lying within the wall of the digestive tract, and
      (2) long reflexes mediated over nerves outside of the tract.
   b. Short reflexes can be excitatory or inhibitory depending on the mediator released at the effector cell by motor and secretoary neurons.
   c. Long reflexes coordinate activites of different regions of the gastrointestinal system and between the system and other body parts: long reflexes involve the CNS and autonomic nervous system.

2. Hormonal Control of Gastrointestinal Processes
   a. Four hormones important in the control of motility and secretion are:
      (1) gastrin,
      (2) cholescystokinin (CKK),
      (3) secretion,
      (4) gastric inhibitory peptide (GIP).
   b. These hormones produced by endocrine cells in the epithelial lining of the tract are released in response to intraluminal stimuli acting directly in the endocrine cells.

II. Chewing, Salivary Secretion, and Swallowing

A. Chewing

* Chewing is accomplished by combined actions of the skeletal muscles of the jaws, lips, cheeks and tongue.
* Chewing is partly reflexive in nature.

B. Secretion of Saliva

* Saliva is secreted by the parotid, submaxillary and sublingual glands in response to chewing.

* Saliva is composed of water, mucus and amylase.
* Secretion of saliva is regulated by long reflexes involving sympathetic and parasympathetic nerves.
* Salivary secretion serves a number of functions including:
  (1) softening and lubricating food;
  (2) neutralizing acids produced by oral bacteria.
* Salivary amylase degrades complex carbohydrates.

C. Swallowing
* Long reflexes mediated through a swallowing center in the brain coordinate actions of smooth and skeletal muscles involved in swallowing the bolus of food.

1. Swallowing Movements
   a. Food is prevented from entering the glottis by the epiglottis.
   b. A bolus of food moves from the pharynx through the relaxed upper sphincter into the esophagus in response to the downward pressure gradient existing through these regions.
   c. A wave of contraction called peristalsis along the esophagus moves the bolus to the stomach through the relaxed lower sphincter.

2. The Swallowing Reflex
   a. The all or none swallowing reflex is activated when a bolus stimulates mechano-receptors in the pharynx.

III. The Processes of Motility and Secretion in the Stomach

A. Motility of the Stomach
* The motor activity of the stomach serves the major functions of:
  (1) mixing food with gastric secretions,
  (2) conversion of large solid food particles to liquid suspension of fine particles,
  (3) emptying of gastric contents into the duodenum, and
  (4) storage.

1. Muscular Movements of the Stomach
   a. The storage function is served by the smooth muscle of the stomach.
   b. The plasticity of smooth muscle allows the stomach to accommodate large volumes with minimal changes in intragastic pressure.
   c. Peristaltic contractions mix food with gastric juice, reduce particle size and expel gastric contents into the duodenum.

2. Regulation of Stomach Motility
   a. The stomach has a basic electrical rhythm which consists of cycles of spontaneous depolarization and repolarization originating in muscle pacemaker cells at the top of the stomach.
   b. When excitatory stimuli are sufficient to produce action potentials, contraction becomes more vigorous.
   c. Neural and hormonal mechanisms are involved in regulating the rate of gastric emptying.
   d. Stretching of stomach mechanorecptors and the presence of gastrin increase gastric motor activity.

e. Inhibitory mechanisms which prevent the small intestine from being overwhelmed by material from the stomach originate in the duodenum.
f. Secretion and gastric inhibitory hormone, released by the duodenum mucosa when contacted by acid and fat, respectively, inhibit gastric motor activity.
g. The enterogastric inhibitory reflex which is initiated by stimulation of receptors in the duodenum also inhibits gastric motility.

B. Secretion of Gastric Juice
* The exocrine secretory glands contain three types of secretory cells:
(1) chief cells which secrete pepsinogen;
(2) parietal cells which secrete HCl and intrinsic factor, a substance necessary for vitamin B12 absorption; and,
(3) mucous cells which produces alkaline mucus that protects the mucosa.

1. Secretion of Acid by Parietal Cells
a. Hydrogen ions are actively transported into the gastric lumen. Chloride ions are actively transported from blood to parietal cells and then to the gastric lumen.
b. Excitation and inhibition of secretion occur in three phases: the cephalic, gastric, and intestinal phases. Both short and long reflexes via the vagus nerve are involved.

2. Secretion of Pepsin by the Chief Cells
a. Pepsinogen, the precursor of pepsin, is synthesized and stored in the chief cells until it is released into the gastric lumen. There it is converted to pepsin by HCl.
b. Secretion of pepsinogen involves short and long reflexes that occur during the cephalic and gastric phases of digestion.
c. Both peptides and acetylcholine play important roles not only in activation of pepsin but also in the maintenance of the highly acidic environment required for optional activity of pepsin.

C. Vomiting
* Vomiting is a reflex act coordinated by a center located in the medulla.

IV. The Process of Secretion in the Exocrine Pancreas
* The pancreatic acinar cells secrete an alkaline juice that contains digestive enzymes.

A. The Secretion of Pancreatic Bicarbonate

B. The Secretion of Pancreatic Enzymes
* The pancreas secretes enzymes capable of digesting proteins, fats, carbohydrates and nucleic acids.

C. The Regulation of Pancreatic Secretion
* The hormones secretin and cholecystokinin, released from the duodenal mucosa during digestion, play the central role in the control of secretion by the pancreas.

V. The Process of Secretion in the Biliary System

* Bile, secreted by liver cells and stored in the gallbladder, plays a role in the digestion and absorption of fat.
* Bile is composed of bile salts, pigments, cholesterol, Iecithin and inorganic ions such as sodium, chloride and bicarbonate.

A. The Gallbladder: The Storage of Bile

* In the gallbladder the organic constituents of bile become concentrated by the removal of sodium and fluid.

B. The Enterohepatic Circulation of Bile Salts

* Bile salts, synthesized from cholesterol by hepatocytes, play an essential role in the digestion and absorption of fat.
* Bile salts are absorbed from the small intestine, returned to the liver and re-secreted in bile. This recycling is called the enterohepatic circulation of bile salts.
* The rate of synthesis of bile salts is regulated by portal blood concentration of these molecules.

C. The Regulation of Bile Secretion

* Bile secretion is regulated by the concentration of bile salts in the portal blood and by secretin which stimulates epithelial cells lining the bile ducts.

VI. The Processes of Motility, Secretion and Absorption in the Small Intestine

A. Motility in the Small Intestine

* Segmenting contraction, the most frequently occurring type of muscular movement, moves the contents of different regions of the small intestine back and forth over small distances. This action mixes the contents with digestive secretions and brings products of digestive activity into contact with the absorptive epithelium.
* Pacemaker cells determine the frequency of these movements.
* Peristaltic movements provide slow transit required for completion of the absorptive processes.
* Chemical and mechanical stimulation of receptors in the intestinal wall initiate long and short reflexes important in regulation of small intestinal mobility. Gastrin increases motor activity of the ileum and relaxes the ileocecol sphincter.

B. Secretion in the Small Intestine

* Fluid moves from blood to the intestinal lumen in response to the hyperosmotic contents of the lumen.
* Mucosal exocrine cells secrete water, inorganic ions and mucus into intestinal lumen.

C. Absorption from the Small Intestine

1. The Absorptive Surface of the Small Intestine
   a. The absorptive surface area is increased greatly by folds, villi, and microvilli.
   b. Water absorption by osmosis occurs secondarily to the absorption of dissolved minerals.
   c. Sodium is actively transported across the brush border membrane into the intestinal cell from which it is extruded into blood by the sodium pump.
   d. Other inorganic ions are actively or passively transported into the blood.
   e. The absorption of iron and calcium is regulated. Iron is absorbed when the body becomes deficient in this cation. Calcium absorption requires parathyroid hormone and vitamin D.

3. Absorption of Carbohydrates from the Small Intestine
   a. Carbohydrates are enzymatically digested into monosaccharide units which may be absorbed by different mechanisms such as:
      (1) facilitated diffusion (fructose),
      (2) active transport by carrier mediated process (glucose), and
      (3) co-transports (glucose, galactose coupled with sodium).

4. Absorption of Protein from the Small Intestine
   a. Amino acids are transported by active processes. Each class of amino acid has its own specific carrier-mediated system in which amino acid transport is coupled with sodium transport.
   b. Dipeptides and tripeptides are also absorbed.
   c. In the newborns of some species proteins are absorbed by pinocytosis.

5. Absorption of Lipid from the Small Intestine
   a. Triacylglycerols are emulsified by bile salts and then digested by pancreatic lipase into a monoglyceride and two free fatty acid molecules. Bile salts render monoglycerides and free-fatty acids water-soluble by facilitating the formation of micelles.
   b. Monoglycerides and free fatty acids are absorbed as individual molecules from the monomolecular dispersion. The micelles serve as a reservoir for these molecules and replenish them in the monomolecular dispersion.
   c. There is a dynamic relationship between the monomolecular dispersion and the micelles.
   d. Inside epithelial cells monoglycerides and free fatty acids are resynthesized to triacylglycerols which aggregate as droplets.
   e. A layer of phospholipid and protein is added to each droplet to form a chylomicron which enters the central lacteal of the villus and the lymphatic system.

VII. The Processes of Absorption, Secretion, and Motility in the Large Intestine
   * The large intestine is subdivided into the cecum (and its appendix), the ascending colon, transverse colon, descending colon, sigmoid colon, rectum, and anus with its internal and external sphincters.

   A. Absorption and Secretion in the Large Intestine
      * The primary absorptive process is the active transport of sodium from the colon which is accompanied by the osmotic absorption of water.
      * The colonic mucosa secretes an alkaline fluid that protects the mucosa from chemical and mechanical trauma and lubricates the fecal mass thus facilitating its passage.

   B. Motility in the Large Intestine
      * Segmenting contractions promote absorption of water and inorganic ions by exposing the contents to the mucosa.
      * Propulsive mass movements may be stimulated by gastrin, the gastrocolonic reflex, and by distention of colemic walls.

   C. The Defecation Reflex
      * Mass contractions move the contents into the rectum whose distension elicits the defecation reflex.
      * Constipation, the accumulation of feces in the large intestine above the normal capacity, occurs when the muscular activity of the large intestine is decreased.

Chapter Learning Objectives

1. Describe the components and cellular arrangements of the gastrointestinal system.
2. Describe general features of the processes of motility, secretion, digestion and absorption.
3. Describe neural control of the gastrointestinal processes of motility and secretion by short and long reflexes.
4. Describe control of gastrointestinal processes by gastrin, cholecystokinin, secretin and gastric inhibitory peptide. (See Table 23.3)
5. Describe the composition and role of saliva.
6. Describe the muscular movements responsible for swallowing and the passage of food into the stomach.
7. Describe the types of motor activity in the stomach and how this motility is regulated neurally and hormonally.
8. Describe the composition of gastric juice and discuss how gastric juice secretion is regulated.
9. Describe the composition of pancreatic juice and discuss how pancreatic juice secretion is regulated.
10. Describe the composition of bile and discuss how its secretion is regulated.
11. Describe the types of movements in the small intestine and how they are regulated.
12. Describe the mechanisms by which the carbohydrates, proteins, and triacylglycerides are digested and absorbed into epithelial cells and then to the blood or lymphatic system.
13. Describe the mechanisms for the absorption of water and inorganic ions from the small intestine.
14. Describe the types of molecules and mechanisms by which these molecules are absorbed in the large intestine.
15. Describe the types of motility in the large intestine and the defecation reflex.

Key Terms

absorption
acini
amylase (salivary, pancreatic)
basic electrical rhythm
bile (salts, pigments)
bilirubin
bolus
cecum
chief cells
cholecystokinin
cholesterol
chylomicron
colon
common bile duct
constipation
defecation reflex
dietary fiber
digestion
duodenum
enterogastric inhibitory reflex
enterohepatic circulation of bile salts
esophagus
flatus
G-cell
gall bladder
gastric inhibitory peptide
gastrin
gastrocolic reflex
hepatocyte
ileum
jaundice
jejunum
lacteal
lipase
liver
long reflexes
mass movement
micelles
microvilli
mixing movements
monoglyceride
monomolecular dispersion
motility
mucin
mucosa
muscularis
pancreas
pancreatis
parietal cells
pepsin
peptidases
peristalsis
plasticity
portal circulation
propulsive movements
receptive relaxation
rectum
retropulsion
salivary glands
secretin
secretion
segmenting contraction
short reflexes
small intestine
sphincter (anal, pyloric, of Oddi, ileocecal, upper and lower esophageal)
splanchnic circulation
stomach
straining movements
terminal ileum
trypsin
ulcer
villus
zymogen granules

Testing Your Understanding

I. Matching. Select the correct word from the Key Terms

________ 1.	epithelial lining of digestive tract
________ 2.	path for blood from stomach and intestines to the liver
________ 3.	secreted by all regions of the digestive tract
________ 4.	reflex mediated through nerve cells lying entirely within digestive tract wall
________ 5.	reflex mediated over nerves outside of the tract
________ 6.	secreted by G cells, stimulates stomach and secretion and gastric emptying
________ 7.	hormone from small intestine, stimulates bicarbonate secretion from pancreas and biliary system
________ 8.	prevents reflux of gastric contents into esophagus
________ 9.	propulsive movement in esophagus
________ 10.	sphincter between stomach and duodenum
________ 11.	secrete pepsinogen
________ 12.	pancreatic exocrine secretory cells
________ 13.	act together to digest triacylglycerides
________ 14.	membranous projections that increase surface area
________ 15.	primary site of water absorption.

II. Complete the Table. For each nutrient indicate the digestive enzyme, the digestive product and the mechanism by which the digestive product is absorbed.

Nutrient/ Source	Digestive Enzyme(s)	Digestive Product(s)	Mechanism of Absorption
Starch			
cellulose			
myosin			
actin			
cream			
hamburger			
roll			
apple			
casein			

CHAPTER 24 THE KIDNEY

Chapter Outline

* Functions of the kidneys include:
  (1) regulation of osmotic pressure of the plasma and extracellular fluids;
  (2) regulation of the excretion of sodium and water and of the volume of extracellular fluid;
  (3) regulation of hydrogen ion concentration;
  (4) elimination of metabolic waste;
  (5) production of hormones and proteolytic enzymes.

I. Functional Anatomy of the Kidney
  * The two parts of the kidney are the
    (1) medulla in which the loops of Henle and medullary collecting ducts are located, and the
    (2) cortex which contains the glomeruli, convoluted tubules and cortical collecting ducts.
  * The kidney is divided into about 12 lobes, each consisting of a pyramid of medullary and cortical tissues.

  A. The Structure of a Nephron
    * The basic unit of kidney structure and function is the nephron which is composed of a renal corpuscle and its attached renal tubule.
    * The renal tubule consists of a tuft of capillaries, the glomerulus, surrounded by a double-walled cup, Bowman's Capsule.
    * The renal tubule is divided into
      (1) proximal convoluted tubule,
      (2) loop of Henle, and
      (3) distal convoluted tubule which lead to collecting ducts.
    * There are two types of nephrons, the cortical nephrons and juxtamedullary nephrons. They differ structurally in the size of their glomeruli, length of limbs, and location. Functional differences are seen in filtration rate, tubular transport properties and renin content.
    * The renal tubule and collecting duct are composed of a single layer of epithelial cells surrounding a tubule lumen. Cell structure and function vary considerably from one segment to another.

  B. The Blood Supply of the Kidney
    * The renal artery divides into smaller arteries which course through the medulla and cortex. The cortical radical arteries supply the afferent arterioles each of which leads to a glomerulus.
    * The efferent arterioles from the glomerule break up into the peritubular capillaries which form an extensive network surrounding the tubules.
    * The peritubular capillaries lead to veins that eventually empty into the renal vein.
    * The glomeruli, in which blood pressure is high, are specialized for filtration while the peritubular capillaries are specialized for uptake of fluid reabsorbed by the tuberlis.

  C. Nerves and Lymphatic Vessels of the Kidney
    * The sympathetic nerves predominantly innervate blood vessels and cause vasoconstriction.
    * Lymphatic vessels are found in the cortex.

D. The Juxtaglomerular Apparatus

* The juxtaglomerular apparatus consists of specialized cells believed to play a role in regulating glomerular blood flow and filtration rate.

E. The Blood Flow of the Kidney

* The high blood flow to the kidneys is necessary to sustain a high rate of filtration in the glomeruli.
* Blood flow is not distributed uniformly within the kidney.
* Renal autoregulation prevents changes of arterial blood pressure from producing large changes in glomerular filtration rate.
* Renal blood flow is affected by hormones, and physiological and physical conditions.

II. Processes Involved in Formation of Urine

* Three basic processes are involved in urine formation:
  (1) glomerular filtration,
  (2) subular reabsorption, and
  (3) tubular secretion.
* Excretion refers to what comes out in the urine that leaves the body.

A. Glomerular Filtration

* Ultrafiltration is a nonselective process in which a filtrate of plasma is pushed out of the glomerulus by high hydrostatic pressure into the Bowman's capsule.

1. The Glomerular Filtration Membrane
   a. The glomular filtration membrane consists of three layers:
      (1) capillary endothelium,
      (2) glomerular basement membrane, and
      (3) podocyte cell layer.
   b. The filtration membrane is a size-selective and electrostatic barrier to the free movement of molecules.

2. Factors that Affect Glomerular Filtration Rate

   a. Glomerular capillary hydrostatic pressure (P_{gc}) is the driving force for filtration.
   b. Filtration is opposed by the hydrostatic pressure in the urinary space in Bowman's capsule (P_{BS}) and by intra-capillary colloid osmotic pressure due to the plasma proteins (π GC).
   c. The net filtration pressure gradient (Δ P) is equal to the difference between pressures favoring and opposing filtration and is expressed by the equation:

$$\Delta P = P_{gc} - P_{BS} - \pi GC$$

   d. The glomerular filtration rate (GFR) is expressed as GFR = K_f x P where K_f equals the glomerular coefficient.
   e. Glomerular filtration rate is high because
      (1) the glomerular filtration membrane has a high fluid permeability,
      (2) the glomerular hydrostatic pressure is unusually high for a capillary bed, and
      (3) of the high rate of renal blood flow.
   f. Glomerular hydrostatic pressure depends mainly on arterial blood pressure and resistance of upstream blood vessels.

3. The Clearance Concept and the Measurement of Glomerular Filtration Rate
   a. The clearance is rate of excretion of a substance (x) which is equal to the product of its urine concentration (Ux) and urine flow rate (V) divided by its plasmic concentration (Px) and is expressed by the equation:

$$Cx = Ux \quad x \ V/Px.$$

   b. The measurement of GFR is important in assessing kidney function.

B. Tubular Reabsorption
   * In this selective process substances are transferred out of the tubular fluid and returned to the peritubular capillaries.
   * Reabsorption may be either active or passive.

1. Reabsorption of Glucose
   a. Glucose is actively reabsorbed by the proximal tubule. It is cotransported with sodium across the luminal cell membrane.
   b. The maximal rate of glucose reabsorption is called the tubular transport maximum (Tm) for glucose (G).
   c. Other sugars are reabsorbed by the same mechanism as glucose.
   d. Sugars may compete for transport.

2. Reabsorption of Amino Acids
   a. There are several distinct transport mechanisms for amino acids, each reabsorbing a group of structurally similar compounds.
   b. Amino acid reabsorption is active, depends on sodium transport, occurs in the proximal tubule, shows a maximal rate of transport and within-group competition.

3. Reabsorption of Uric Acid
   a. Reabsorption and secretion of uric acid occur in the proximal tubule by carrier-mediated processes.

4. Reabsorption of Urea
   a. Eighty percent of urea, the major nitrogen-containing end product of metabolism, is reabsorbed by the inner medullary collecting duct.

5. Reabsorption of Proteins
   a. The proximal tubules reabsorb a variety of proteins by pinocytosis
   b. Many other organic compounds are reabsorbed by the kidney tubules.

C. Tubular Secretion
   * In this process substances move from the peritubular capillaries into the tubular fluid.
   * The two secretory mechanisms transport a variety or organic anions, and cations, are present in the proximal tubule and are active. They also show maximal transport rate at high plasma levels and show within-group competition for transport.

III. Tubular Transport of Mineral Eletrolytes

A. Tubular Transport of Sodium
   * Sodium reabsorption is the major driving force for water reabsorption, is coupled to the reabsorption of both organic and inorganic substances and is related to the secretion of hydrogen and potassium ions.

1. Sodium Transport in the Proximal Convoluted Tubule
   a. The proximal convoluted tubule absorbs 70% of the filtered sodium and water.
   b. Sodium moves into the cell along chemical and electrical gradients. Its entry is coupled to the movement of other solutes like glucose, amino acids, phosphate ions and chloride ions.
   c. The intracellular concentration is low because sodium is actively transported out the basolateral membrane.
   d. Reabsorbed fluid is taken into the peritubular capillaries by a difference in hydrostatic and colloid osmostic pressures.

2. Sodium Transport in More Distal Nephron Segments
   a. The loop of Henle absorbs about 20% of filtered sodium and 10% of the filtered water.
   b. The ascending limb is impermeable to water but resorbs salt by a coupled sodium-potassium-chloride transporter in the terminal cell membrane and a sodium-potassium pump in the basolateral cell membrane.
   c. Most of the remaining salt and water is resorbed in the distal collecting tubule and collecting duct by action transport for sodium.
   * The collecting ducts are the site of fine control for sodium and water reabsorption by the hormones aldosterone and ADH respectively.

B. Tubular Transport of Potassium
   * Potassium is reabsorbed primarily in the proximal convoluted tubule and loop of Henle. It is secreted by the collecting ducts under normal conditions or with potassium excess.
   * Potassium is taken up into the cortical collecting duct principal cell by the basolateral membrane sodium-potassium pump and then diffuses across the luminal cell membrane into the lumen.
   * The concentration of potassium in the cell is affected by aldosterone and the extracellular potassium concentration. Aldosterone increases luminal membrane permeability to sodium and potassium.
   * Across many nephron segments is a transtubular potential difference which is lower in the luminal side than at the basolateral side of the cell. This favors potassium secretion into the lumen.

C. Tubular Transport of Calcium
   * Renal excretion of calcium represents only about 10% of total daily output from the body. The rest passes out of the body in the feces.
   * About 60% of filtered calcium is reabsorbed in the proximal convoluted tubule and most of the rest in the thick ascending limb, distal convoluted tubule and collecting ducts.

D. Tubular Transport of Magnesium
   * About 20-30% fliltered magnesium is reabsorbed in the proximal convoluted tubule and 50-60% reabsorbed in the Loop of Henle. Only about 3-5% is excreted in the urine. About two thirds of dietary magnesium is lost in the feces.
   * The kidneys play a major role in regulating plasma magnesium concentration.

E. Tubular Transport of Phosphate

* The kidneys play an important role in regulating the plasma concentration of inorganic phosphate.
* Filtered phosphate is reabsorbed by sodium-dependent, secondary active transport in the proximal tubule.
* Phosphate excretion depends on the Tm for phosphate which is normally close to the filtered phosphate load. Thus Tm will be exceeded more than usual and phosphate excretion will increase. If filtered phosphate amounts are decreased, all will be reabsorbed.

IV. Tubular Reabsorption of Water

* The rate of water excretion in the urine depends on the glomerular filtration and tubular reabsorption rates.

A. Production of Hyperosmotic Urine to Save Water

* The ability to produce a hyperosmotic urine or concentrated urine depends on the length of the loop of Henle, i.e. the longer the loop, the greater the ability to produce hyperosmotic urine.

B. The Countercurrent Hypothesis for the Formation of Osmotically Concentrated Urine.

* The Loops of Henle act as countercurrent multipliers in setting up an increasing gradient of osmolality from the junction of the cortex and medulla to the tip of the renal papillae.
* The blood vessels of the medulla acting as passive countercurrent exchangers help preserve the gradient.
* The collecting ducts acting as osmotic equilibrating devices alter the osmolality of the urine depending on the plasma level of ADH.
* Countercurrent multiplication is an energy-consuming process.
* The osmotic gradient along the Loop of Henle can be established by salt transport between ascending and descending limbs.
* The osmolality of the tubular fluid changes as the fluid passes through the descending and ascending limbs, and the collecting ducts in the outer and inner medulla.

C. A Special Role for Urea in Producing a Concentrated Urine.

* Urea plays an important role in the concentrating mechanism in the inner medulla. It is added to the inner medulla from the collecting ducts and from the calyceal urine bathing the papilla.
* The osmotic pressure due to urea sets up a concentration gradient for sodium in the inner medulla.

D. The Role of the Vasa Recta in Producing a Concentrated Urine

* The vasa recta act as countercurrent exchangers and are responsible for removing water from the medulla by plasma called osmotic pressure mechanism.

E. Factors Affecting Urinary Concentrating Ability

* Factors affecting urinary concentrating ability include:
  (1) antidiuretic hormone (ADH),
  (2) adequate delivery to and reabsorption of salt along the ascending limb,
  (3) adequate delivery of fluid to the collecting duct,
  (4) adequate urea concentration, and
  (5) length of the Loop of Henle.

F. Production of an Osmotically Dilute Urine
   * Production of an osmotically dilute urine results from the reabsorption of solute across a relative water impermeable membrane, with water left behind.
   * The degree of water-permeability of the collecting ducts depends on the presence of ADH.

Chapter Learning Objectives

1. Draw and identify parts of the kidney and a nephron.
2. Describe the general function of each part of the kidney and nephron.
3. Describe an epithelial cell from the proximal convoluted tubule.
4. Trace the flow of blood through the kidney from the renal artery to the renal vein.
5. Describe the structure and function of the juxtoglomerular apparatus.
6. Describe renal autoregulation of blood flow to the kidney.
7. Describe glomerular filtration as to where and how it occurs, factors affecting glomerular filtration rate, and the selectivity of the process.
8. Definc clearance and describe how glomerular filtration rate is measured.
9. Describe tubular reabsorption as to where and how it occurs, the selectivity of the process, and factors affecting reabsorption.
10. Describe the reabsorption of glucose, amino acids, uric acid, urea, and proteins as to the transport processes involved for each type of molecule, where each is reabsorbed, and the affects of competition and concentration on reabsorption.
11. Describe the types of molecules and transport processes by which these molecules are secreted, where they are secreted and factors affecting their secretion.
12. Describe the transport of sodium through the proximal convoluted tubule, loop of Henle, distal convoluted tubule, and collecting ducts. Describe where and how reabsorption occurs and the effect of sodium reabsorption on water reabsorption.
13. Describe the conditions and processes by which potassium and phosphate are secreted and reabsorbed.
14. Describe the processes by which water is reabsorbed and factors affecting these processes.
15. Describe how hyperosmotic urine is produced. Discuss the roles of the loops of Henle and urea in the production of concentrated urine.
16. Describe several factors affecting urinary concentrating ability.

Key Terms

aldosterone
antidiuretic hormone (ADH)
basement membrane
basolateral membrane
Bowman's capsule
calyx (major, minor)
clearance formula (Cx=Ux x V/Px)
colloid osmotic pressure
convoluted tubule (distal, proximal)
cortex
cortical collecting ducts
countercurrent exchanger
countercurrent hypothesis
countercurrent multiplier
diabetes insipidus
diluting segment
glomerular filtration rate (GFR)
glomerular filtration membrane
glomerular hydrostatic pressure (Pgc)
glomerulus
hydrostatic pressure
insulin
juxtaglomerular apparatus
juxtamedullary nephron
Loop of Henle (ascending, descending limbs)
luminal membrane
medulla (outer, inner)
medullary collecting duct (outer,inner)
nephron
osmotic equilibrating device
renal autoregulation
renal corpuscle
renal pelvis
renal plasma clearance
renal tubule
slip pore
transtubular potential difference
tubular reabsorption
tubular secretion
tubular transport maximum (Tm)
tubuloglomerular feedback hypothesis
urea
ureter
urethra
uric acid
vasa recta

excretion
fenestra
filtration coefficient (Kf)
glomerular filtration
peritubular capillaries
podocyte
proteinuria

Testing Your Understanding

I. Matching. Selecte the correct word from the Key Terms.

__________1. tuft of capillaries in renal corpuscle
__________2. major site of reabsorption of glucose, amino acids
__________3. tube draining kidney
__________4. have large glomeruli and long loops of Henle
__________5. membrane through which solutes in tubular fluid pass
__________6. surround tubules and specialized for uptake of fluids reabsorbed by tubules
__________7. may play a role in regulating glomerular blood flow and filtration rate at level of single nephron
__________8. forces fluid from renal corpuscle into renal tubule
__________9. hole in endothelial cell layer lining capillaries
__________10. exceeded for glucose in diabetes mellitus
__________11. function as countercurrent multipliers
__________12. passive countercurrent exchangers in medulla
__________13. increases with increase in concentration of serum proteins
__________14. affects water-permeability of collecting tubules
__________15. primary nitrogenous waste product

II. Complete the Table. For each condition, indicate the effect on glomerular filtration rate.

Condition	Glomerular filtration rate
1. increase in length of Loop of Henle	
2. decreased glomerular hydrostatic pressure	
3. decrease in renal blood flow	
4. concentration of glucose above Tm	
5. decrease in sodium reabsorption	
6. constriction of afferent arterioles	
7. increase in hydrostatic pressure in Bowman's space	
8. decrease in plasma colloid osmotic pressure	

III. Complete the Table. For each condition indicate the effect on tubular reabsorption of glucose, sodium, and/or water.

Condition	Effect on Tubular Glucose	Reabsorption Sodium	Water
1. high concentration of fructose			
2. low plasma concentration of sodium			
3. low plasma osmolality			
4. presence of aldosterone			
5. pressure of antidiuretic hormone			
6. diabetes mellitus			
7. deficiency of dietary protein			
8. decrease in length of loop of Henle			

CHAPTER 25 REGULATION OF FLUID AND ELECTROLYTE BALANCE

Chapter Outline

I. Body Fluids and Fluid Compartments

A. Body Water and Its Divisions
- * The percentage of total body weight that is water varies from 45% to 75% and is related to the amount of body fat.
- * Two thirds of body water is contained in the intracellular fluid compartment and one third in the extracellular fluid compartment which is subdivided into the blood plasma, interstitial fluid and lymph, and transcellular fluid subcompartments.

B. Electrolyte Composition of the Body Fluids
- * Electrolytes contribute most to the osmotic pressure of the body fluids and are crucial in the distribution of body water.
- * Concentrations of electrolytes are expressed in terms of milliequivalents per liter solution.
- * Sodium is the major cation and chloride and bicarbonate the major anions in the plasma.
- * The differences in concentrations of small ions between the plasma water and interstitial fluid arise because of differences in protein concentration between these two fluids.
- * The distribution of potassium and sodium ions is maintained by the sodium-potassium pump while that of chloride and bicarbonate is accounted for by the membrane potential difference.
- * The intracellular distribution of ions is not uniform; different organelles may have different ion concentrations.

C. Distribution of Water Between Cellular and Extracellular Fluids
- * Osmotic pressure is of prime importance in determining the distribution of water between cells and extracellular fluid and is directly related to osmolality.
- * In extracellular fluid the amount of sodium is a major determinant of the volume of water present. Sodium, chloride, and bicarbonate are the osmotically active solutes in the extracellular fluid.
- * In the intracellular fluid compartment, potassium is the major osmotically active solute.
- * The sodium-potassium pump plays a key role in regulation of cell volume.
- * The normal distribution of water between the cellular and extracellular compartments changes in a variety of circumstances.

D. Distribution of Water Between Blood Plasma and Interstitial Fluid
- * The relative volumes of plasma and interstitial fluids are determined by the balance between capillary and tissue hydrostatic and collard osmotic pressures.
- * An increase in capillary hydrostatic pressure favors net movement of fluid out of the vascular system while a decrease would favor movement of interstitial fluid into the circulation.

II. The Concept of Fluid and Electrolyte Balance
- * The composition of body fluids remains constant despite varying dietary intake of food and water.
- * The kidneys play a major role in maintaining balance with respect to water, mineral electrolytes, hydrogen ions, and various organic compounds.

A. The Regulation of Water Balance

* The regulation of body water balance involves two basic mechanisms:

(1) the thirst sensation, and

(2) control of renal water excretion by the antidiuretic hormone (ADH).

1. Thirst and the Regulation of Fluid Intake
   a. Thirst is controlled by centers in the hypothalamus which relay information to the cerebral cortex where thirst becomes a conscious sensation. The hypothalamus controls the release of ADH.
   b. Cellular dehydration is detected by osmoreceptors in the anterior hypothalamus which signals the cerebral cortex to give rise to the thirst sensation.
   c. Extracellular dehydration or a decrease in effective circulatory blood volume is detected by various baroreceptors such as arterial baroreceptors in the carotid sinus and aortic arch and stretch receptors in large veins in the thorax. Impulses are sent to the thirst control centers in the hypothalamus.
   d. The kidneys also act as volume receptors.

2. Antidiuretic Hormone and the Regulation of Fluid Output
   a. ADH facilitates water reabsorption by the collecting ducts.
   b. Cellular and extracellular dehydration stimulate the release of ADH.

3. Renal Responses to Extra Water Intake or to Dehydration
   a. Renal excretion of water is continuously adjusted by changes in plasma ADH levels so plasma osmolality and extracellular fluid volume are kept at normal levels.

B. The Regulation of Sodium Balance

1. Sodium Input and Output
   a. The kidneys are the major site of control of sodium output and normally adjust excretion so as to maintain balance.
   b. Sodium balance is related to regulation of extracellular fluid volume.

2. The Renal Response to Changes in Dietary Intake of Sodium
   a. Changes in dietary input lead to appropriate changes in sodium excretion by the kidneys.

3. Effector Mechanisms Activated by Altered Extracellular Fluid Volume.
   a. Effector mechanisms include changes in:
      (1) glomerular filtration rate,
      (2) plasma aldosterone levels,
      (3) peritubular capillary Starling forces,
      (4) renal sympathetic nerve activity
      (5) intrarenal blood flow distribution, and
      (6) plasma atrial natriuretic factor.
   b. Aldosterone increase sodium reabsorption by a variety of epithelial tissues and the collecting ducts.
   c. The renin-angiotensin system controls aldosterone secretion.
      (1) Volume depletion stimulates the release of renin from granular cells of the juxtaglomerular apparatus.
      (2) Renin acts on the plasma protein angiotensinogen to produce angiotensin I which is converted enzymatically to angiotensin II.

(3) Angiotensin II raises blood pressure, stimulates the synthesis and release of aldosterone, stimulates the hypothalamic thirst centers and the release of ADH.

d. Atrial natriuretic factor is released by the atria in response to an increase in blood volume. It increases sodium excretion by increasing glomerular filtration rate and inhibiting sodium reabsorption.

4. The Nature of the Stimuli and the Location of Receptors Affecting Sodium Excretion
   a. Effective arterial blood volume is believed to be the controlled variable affecting sodium excretion.
   b. Volume receptors are located in the wall of the left atrium, in intrathoracic veins, and in the kidneys.
   c. Changes in effective arterial blood volume can elicit the appropriate renal response by three possible mechanisms.
      (1) A change in blood volume affects changes in glomerular blood flow and capillary pressure which affect glomerular filtration rate.
      (2) A change in blood volume is detected by an intrarenal baroreceptor which then affects release of renin.
      (3) A change in blood volume could change peritubular capillary Starling forces.

5. Other Factors That Influence Sodium Excretion
   a. Other factors affecting sodium excretion include
      (1) glucocorticoids,
      (2) estrogen,
      (3) osmotic diuretics,
      (4) poorly reabsorbed anions, and
      (5) diuretic drugs.

C. The Regulation of Potassium Balance

* Potassium plays a number of important roles in the body. It
  (1) influences the electrical excitability of cells.
  (2) is the major osmotically active solute in cells.
  (3) affects acid-base balance.
  (4) affects cell metabolism.
* The kidneys are the major site of potassium loss and control of potassium balance
* Several factors affect the distribution of potassium between cells and extracellular fluid. These include:
  (1) the activity of the sodium-potassium pump,
  (2) acid-base status of body fluids,
  (3) the availability of insulin,
  (4) cellular breakdown due to trauma, infection, ischemia and heavy exercise.
* The regulation of plasma potassium involves
  (1) hormones like insulin, epinephrine and aldosterone, and
  (2) the kidneys.
* Factors affecting potassium excretion include
  (1) intracellular potassium concentration,
  (2) aldosterone,
  (3) excretion of anions, and
  (4) urine flow rate.

III. Kidney Failure and Its Treatment

* Kidney disease results from a loss of nephrons. A symptom of renal failure is uremia.

A. Disturbances in Renal Failure

* Disturbances occurring in uremia include:
  (1) anemia resulting from a deficiency of erythroporetin,
  (2) azotemia,
  (3) alterations in calcium and phosphate metabolism,
  (4) hypertension,
  (5) metabolic acidosis,
  (6) altered potassium and sodium balance
  (7) impairment of urinary concentrating ability.

B. Treatment by Dialysis

* Most of the signs and symptoms of uremia can be relieved by dialysis.

C. Transplantation of the Kidney

IV. Functions of Ureters and Urinary Bladder

A. The Ureter

* The ureter carries urine from the kidney pelvis to the urinary bladder. Urine is forced along the ureters by peristaltic movements.

B. The Urinary Bladder

* The bladder has two functions:
  (1) to serve as a distensible reservoir for urine, and
  (2) to empty its contents at suitable intervals

C. Micturition

* Miturition, the periodic complete emptying of the bladder, involves several reflexes that can be facilitated or inhibited by higher centers of the brain.

Chapter Learning Objectives

1. Describe the three fluid compartments in the body.
2. Compare the interstitial, cellular and plasma fluids as to distribution of major electrolytes.
3. Describe factors affecting the distribution of water between cellular and extracellular fluids and between blood plasma and interstitial fluid.
4. Describe mechanisms that regulate water balance.
5. Describe body response to cellular dehydration and extracellular dehydration.
6. Discuss how ADH affects fluid output.
7. Describe body responses to changes in dietary intake of sodium.
8. List important roles of potassium in the body.
9. Discuss factors affecting the distribution of potassium between cells and extracellular fluid and potassium excretion.
10. List disturbances occurring in response to uremia.
11. Describe the functions of the ureters and urinary bladder.

Key Terms

aldosterone
angiotensin (I, II)
antidiuretic hormone (ADH)
atrial natriuretic factor
azotemia
baroreceptor
detrusor
dialysis (peritoneal)
diuretic
Donnan equilibrium
effective arterial blood volume
effective osmotic pressure
extracellular fluid
glomerulotubular balance
hemodialysis
hyperkalemia
hypertension
hypokalemia
hyponatremia
hypovolemia
insensible water loss
intracellular fluid
micturition
milliequivalent (mEq)
negative balance
osmoreceptor
osmotic diuretic
positive balance
renin
sodium appetite
transcellular fluid
ureter
urethra
urinary bladder
water diuresis

Testing Your Understanding

I. Matching. Select the correct word from the Key Terms.

________ 1. occurs when input exceeds output
________ 2. detects cellular dehydration
________ 3. detects hypovolemia
________ 4. low sodium concentration in the blood
________ 5. increases the water permeability of the collecting ducts
________ 6. urination
________ 7. carries urine outside body
________ 8. increases reabsorption of sodium by collecting ducts
________ 9. increases sodium excretion by increasing glomerular filtration rate
10. increase excretion of water
________ 11. below normal level of plasma potassium
________ 12. high blood pressure
________ 13. accumulation of nitrogenous waste products
________ 14. uses artificial kidney
________ 15. smooth muscle in urinary bladder wall

II. Complete the Table. For each condition indicate the effect on water intake and release of antidiuretic hormones.

Condition	Water Intake	ADH Release
1. ingestion of excess salt		
2. decreased function of adrenal cortex		
3. excessive sweating		
4. activation of thirst sensation		
5. decrease in plasma osmolality		
6. cellular dehydration		
7. hypovolemia		
8. presence of renin in the plasma		
9. presence of ADH		
10. decrease in effective arterial blood volume		

III. Complete the Table. For each condition indicate the effect on sodium reabsorption.

Condition	Sodium Reabsorption
1. presence of ADH	
2. heavy exercise	
3. diarrhea	
4. congestive heart failure	
5. ingestion of salty potato chips	
6. increase in glomerular filtration rate	
7. hemorrhage	
8. presence of aldosterone	
9. stimulation of renal sympathetic nerves	
10. increase in peritubular capillary hydrostatic pressure	
11. decrease in colloid osmotic pressure	
12. presence of atrial natriuretic factor	
13. osmotic diuretic	
14. hyperkalemia	

CHAPTER 26 REGULATION OF ACID-BASE BALANCE

Chapter Outline

I. Principles of Acid-Base Physiology
 * Hydrogen ion concentration influences
  (1) the speed of chemical reactions catalyzed by enzymes,
  (2) cell permeability properties, and
  (3) cell structure.

A. Definition of Acid and Base
 * An acid is a substance that can donate hydrogen ions.
 * A base is a substance that can accept or bind hydrogen ions.

B. The Neutralization Reaction
 * In a neutralization reaction an acid reacts with a base to form a salt and water.

1. Quantifying Acids and Bases: Milliequivalents
 a. The amount of acid or base is expressed in terms of equivalents or milliequivalents (mEq).
 b. One equivalent of acid will neutralize one equivalent of base.

2. Amphoteric Substances
 a. Amphoteric substances can function as an acid or base. They include amino acids and proteins.

C. The Acid Dissociation Constant
 * When an acid (HA) is added to water, it dissociates

$$HA \rightleftharpoons H^+ + A^-$$

 * The rate of disocciation is equal to the concentration of HA and the dissociation rate constant k_1.
 * The rate of association ($A^- + H^+ \rightarrow HA$) is equal to the product of the concentrations of H^+ and A^- and the association rate constant k_2.
 * At equilibrium $\frac{[H^+] \times [A^-]}{[HA]} = \frac{k_1}{k_2}$ $k_1/k_2 = ka$.

 Ka is the equilibrium constant or dissociation constant for this reaction. The higher the acid dissociation constant, the more completely an acid is dissolved.
 * Acid dissociation constants are often expressed in a logarithmic form. pKa is defined as the negative logarithm to the base 10 of Ka or pKa = -log ka.

D. pH Values of Aqueous Solutions
 * pH is defined as the negative logarithm to the base 10 of the molar activity (concentration) of hydrogen ions or

$$pH = -\log [H^+]$$

1. The Henderson-Hasselbalch Equation
 a. The Henderson-Hasselbalch equation relates pH to the acid dissociation constant and is expressed as

$$pH = pKa + \log ([A^-]/[HA])$$

2. The Ion Product of Water
 a. The dissociation constant (K) for water is equal to

$$K = [H^+] \times [OH^-]/[H_2O]$$

 b. The ion product of water (Kw) is $Kw = [H^+] \times [OH^-]$

E. Buffer Systems: General Principles

* A pH buffer minimizes a change in pH when either acid or base is added to a solution.
* A chemical buffer consists of a weak acid and its conjugate base or a weak base and its conjugate acid.
* The equilibrium expression for dissociation of an acid can be written in the Henderson-Hasselbalch equation form:

$$pH = pKa + \log([\text{conjugate base}])/_{[\text{acid}])}$$

* For a specific buffer the pH change for a given amount of added acid or base will be least near the pKa of the buffer.
* The effectiveness of a buffer in minimizing pH changes depends on two factors:
  (1) the pKa of the buffer in relation to the desired pH, and
  (2) the amount or concentration of buffer present.

F. Sources of Hydrogen Ions for the Body

* The metabolism of food in our diet is usually the major source of hydrogen ions.

1. Metabolic Production of CO_2 as a Source of Hydrogen Ions
   a. Carbon dioxide reacts with water to produce carbonic acid (H_2CO_3) which dissociates with H^+ and HCO_3^-.
   b. As long as CO_2 is expressed, there is no acid burden imposed on the body.

2. Metabolism of Carbohydrates and Fatty Acids as a source of Hydrogen Ions
   a. If carbohydrates and fatty acids are completely oxidized, there is no acid burden imposed on the body.
   b. Incomplete oxidation increases the acid burden on the body.

3. Metabolism of Proteins as a Source of Hydrogen Ions
   a. The metabolism of dietary proteins results in production of strong acids.
   b. To some extent these acid-producing reactions are neutralized by acid-consuming reactions.

II. Regulation of Extracellular pH: Buffering Mechanisms in the Body

* pH is stabilized in the body by chemical buffers in extracellular and intracellular fluids and in bone, by the lungs which dispose of CO_2, and by the kidneys which buffer blood pH by excreting hydrogen ions.

A. Chemical pH Buffers

* Chemical pH buffers include
  (1) phosphates,
  (2) proteins, and
  (3) the bicarbonate-CO_2 system
* Chemical buffers consist of conjugate acid-base pairs that bind or release hydrogen ions when acid or base is added.

1. Phosphate as a Chemical Buffer
   a. Phosphate with pK of 6.8 is a good buffer for stabilizing blood pH close to its normal value of 6.8.
   b. Phosphate is found in phosphate salts in bone and in organic phosphate compounds in the cell.

2. Proteins as Chemical Buffers
   a. Proteins constitute the largest pool of buffers and contain many different ionizable groups.

3. The Bicarbonate-CO_2 System as a Chemical Buffer
   a. The bicarbonate-CO_2 system is of special importance in pH buffering in extracellular fluids.
   b. The bicarbonate-CO_2 system is represented by the following reaction:

$$CO_2 + H_2O \rightleftharpoons H_2CO_3 \rightleftharpoons H^+ + HCO_3^-$$

   c. The concentration of dissolved CO_2 in the plasma is related to P_{CO_2}. The concentration of H_2CO_3 is directly proportional to the P_{CO_2} by way of dissolved CO_2.
   d. The pK of bicarbonate - CO_2 buffer pair is 6.10 but the buffer pair operates in an open system. CO_2 can be exhaled which lowers its level in plasma.
   e. The bicarbonate-CO_2 system is effective because of the ability of the body to change the amounts of components of this particular buffer pair.

4. The Isohydric Principle
   a. In any fluid compartment all the buffer systems are in equilibrium with the same hydrogen ion concentration, a concept called the isohydric principle.

B. Physiological Barriers

1. The Respiratory System as a Buffer System: Control of the P_{CO_2}.
   a. CO_2 is expired at the same rate as it is produced from metabolism and the P_{CO_2} remains constant under normal conditions.
   b. In a state of hyperventilation, CO_2 is exhaled at a rate greater than the rate at which it is produced in the body. The results in the bicarbonate-CO_2 equation (See II.A.3.b) shifting to the left and the blood becoming more alkaline.
   c. During hypoventilation, CO_2 is exhaled at a rate slower than the rate at which it is produced. This results in the bicarbonate-CO_2 equation shifting to the right and blood becoming more acidic.
   d. Peripheral and central chemoreceptors detect changes in blood pH which stimulates the appropriate changes in ventilation.

2. The Kidneys as a Buffer System: Acidification of Urine
   a. The kidneys get rid of acid or base in the urine when there is an excess or deficit of hydrogen ions in the body.
   b. Most of the hydrogen ions excreted in the urine are combined with urinary buffers which include titratable acids and ammonia.
   c. Urine is acidified by the secretion of H^+ by the tubular epithelium.
   d. Bicarbonate ions in the tubular filtrate are reabsorbed into the peritubular capillaries.
   e. In the proximal convoluted tubule hydrogen ions secreted into tubular urine combine with bicarbonate ions to form H_2O. CO_2 enters the tubular cell and associates with H_2O to form H_2CO_3 which then dissociates to form bicarbonate. The filtered bicarbonate is reabsorbed indirectly by hydrogen ion secretion.
   f. Filtered phosphate is incompletely reabsorbed and the unreabsorbed phosphate acts as a pH buffer in the urine.
   g. Ammonia produced by kidney tubule cells diffuses into the urine where it combines with H^+ to form the ammonium ion. The ammonium ion is trapped in the urine. For each H^+ exerted as part of the ammonium ion an equivalent

quantity of new bicarbonate is added to the blood.

h. A high blood P_{CO_2} favors generation and increased excretion of H^+ combined with titrable acids and ammonia and more complete reabsorption of filtered bicarbonate. A low blood P_{CO_2} results in a lower rate of hydrogen ion secretion, less complete reabsorption of bicarbonate and the excretion of an alkaline urine.

i. The kidneys regulate plasma pH by changing plasma bicarbonate concentration in the appropriate direction.

III. Disturbances of Acid-Base Balance

* There are four fundamental types of acid-base disturbance:
  (1) respiratory acidosis,
  (2) respiratory alkalosis,
  (3) metabolic acidosis, and
  (4) metabolic alkalosis.

A. Respiratory Acidosis: Accumulation of CO_2

* Respiratory acidosis is characterized by accumulation of CO_2 due to inadequate alveolar ventilation.
* Plasma concentrations of bicarbonate and hydrogen ions increase.
* The kidneys compensate for respiratory acidosis by secreting hydrogen ions into tubular urine and reabsorbing all the filtered bicarbonate.
* The bicarbonate added to the blood diminishes the severity of the acidemia.

B. Respiratory Alkalosis: Loss of CO_2

* The excessive loss of CO_2 by alveolar hyper-ventilation leads to a fall in plasma hydrogen ion concentration and a decline in plasma bicarbonate.
* Chemical buffers release H^+.
* The kidneys compensate by excreting bicarbonate in the urine and a decreased hydrogen in secretion by the tubular epithelium.

C. Metabolic (Nonrespiratory) Acidosis: Gain of Fixed Acid or Loss of Bicarbonate.

* Metabolic acidosis, characterized by a gain of fixed acid or loss of bicarbonate, can result from diarrhea, abnormal excretion of bicarbonate in the urine, ingestion of certain acidifying agents, disease conditions and heavy exercise.
* Respiratory compensation is rapid but usually does not restore blood to normal pH. Renal compensation is slower but more complete.

D. Metabolic (Nonrespiratory) Alkalosis: Gain of Strong Base or Bicarbonate or Loss of Acid.

* Metabolic alkalosis, characterized by gain of strong base or bicarbonate or loss of acid, can result from ingestion of excess sodium bicarbonate, oxidation of organic anions, and vomiting.
* Metabolic alkalosis leads to an increase in plasma bicarbonate, a rise in pH and a compensatory rise in P_{CO_2}.
* Chemical buffers release H^+. Respiratory compensation is alveolar hypoventilation. Renal compensation involves increased excretion of bicarbonate.

E. Analysis of Acid-Base Data from Blood

* Identification of the type of acid-base disturbance requires clinical evidence and laboratory data on pH, P_{CO_2} and plasma bicarbonate concentration.

IV. Regulation of Intracellular pH

* Intracellular pH is generally lower than extracellular pH.
* Cells buffer acid in three ways:
  (1) by chemical buffers like proteins, organic phosphates, and bicarbonate,
  (2) by biochemical reactions which use or release H^+, and
  (3) by intracellular transfer of H^+

Chapter Learning Objectives

1. Define pKa, pH, and write the Henderson-Hasselbalch equation.
2. Describe how buffers minimize changes in pH.
3. Describe four sources of hydrogen ions.
4. List three chemical buffers and describe how each operates as a buffer.
5. Describe how and under what conditions the respiratory system acts as a physiological buffer.
6. Describe how and under what conditions the kidneys act as a physiological buffer.
7. Compare respiratory and metabolic acidoses and respiratory and metabolic alkalosis as to cause, characteristics, the nature of the abnormal process and how buffering mechanisms in the body act to minimize deviations from normal pH.
8. Describe three ways cells can buffer acid.

Key Terms

acid
amphoteric substance
association rate constant, k_2
association reaction
base
bicarbonate
bicarbonate-CO_2 system
buffer (chemical, physiological)
chemoreceptor (peripheral, central)
conjugate base
dehydration reaction
diffusion trapping
dissociation constant, Ka
dissociation rate constant, k_1
dissociation reaction
Henderson-Hasselbalch equation
hydration reaction
hydrogen in concentration $[H^+]$
ion product of water, Kw
isohydric principle
metabolic acidosis
metabolic alkalosis
milliequivalent (mEq)
neutralization
pH
pKa
respiratory acidosis
respiratory alkalosis
titratable acid

Testing Your Understanding

I. Matching. Select the correct word from the Key Terms

________1. donates hydrogen ions
________2. accepts or binds hydrogen ions
________3. describes substance that can donate and accept hydrogen ions
________4. describes reaction $HA \rightleftharpoons H^+ + A^-$
________5. describes reaction $H^+ + A^- \rightleftharpoons HA$
________6. substance that minimizes a change in pH when acid or base is added to solution
________7. detects change in blood pH
________8. characterized by accumulation of CO_2
________9. characterized by loss of CO_2
________10. characterized by gain of fixed acid or loss of bicarbonate

II. Complete the Table. For each condition indicate the effect on secretion of H^+, the reabsorption of bicarbonate and blood pH

Condition	Secretion of H^+	Reabsorption of HCO_3^-	Concentration of plasma H^+
1. hyperventilation			
2. hypoventilation			
3. metabolic acidosis			
4. metabolic alkalosis			
5. respiratory acidosis			
6. respiratory alkalosis			
7. uncontrolled diabetes mellitus			
8. excessive ingestion of sodium bicarbonate			

CHAPTER 27 CALCIUM, PHOSPHATE AND BONE METABOLISM

Chapter Outline

I. Overview: Functions of Calcium and Phosphate
   * Calcium is involved in a number of different physiological processes. These include:
     (1) maintaining normal sodium permeability in nerves,
     (2) triggering the release of acetylcholine from nerve endings at the neuromuscular junction,
     (3) acting as a signal for excitation-contraction coupling in muscle,
     (4) acting as an intracellular signal or second messenger for normal activity,
     (5) serving as a cofactor for enzymes and hormones,
     (6) playing a structural role as a component of bone.
   * The physiological actions of phosphate include:
     (1) functioning as part of the intracellular buffer system,
     (2) serving as a constituent of nucleic acids, phospholipids, and other macromolecules,
     (3) regulating metabolic processing by phosphorylation, and dephosphorylation of key regulatory enzymes.

   A. The Distribution of Calcium and Phosphate in Tissues
      * About 99% of total body calcium is located in bone. The rest is in muscle (0.3%) and in cells and extracellular fluid.
      * About 85% of total body phosphate is located in bone.
      * Bone contains other inorganic minerals, water, and carbonate which can be released to combat acidosis.

   B. The Forms of Calcium and Phosphorus in the Blood

      1. Forms of Calcium in the Blood
         a. The two major forms of calcium in the plasma are:
            (1) filterable calcium which can be subdivided into ionized and complexed forms, and
            (2) protein-bound calcium.
         b. Filterable calcium comprises those forms readily filtered in the glomerulus and reabsorbed in the renal tubules.
         c. Ionized calcium (Ca^{2+}), the physiologically active form, can diffuse across plasma membranes and is the form that is regulated in the plasma.
         d. Complexed calcium may be bound to bicarbonate or citrate.
         e. Protein-bound calcium is not filtered in the kidney and is bound mainly to albumin.
         f. The plasma calcium concentration is normally regulated within very narrow limits.

      2. Forms of Phosphorus in the Blood
         a. The plasma phosphate concentration fluctuates daily.
         b. Phosphorus exists as orthophosphate (PO_4) in the plasma. In its ionized form phosphorus diffuses readily acorss membranes and is filterable in the kidney.
         c. Phosphorus may also be present in organic form.

II. Pathways of Calcium and Phosphate Homeostasis

   A. Pathways of Calcium Homeostasis
      * The diet is the ultimate source of calcium and phosphorus. Plasma concentrations are determined by the intestines, bone, and the kidneys.

* The majority of ingested calcium is not absorbed and some body calcium is lost to the intestines.
* Ninety-nine percent of filtered calcium is reabsorbed and returned to the blood.
* There is dynamic flux of calcium into and out of bone.
* The processes of calcium absorption from the intestines, calcium reabsorption by the kidneys, and bone mineral formation and resorption, are precisely controlled.

B. Pathways of Phosphate Homeostasis
   * Most of ingested phosphate is absorbed in the intestines but a small amount is also secreted into the intestines each day.
   * Phosphate ion is reabsorbed from the filtrate and returned to the plasma.
   * There is a dynamic flux of phosphate into and out of the bone each day.

III. Mechanisms Involved in Calcium and Phosphate Homeostasis

A. Absorption of Calcium and Phosphate in the Gastrointestinal Tract

1. Calcium Absorption in the Gastrointestinal Tract
   a. Calcium is absorbed by active transport which occurs predominantly in the duodenum and jejunum and passive diffusion which occurs predominantly in the ileum.
   b. Calcium uptake from the intestines is regulated through the regulation of active calcium transport mechanisms.

2. Phosphate Absorption in the Gastrointestinal Tract
   a. Phosphate absorption occurs by active transport and passive diffusion.
   b. Active transport of phosphate is in part coupled to that of calcium.
   c. Phosphate absorption is only slightly regulated, if at all.

B. Reabsorption of Calcium and Phosphate in the Kidney

1. Calcium Reabsorption in the Kidney
   a. Reabsorption of calcium in the kidney occurs by tubules, and by passive diffusion from the ascending limb of the loop of Henle.
   b. Calcium reabsorption is regulated in the distal tubule by the action of parathyroid hormone.

2. Phosphate Reabsorption in the Kidney
   a. About 85% of filtered phosphate is reabsorbed by active transport processes operating primarily in the proximal tubule but also in the distal tubule.
   b. Phosphate reabsorption in the proximal tubule is inhibited by parathyroid hormone.

C. Homeostasis of Calcium and Phosphate in the Bone

1. The Composition of Bone
   a. Mature bone consists of inorganic bone mineral deposited in a framework of organic support material.
   b. The mineral is largely calcium phosphate in the form of hydroxyapatite crystals.
   c. The organic matrix, known as osteoid, is composed of collagen (95%) and ground substance (5%) which consists of a mixture of various proteoglycans.

2. Bone Cells
   a. Osteoblasts synthesize osteoid which is deposited on the surface of the bone.
   b. Osteocytes are osteoblasts which have lost their bone-forming capability. They communicate via channels known as canaliculi.
   c. Osteoclasts reabsorb bone by secreting both acids and proteolytic enzymes into extracellular space adjacent to the bone.

3. The Formation of Bone
   a. The fetal skeleton consists of cartilage which serves as the template for the development of the bony skeleton.
   b. The process of cartilage replacement begins in the middle and progresses outward toward the ends where the epiphyseal plate is located.
   c. At the epiphyseal plate, as a result of the continuing process of cartilage synthesis by chondrocytes, calcification and later erosion of cartilage, osteoblast invasion and replacement of cartilage by bone, the zone of active bone formation moves outward.
   d. Somatomedin, produced in the liver in response to growth hormone, stimulates chondrocyte activity. Insulin and thyroid hormones also stimulate chondrocyte activity and promote bone growth.
   e. Around puberty the epiphyseal plates of long bones become unresponsive to hormonal stimuli.
   f. Remodeling of bones is a continuous process and serves to meet the changing mechanical needs occurring throughout life.

IV. Regulation of Calcium and Phosphate Concentrations in the Plasma

A. Nonhormonal Mechanisms for Calcium and Phosphate Regulation
   * About 1% of calcium in bone exists in a readily exchangeable form that can move rapidly between bone and extracellular fluid. The free ionized calcium in extracellular fluid exists in chemical equilibrium with calcium present in the crystal matrix.

B. Hormonal Mechanisms for Calcium and Phosphate Regulation
   * Three hormones are involved in the regulation of calcium ion concentrations in the extracellular fluid:
     (1) parathyroid hormone,
     (2) calcitonin, and
     (3) metabolites of vitamin D.

1. Chemistry and Regulation of Hormone Production and Secretion
   a. Parathyroid hormone (PTH) produced by the parathyroid glands is released in response to a decrease in the concentration of ionized calcium in the plasma.
   b. Calcitonin (CT) produced by parafollicular cells in the thyroid is secreted in response to an increase in the plasma concentration of ionized calcium. It is also secreted in response to several gastrointestinal hormones, particularly gastrin.
   c. Metabolites of vitamin D such as 1,25-dihydroxy-vitamin D_3, are the hormonally active forms which regulate plasma calcium concentrations.

(1) These metabolites are formed from D vitamins, D_3 and D_2, which are enzymatically modified and activated in the liver and kidney.

(2) The primary site of regulation of the formation of the active form is the proximal tubule where the enzyme 1 α - hydroxylase catalyzes the conversion of 25-hydroxy-vitamin D_3 to 1,25-dihydroxy-vitamin D_3, the active form.

(3) The activity of the enzyme is increased by PTH and indirectly as a result of changes in plasma calcium concentration.

(4) The activity of the enzyme is also increased by a decrease in plasma phosphate concentration.

2. Actions of Hormones Involved in Regulating Calcium and Phos-Phate Homeostasis

* Parathyroid hormone is essential in the regulation of plasma calcium concentration while calcitonin provides a "fine tuning" for the regulation of calcium and phosphate metabolism.

a. The effects of PTH on the kidney include:
   (1) increasing the activity of 1α-hydroxylase to form the active metabolite of vitamin D,
   (2) stimulation of the active transport mechanism for calcium reabsorption in the distal tubules, and
   (3) decreasing the proximal tubular reabsorption of phosphate.

b. The effects of PTH on the bone include:
   (1) stimulation of dissolution of bone by increasing activity of osteoclasts,
   (2) stimulation of maturation of immature osteoclasts, and
   (3) decreasing collagen synthesis in osteoblasts.

c. The effects of calcitonin include:
   (1) decreasing tubular reabsorption of calcium and phosphate, and
   (2) decreasing resorption of calcium by inhibiting activity of osteoclasts.

d. The effects of the active form of vitamin D include:
   (1) increasing the tubular reabsorption of both calcium and phosphate,
   (2) promoting the actions of PTH in the bone, and
   (3) stimulation of both calcium and phosphate absorption in the small intestine.

V. Abnormalities of Bone Mineral Metabolism

* The two major categories of metabolic bone disease are
  (1) osteoporosis, and
  (2) osteomalacia and rickets

A. Osteoporosis

* Osteoporosis is a disease in which there is a reduction in overall bone mass with equal losses of both mineral and organic matrix.
* Among the factors contributing to osteoporosis are:
  (1) long-term calcium deficiency,
  (2) pronounced vitamin C deficiency,
  (3) immobilization, and
  (4) advancing age.

B. Osteomalacia and Rickets

* Both diseases are characterized by inadequate mineralization of new bone matrix, such that the ratio of mineral to organic matrix is lower than normal.

* The disorder in children is called rickets and called osteomalacia in adults.
* Rickets and osteomalacia are most commonly caused by a deficiency in vitamin D activity as a result of one of three general causes:
  (1) combined dietary deficiency of vitamin D and insufficient exposure to sunlight,
  (2) impairments in the conversion of vitamin D in the liver and kidney to its hormonally active form, resulting from liver disease, kidney disease or absence of PTH, and
  (3) inability of the active form of vitamin D to act in its target tissues.

Chapter Learning Objectives

1. Describe physiological actions of phosphate and calcium.
2. Describe the forms in which calcium and phosphorus exist in the plasma.
3. Describe the pathways of calcium and phosphorus homeostasis.
4. Describe where and how calcium and phosphorus are absorbed in the gastrointestinal tract.
5. Describe where and how calcium and phosphorus are reabsorbed in the kidney.
6. Describe bone structure and formation.
7. Describe nonhormonal mechanisms for calcium and phosphate regulation.
8. Describe the synthesis and release of parathyroid hormone, calcitonin, and the active forms of vitamin D.
9. Describe the actions of PTH, calcitonin, and the active forms of vitamin D.
10. Discuss factors contributing to the development of osteoporosis.
11. Discuss factors contributing to the development of rickets and osteomalacia.

Key Terms

albumin
calcification
calcitonin
canaliculi
chondrocyte
collagen
complexed calcium
demineralized
1,25-dihydroxy-vitamin D_3
epiphyseal plate
filterable calcium
ground substance
hydroxyapatite crystal
1alpha hydroxylase
hypocalcemic tetany
inadequate mineralization
ionized calcium
orthophosphate
osteoblast
osteoclast
osteocyte
osteoid
osteomalacia
osteoporosis
parafollicular cells
parathyroid hormone
phosphaturia
postmenopausal osteoporosis
protein-bound calcium
proteoglycan
remodeling
rickets
tetany
vitamin D_2 (ergocalciferol)
vitamin D_3 (cholecalciferol)

Testing Your Understanding

I. Matching. Select the correct word from the Key Terms.

_________1. represents 60% of total body calcium
_________2. results from apostic contractions of muscles
_________3. mineral fraction of bone
_________4. organic matrix of bone
_________5. synthesize and secrete organic matrix of bone
_________6. involved in bone resorption
_________7. site of elongation or growth of bone after birth
_________8. synthesize cartilage
_________9. synthesize and secreted in response to decrease in plasma calcium; most important regulator for calcium

________ 10. synthesize by parafollicular cells
________ 11. active form of vitamin D
________ 12. component of organic matrix of bone
________ 13. results from increased phosphate excretion
________ 14. characterized by decrease in overall bone mass
________ 15. characterized by inadequate mineralization

II. Complete the Table. For each condition, indicate the effect on calcium and/or phosphate reabsorption and on plasma calcium level.

Condition	Plasma level	Effect on Calcium Reabsorption	Effect on Phosphate Reabsorption
1. presence of PTH			
2. presence of calcitonin			
3. presence of 1,25-dihydroxy-vitamin D_3			
4. absence of PTH			
5. living in a cave			

CHAPTER 28 REGULATION OF BODY TEMPERATURE

Chapter Outline

I. Normal Body Temperature
- * Body temperature is regulated within a relatively narrow range to ensure the capacity for rapid metabolism.
- * Fluctuations in body temperature produced by changes in atmospheric temperature are greater at the body surface than in the "homeothermic" core which ranges from 36-39 degrees centigrade.

A. Core Temperature
- * Core temperature exhibits temperature gradients from 0.2 to 1.2 degrees C. Rectal temperature can be regarded as representative of the body core.
- * Normal body temperature should be conceived as a range of core temperatures that may be expected in a group of normal subjects under various conditions.
- * The lower and upper limits to the range are 35° C and 41° C.

B. Skin Temperature
- * Skin temperature is representative of the temperature of the body shell and varies at different body sites and at different atmospheric temperatures.

1. Mean Skin Temperature
   a. Mean skin temperature is regarded as representative of the temperature of the body shell and is calculated as the mean of the temperature at several representative body sites.
   b. Mean skin temperature is about 33° C to 34° C.

2. Thermography
   a. In thermagraphy an infrared camera is used to measure infrared rays emitted from the skin, which are directly related to the temperature of the skin.

C. Mean Body Temperature
- * Mean body temperature is estimated by the fractional sum of the core and shell and is estimated from the equation:

Mean body temperature = 0.3x mean skin temperature + 0.7 x rectal temperature.

D. Factors Affecting Body Temperature
- * Body temperature is affected by
  (1) exercise,
  (2) circadian rhythms,
  (3) menstrual cycles,
  (4) age, and
  (5) disease

1. Exercise and Body Temperature
   a. Exercise can increase the core temperature by 2°C or more but decrease the skin temperature.

2. Circadian Rhythms and Body Temperature
   a. Body temperature cycles with a circadian or diurnal rhythm and with fluctuations in temperature averaging 1°C.

3. The Menstrual Cycle and Body Temperature
   a. Changes in temperature associated with the menstrual cycle are superimposed on the diurnal temperature changes.
   b. Temperature drops about 0.6°C prior to ovulation after which it rises quickly about 1°C and remains at the normal level until the onset of the next cycle.

4. Age and Body Temperature
   a. Body temperature in premature infants and the elderly tends to fluctuate with atmospheric temperature.

5. Disease and Body Temperature
   a. Abnormal body temperature is associated with fever, hyperthyroidism and tumors of the adrenal gland

II. The Balance Between Heat Production and Heat Loss
   * Thermal homeostasis is maintained by physiological regulatory mechanisms that operate to keep heat production and heat loss approximately equal.

A. Heat Production by the Body

1. Metabolic Rate and Heat Production
   a. Heat is produced continuously as a by-product of the catabolism of food.
   b. Metabolic rate is the amount of food energy converted per unit time.
   c. Eighty percent of food energy is liberated as metabolic heat.

2. Factors Affecting Metabolic Rate
   a. Some factors affecting metabolic rate are:
      (1) exercise,
      (2) ingestion of food,
      (3) hormones like catecholamines and thyroxin,
      (4) body size, age, and sex, and
      (5) temperature.

3. The Basal Metabolic Rate
   a. Basal metabolic rate (BMR) is a standard measure for determining metabolic rate that allows comparison between individuals.
   b. Measurement of BMR is made under specified conditions.

4. Measurements of Metabolic Rate
   a. Metabolic rate is a measure of the total energy used by the body per unit time and can be determined by measuring the heat given off from the body in a defined time period.
   b. A person's metabolic rate can be measured by direct or indirect calorimetry.
   c. In indirect calorimetry metabolic rate is based on the determination of a person's oxygen consumption per unit of time which is measured by a respirometer.

B. Heat Loss from the Body
   * The body exchanges heat with its surroundings through four physical processes:
   (1) radiation,
   (2) conduction,
   (3) convection, and
   (4) evaporation.

1. Heat Loss by Radiation
   a. Radiation is heat transfer by electromagnetic radiation between objects not in contact.
   b. Radiant heat exchange is affected by the temperature difference between objects and the body's position.

2. Heat Loss by Conduction
   a. Conduction is heat exchange in the form of kinetic energy between molecules of objects in direct contact.
   b. Heat exchange by conduction is affected by the temperature difference between the objects.

3. Heat Loss by Convection
   a. Convection is the transfer of heat between the body and a moving gas or liquid. Conduction is part of the convective process.
   b. Forced convection increases the rate of heat exchange by the body.

4. Heat Loss by Evaporation
   a. Evaporation is the process of converting water from a liquid to a gas. Thermal energy is required to transform water to a gas.
   b. Evaporation is a continuous heat loss mechanism.

5. Heat Loss from Sweating
   a. Sweating involves active secretion of water by specialized glands in the skin.
   b. Evaporation of sweat is the only way to lose heat in hot environments.

C. Heat Transfer Within the Body
   * The transfer of heat within the body is accomplished by a combination of internal conduction and circulatory convection.

1. Heat Transfer by Internal Convection
   a. Heat transfer by convection is slow because of the small temperature difference between cells.

2. Heat Transfer by Circulatory Convection
   a. Forced convection by the circulatory system is very important for thermal balance.
   b. Vasomotor responses regulate peripheral blood flow to achieve thermal balance.

III. Regulation of Body Temperature
   * The control of body temperature is dependent on the coordinated activites of several subsystems, including:
     (1) sweating,
     (2) vasomotor control, and
     (3) metabolic rate.
   * The physiological control system that coordinates the responses for effective regulation of body temperature is a negative feedback system and has at least three components:
     (1) temperature receptors to sense existing body temperature,
     (2) effector organ systems to determine heat production and loss, and
     (3) an integrator or controller to compare sensed temperature to a reference temperature, and to activate appropriate effector systems to return temperature to normal.

A. Peripheral Thermoreceptors in Temperature Regulation
   * Thermoreceptors are located just beneath the skin.
   * Cold receptors are more numerous than warm receptors.

B. Central Thermoreceptors in Temperature Regulation
   * Central thermoreceptors, located in the hypothalamus, spinal cord, abdominal viscera, and great veins, include both cold and warm receptors.
   * Nerve impulses from central thermoreceptors are integrated with those from peripheral thermoreceptors in the brain.

C. Central Integration of Thermal Information
   * The hypothalamus, the brain center for body temperature regulation, acts as a thermostat to prevent excessive body heating or cooling.

IV. Diseases that Affect Temperature Regulation

A. Fever: A Regulated Increase in Body Temperature
   * Fever is usually caused by pyrogens which appear to reset the hypothalamic thermostat at a higher temperature level.
   * The hypothalamus activates heat production and conservation responses and inhibits heat loss responses as long as the pyrogen is present.

B. Hyperthermia: Unregulated Increases in Body Temperature

   1. Heat Stroke
      a. Heat stroke, a form of heat illness associated with a breakdown of the body's temperature regulating system, may occur if body temperature rises beyond 41-42°C.

   2. Heat Exhaustion
      a. Heat exhaustion, a less serious heat illness, is caused by circulatory insufficiency and hypotension.

C. Hypothermia: Unregulated Decreases in Body Temperature
   * Cold illnesses usually involve peripheral circulatory or cardiac defects.

<u>Chapter Learning Objectives</u>

1. Describe various methods for measuring core body and skin temperatures.
2. Describe how mean body temperature is determined.
3. List several factors affecting body temperature and describe how each acts.
4. Define metabolic rate and describe several factors affecting metabolic rate.
5. Describe methods for measuring metabolic rate.
6. Describe four physical processes by which the body loses heat.
7. Describe heat transfer within the body.
8. Describe how body temperature is regulated.
9. Describe the cause of and effect on the body of fever, heat stroke, heat exhaustion, and hypothermia.

Key Terms

antidrop response
antirise response
basal metabolic rate (BMR)
circadian (diurnal) rhythm
circulatory convection
conduction
convection (free, forced)
core temperature
effector organ system
evaporation
fever
heat exhaustion
heat stroke
homeotherm
human calorimeter
hyperthermia
hypothalamus
hypothermia
insensible perspiration
integrator
internal conduction
longitudinal temperature gradient
malignant hyperthermia
mean body temperature
mean skin temperature
metabolic heat
metabolic rate
negative feedback system
poikilotherm
pyrogen
radial temperature gradient
radiation
respirometer
shell temperature
specific dynamic action
sweating
temperature (rectal, oral, axillary)
thermal homeostasis
thermography
thermoreceptors (central, peripheral)

Testing Your Understanding

I. Matching. Select the correct word from the Key Terms.

_________1. animal whose body temperature fluctuates with changes in ambient temperature
_________2. temperature regarded as representative of core temperature
_________3. representative temperature of body shell
_________4. technique of determining mean skin temperature by measuring infrared radiation
_________5. equals 0.3x mean skin temperature plus 0.7 x rectal temperature
_________6. amount of food energy converted per unit of time
_________7. maintenance of normal body temperature
_________8. insulated chamber for measuring metabolic rate
_________9. measures oxygen consumption
_________10. heat transfer by electromagnetic radiation
_________11. process of converting water to a gas
_________12. heat transfer between the body and a moving gas or liquid
_________13. vasodilation and sweating
_________14. caused by circulatory insufficiency and hypotension
_________15. drop in body temperature to abnormal level

II. Complete the Table. For each condition, indicate the likely effect on the body temperature.

Condition	Effect on body temperature
1. luteal phase of menstrual cycle	
2. sleep	
3. exercise	
4. presence of pyrogens	
5. ambient temperature of 44°C	
6. exposure to cold water	
7. shivering	
8. vasodilation and sweating	
9. heavy work under hot, humid conditions	

CHAPTER 29 PHYSIOLOGY OF EXERCISE

Chapter Outline

* Exercise is often classified as either dynamic or static. In positive dynamic exercise the muscles act as a "motor" while in negative dynamic exercise muscles act as "brakes." Static exercise is performed during isometric muscle contraction.
* Elevated metabolic demand is the common feature of all types of exercise.

I. Metabolic Aspects of Exercise

A. Energy Requirements of Muscular Contraction
* High energy phosphate compounds are the primary energy source for skeletal muscle contraction.
* Energy is provided by three metabolic systems:
(1) the phosphagen system,
(2) the glycogen-lactic acid system, and
(3) the aerobic system

1. The Phosphogen Energy System
a. The phosphagen energy system includes ATP and phosphocreatine which has more energy than ATP and can donate phosphate groups to AMP and ADP to form ATP.
b. The phosphagen energy system is used for short bouts of maximal exercise.

2. The Glycogen-Lactic Acid System
a. This system which occurs under anaerobic conditions is used as a rapid source of energy for muscle contraction.

3. The Aerobic Energy System
a. Aerobic metabolism is the source of energy for prolonged light work.
b. During heavy exercise part of the energy is obtained anaerobically.

B. Oxygen Consumption During Exercise
* During exercise oxygen consumption increases during the first few minutes then reaches a steady state in which uptake corresponds to demand.
* Maximal oxygen consumption (VO_2max) occurs at the point where the maximum for oxygen transport and uptake in tissues is reached and a plateau is attained.
* VO_2 max represents a person's maximal aerobic power and can be affected by age, activity level, and training.

C. Oxygen Debt During Exercise
* During light exercise oxygen debt remains constant after a steady state is reached.
* During heavy exervise oxygen debt builds up until the exercise ends
* The repayment of the oxygen debt occurs in two stages:
(1) alactacid oxygen debt, which is usually repaid within 2-3 minutes after exercise and
(2) lactic acid oxygen debt which is repaid very slowly.

D. The Use of Nutrients During Exercise
* The type of nutrient used during exercise depends on the intensity and duration of the exercise and the availability of the stored fuels. At low rates of exercise of short duration lipids supply a large proportion of the required energy.
* Diet affects the type of nutrient used and glycogen recovery following exhaustive exercise.

II. Respiration During Exercise

A. Pulmonary Ventilation During Exercise
* During exercise increased pulmonary ventilation is proportional to metabolic demands (O_2 consumption).

B. The Diffusing Capacity of the Lung During Exercise
* The diffusing capacity provides an index of the dimensions of the pulmonary capillary bed, the pulmonary membrane, and overall efficiency of the system in gas exchange.
* The increased diffusing capacity in the lung results from increased pulmonary flow.

C. Control of Pulmonary Ventilation During Exercise
* The mechanisms controlling ventrilation at rest cannot explain the increased ventilation or hyperpnea during exercise.
* The time course of ventilation changes before and during moderate steady state exercise can be divided into three components:
(1) a rapid rise occurring just before exercise starts,
(2) a slower rise, and
(3) development of steady state ventilation
* Neural and chemical stimuli control ventilation but the mechanisms are unknown.

1. Chemical Stimulation of Pulmonary Ventilation
a. Neither PCO_2 alone, lactic acid or H^+ concentration nor hypoxemia appear to provide the primary stimulus for increased ventilation during exercise.

2. Neural Stimulation of Pulmonary Ventilation
a. Neural stimuli acting alone cannot explain hyperventilation

III. Circulation During Exercise

A. Muscle Blood Flow During Exercise
* About 50% of the increase in muscle blood flow results from local vasodilation caused by direct effects of increased muscle metabolism.
* The increase in muscle blood flow is also attributed to a moderate increase in arterial blood pressure.

B. Cardiac Output During Exercise
* Cardiac output parallels oxygen consumption and work output.
* In trained individuals increased cardiac output is due mainly to hypertrophy of the heart.

C. Stroke Volume and Heart Rate During Exercise
* A trained athlete has a greater stroke volume and lower heart rate at rest and during maximum exercise than an untrained individual.
* Because stroke volume reaches a maximum when cardiac output approaches 15 liters per minutes, further increases in cardiac output result from increases in heart rate.
* The capacity of the cardiovascular system is normally a limiting factor in terms of maximal oxygen consumption and exercise performance.

D. Local Blood Flow to Organs During Exercise
* During exercise brain blood flow is maintained, splanchnic and renal blood flow is decreased, and blood flow to skeletal muscles, heart and skin is increased.

IV. Body Temperature in Exercise

* The mechanical efficiency of the human body is less than 25%. More than 75% of metabolic energy of exercise is converted to heat.
* Body temperature rises during exercise and levels off at a few degrees above normal regardless of atmosphere temperature.
* Nonregulated increases in body temperature exceeding 42° C can cause heat stroke.

V. Hormonal Responses to Exercise

* Exercise stimulates the secretion of numerous hormones particularly
  (1) catecholamines by the adrenal medulla, and
  (2) adrenocortical-stimulating hormone by the anterior pituitary.
* The secretion of catecholamines (epinephrine and norepinephrine) is stimulated by the sympathetic nervous system as an anticipatory response. Catecholamines play a role in regulating the availability of nutrients during exercise and in cardiovascular adjustments in exercise.
* The secretion of ACTH stimulates the release of corticosteroids from the adrenal cortex. Corticosteroids are believed to play a role in regulating nutrients during exercise.

Chapter Learning Objectives

1. Describe the three metabolic systems that supply energy for muscle contraction. For each system indicate the type of exercise utilizing that energy system.
2. Draw a graph showing oxygen uptake during increasing levels of steady state exercise.
3. Define maximal oxygen consumption (VO_2max) and describe factors affecting it.
4. Define oxygen debt and describe how it is repaid.
5. Describe the utilization of nutrients during exercise, the relationship between diet and availability of nutrient and the rate of replenishment as it is affected by diet.
6. Draw a graph relating O_2 consumption and total ventilation.
7. Define diffusing capacity of the lung and describe changes occurring during exercise.
8. Describe chemical and neural stimuli that have been considered as controlling agents for ventilation.
9. Compare untrained and trained individuals at rest and during exercise as to heart rate, cardiac output, and stroke volume.
10. Describe how the body regulates temperature during exercise.

Key Terms

aerobic energy system
alactic acid oxygen debt
anaerobic
diffusing capacity of the lung
dynamic exercise (positive, negative)
glycogen-lactic acid system
hyperpnea
hypoxemia
lactic acid oxygen debt
maximal aerobic power
maximal oxygen consumption (VO_2max)
oxygen debt
phosphagen energy system
phosphocreatine
static exercise

Testing Your Knowledge

I. Matching. Select the correct word from the Key Terms.

________1. energy system used for short bouts of maximal exercise
________2. exercise performed during isometric muscle contraction
________3. plateau of oxygen uptake during exercise
________4. oxygen debt usually repaid within 2-3 minutes after exercise ends
________5. amount of gas moving across pulmonary membrane per minute per millimeter of Hg pressure difference between alveolar air and pulmonary blood

II. Complete the Table. For each condition, indicate the effect on oxygen uptake or consumption.

Condition	Effect on O_2 Uptake
1. increased blood lactic acid	
2. sedentary aging adult	
3. 6 weeks of athletic training	
4. decreased cardiac output	
5. increased body temperature	

CHAPTER 30 REPRODUCTIVE PHYSIOLOGY

Chapter Outline

I. Reproductive Physiology in the Male

A. Male Reproductive Anatomy

1. Anatomy of the Male External Genitalia
   a. The external reproductive organs are the penis and scrotum
   b. The testes, epididymus and spermatic cord are in the scrotum.

2. Anatomy of the Male Internal Genitalia
   a. The testes have two major functions:
      (1) production of sperm,
      (2) production of male sex hormones.
   b. Each testis is composed of two areas:
      (1) the seminiferous tubules in which sperm are produced, and
      (2) the interstitial space which contains blood vessels, lymphatics, nerve fibers, connective tissue, extracellular fluid and the testosterone producing Leydig cells.

B. Spermatogenesis: The Formation of Sperm
   * Spermatogenesis which begins at puberty and continues throughout the male's life, occurs in the seminiferous tubules. The process takes 70-80 days.

1. Differentiation of Germ Cells
   a. Two types of cells are involved in spermatogenesis:
      (1) spermatogenic cells from which mature sperm arise, and
      (2) Sertoli cells which provide mechanical and nutritional support for the spermatogenic cells.
   b. Spermatogenia cells either divide mitotically to replenish their supply or differentiate into primary spermatocytes which then divide meiotically and give rise to sperm.
   c. During meiosis homologous chromosomes exchange chromosomal segments in a process known as crossing over.
   d. Spermatogenesis involves the following steps:

spermatogonium (46 chromosomes) $\xrightarrow{\text{enlarges}}$ primary spermatocyte (46 chromosomes)

primary spermatocyte $\xrightarrow[\text{division}]{\text{1st meiotic}}$ 2 secondary spermatocytes

each secondary spermatocyte (23 chromosomes) $\xrightarrow[\text{division}]{\text{2nd meiotic}}$ spermatid (23 chromosomes)

each spermatid (23 chromosomes) $\xrightarrow{\text{spermiation}}$ sperm (23 chromosomes)

2. Physiology of the Mature Sperm
   a. In a process called spermiation spermatids differentiate into mature sperm.
   b. Each sperm consists of
      (1) a head containing chromatic, and on top of which is the acrosome,
      (2) the tail, and
      (3) the body which contains mitochondria.

3. Functions of the Sertoli Cells
   a. Sertoli cells are joined to each other by tight junctions which form a blood-testes barrier.
   b. Sertoli cells secrete fluid containing proteins, nutrients, androgens and ions into the lumen.
   c. Sertoli cells synthesize two proteins:
      (1) androgen binding protein which bends to testosterone and increases its concentration, and
      (2) inhibin which regulates the secretion of follicle stimulating hormone.

C. Sperm Transport through the Internal Reproductive Structures
   * Sperm move from seminiferous tubules through the rete testis into the epididymis where they become mature and mobile.

1. Storage of Mature Sperm in the Vas Deferens
   a. Sperm move from the epididymus to the vas deferens and then to the ejaculatory duct which runs through the prostate gland.
   b. The wall of the vas deferens is composed of smooth muscle and innervated by sympathetic nerves.

2. Addition of Nutrient Fluid by the Seminal Vesicles
   a. Secretory ducts from the seminal vesicles empty into the vas deferens where they join the ejaculatory duct.
   b. Secretions from the seminal vesicles contain prostaglandins, fructose and other nutrients.

3. Addition of Alkaline Fluid by the Prostate Gland
   a. The prostate gland secretes an alkaline liquid, containing citric acid, calcium, and various enzymes, which neutralizes the acidity in the vagina.

4. Addition of Lubricant Fluid by the Bulbourethral Glands
   a. Semen containing sperm and the secretions from the seminal vesicles and prostate passes from the ejaculatory duct into the urethra where it is joined by secretions from the bulbourethral glands.
   b. The fluid from these glands may appear at the tip of the penis prior to ejaculation.
   c. Ejaculation results from stimulation by sympathetic nerves of the smooth muscle in the epididymus, vas deferens, prostate, and seminal vesicles.

D. Neuroendocrine Control of Reproduction in the Male.

1. Neuroendocrine Control of Spermatogenesis
   a. Follicle stimulating hormone (FSH) stimulates the conversion of spermatogonia into primary spermatocytes and luteinizing hormone stimulates Leydig cells to synthesize and secrete testosterone.
   b. The production of FSH and LH occurs via the sequence:
      (1) hypothalamus secretes gonadotropin releasing hormone (GnRH),
      (2) GnRH stimulates the anterior pituitary to produce and release FSH and LH.

2. Feedback Regulation of Neuroendocrine Function
   a. The constancy of secretions of GnRHq LH and FSH is due to the presence of a continuous feedback loop between the hypothalamus, anterior pituitary, and testes.

3. Control of Neuroendocrine Function by Sensory Stimuli
   a. Sensory stimuli can alter the release of GnRH from the hypothalamus and hence the release of LH, FSH and testosterone.

E. Effects of Testosterone in the Male
   * In the blood testosterone is bound to albumin and to another plasma protein, sex steroid-binding globulin (SSBG).
   * Testosterone acts directly on some tissues like muscle, kidney, and bone. It is transformed into dihydrotestosterone before acting on tissues like the prostate and seminal vesicles. In the brain testosterone is converted into estrogen.

   1. Effects of Testosterone at Puberty
      a. At puberty the hypothalamus secretes increasing amounts of GnRH.
      b. The increase in testosterone results in the enlargement of the penis, scrotum, and testes and stimulates the development of male secondary sex characteristics.

   2. Effects of Testosterone on Spermatogensis
      a. Spermatogenesis requires the presence of high levels of testosterone in the seminiferous tubules.

II. Reproductive Physiology in the Female

A. Female Reproductive Anatomy

   1. Anatomy of the Female External Genitalia
      a. The external genitalia, collectively called the vulva, include the labia minora, labia majora, the clitoris, and the vaginal opening.

   2. Anatomy of the Female Internal Genitalia
      a. The internal reproductive organs include the vagina, uterus, fallopian tubes, and ovaries.
      b. The ovaries produce ova, the germ cells, and hormones.

B. Oogenesis: The Formation of Ova
   * Of the 7 million oocytes formed in the ovary during embryonic development, only about 400 will reach maturity and be released from the ovary.
   * A major difference between growth patterns of germ cells in the male and female is the length of time for maturation of the sperm or ova from the primary spermatocyte or oocyte.
   * The sequence of events in oogenesis is the following:
     (1) oogenia $\xrightarrow{\text{conversion}}$ primary oocyte during second and third month embryonic life
     (2) primary oocyte surrounded by layer of cells primordial follicle
     (3) primordial follicles $\xrightarrow{\text{differentiate}}$ primary follicles in fifth and sixth months of fetal life.
     (4) primary follicles remain in first stage of meiosis until puberty
     (5) primary oocyte $\xrightarrow{\text{1st meiotic division}}$ secondary oocyte just before ovulation
     (6) secondary oocyte $\xrightarrow{\text{2nd meiotic division}}$ mature ovum if fertilized.

C. Ovulation

   1. Growth of the Follicle
      a. Each month 6-20 primary follicles begin to develop but only one reaches maturation and becomes a Graffian follicle.

b. A mature follicle is surrounded by granulosa cells which secrete fluid containing proteins, electrolytes, polysaccharides, and hormones.
c. The antrum contains fluid and the ovum.
d. The mature follicle forms a bulge on the outer surface of the ovary.
e. Around ovulation the follicle secretes proteolytic enzymes which break down the ovarian surface.
f. The ovum released at ovulation enters the fallopian tube.

2. Growth of the Corpus Leuteum
   a. The remaining follicle cells after ovulation become the corpus luteum and secrete estrogen and progesterone.
   b. If fertilization and implantation do not occur, the corpus luteum degenerates between days 8 to 21 following ovulation.

D. Neuroendocrine Control of Reproduction in the Female
   * Neuroendocrine control depends on a continuous interaction between the hypothalamus, anterior pituitary, and the ovaries.
   * The hypothalamus secretes GnRH which stimulates the anterior pituitary to produce FSH and LH that stimulate germ cell development and hormone secretion.
   * The effects of LH and FSH vary during different phases of the ovarian cycle. The three phases are the:
     (1) follicular (lasting about 12 days),
     (2) luteal (lasting about 11 days), and
     (3) menstrual (lasting about 5 days).

1. Neuroendocrine Control of the Follicular (Pre-ovulatory) Phase
   a. Just after menstruation follicular growth and development is stimulated by FSH.
   b. The granulosa cells secrete estrogen which stimulates GnRH secretion and acts in the granulosa cells to increase the number of receptors for both estrogen and FSH. Estrogen has an autocrine action on granular cells.
   c. Estrogen stimulates the pituitary to release LH which stimulates granulosa cells to secrete progesterone.

2. Neuroendocrine Control of Ovulation
   a. The preovulatory surge of LH induces changes in follicular structure resulting in ovulation.
   b. LH-induced changes include
      (1) increase in production of antral fluid,
      (2) protrusion of the follicle against the wall of the ovary,
      (3) enzymatic degradation of the ovarian wall, and
      (4) release of antral fluid and the ovum.

3. Neuroendocrine Control of the Luteal (Postovulatory) Phase
   a. Luteinization, the formation of the corpus luteum, is stimulated by LH.
   b. Estrogen and progesterone secreted during the luteal phase inhibit GnRHg LH and FSH secretion.
   c. As the corpus luteum degenerates, the levels of estrogen and progesterone fall. This releases the inhibition of GnRH, LH and FSH so blood levels of these hormones begin to rise and a new follicular cycle begins.

4. Neuroendocrine Control of the Menstrual Phase
    a. Estrogen stimulates proliferation of the uterine endometrium and the number of progesterone receptors in the uterus.
    b. Estrogen and progesterone secreted in the luteal phase stimulate growth and proliferation of endometrial blood vessels and the accumulation of glycogen and enzymes in endometrial glands.
    c. In the absence of estrogen and progesterone, the endometrium becomes necrotic and menstrual flow occurs.

E. Effects of Estrogen and Progesterone in the Female

1. Effects of Estrogen at Puberty
    a. Estrogen stimulates the development of sex organs, and the appearance of secondary sex characteristics.

2. Metabolic Effects of Estrogen
    a. Estrogen interacts with a variety of other hormones that control metabolic processes.

3. Effects of Progesterone
    a. Progesterone is an androgen antagonist and prevents target tissues from responding to normally low levels of circulatory androgens in the female.

F. Menopause
* Menopause, the cessation of menstruation in the female, occurs on the average at age 50.

<u>Chapter Learning Objectives</u>

1. Describe the anatomy of male internal and external genitalia.
2. Outline the steps in spermatogenesis and spermiation.
3. Describe functions of the Sertoli cells.
4. Describe the pathway traveled by sperm for their site of production to outside the body, and the secretions of the prostate, seminal vesicles and bulbourethral glands.
5. Describe the relationship and feedback loop between the hypothalamus, anterior pituitary and testes regarding the production of sperm and testosterone.
6. Describe the effects of testosterone in an adult male, in a boy beginning puberty.
7. Describe the anatomy and function of female internal and external reproductive structures.
8. Outline the steps in the production of a mature ovum from a primordial germ cell.
9. Compare spermatogenesis and oogenesis as to timing, location and role of hormones.
10. Describe the relationship and feedback loop of the hypothalamus, anterior pituitary and ovaries in the production of hormones and mature ova.
11. Describe the events of the follicular, luteal and menstrual phases of the ovarian cycle.
12. Describe the autocrine action of estrogen in the maturation of the follicle.
13. Describe the effects of estrogen and progesterone on the preparation of the uterine endometrium.
14. Describe the effects of estrogen in a female at puberty and an adult female.
15. Describe changes associated with menopause.

Key Terms

acrosome
amenorrhea (primary, secondary)
androgen-binding-protein
antrum
atresia
autocrine
blood-testes barrier
bulbourethral glands
cervix
clitoris
continuous feedback loop
corpus luteum
dihydrotestosterone
dysmenorrhea
ejaculation
ejaculatory duct
endometrium
epididymis
erectile tissue
estrogen
fallopian tubes (oviducts)
follicle stimulating hormone (FSH)
follicular phase
gonadotropin-releasing hormone (GnRH)
Graafian follicle
granulosa cells
hemorrhagic change
hyperplasia
hypothalamic-pituitary portal vessel
hypothalamus
inhibin
labia (majora, minora)
Leydig cells
luteal phase
luteinizing hormone (LH)
menopause
menstrual phase
menstruation
myometrium
necrotic
oocyte (primary, secondary)
oogenesis
osteoporosis
ova
ovarian cycle
ovaries
ovulation
paracrine
penis
pituitary gland
primary follicle
primordial follicle
progesterone
prostaglandin
prostate
puberty
scrotum
seminal vesicles
seminiferous tubules
Sertoli cells
sex steroid-binding globulin
sperm
spermatid
spermatocyte (primary, secondary)
spermatogenesis
spermatogonia
spermiation
spindle cells
testis
testosterone
Theca interna
urethra
uterus
vagina
vas deferens
vulva
zona pellucida

Testing Your Understanding

I. Matching. Select the correct word from the Key Terms.

__________1. releases testosterone
__________2. secretes progesterone
__________3. secretes estrogen
__________4. site of sperm production
__________5. triggers ovulation
__________6. stimulates sperm production and maturation of primary follicle
__________7. produces alkaline fluid
__________8. part of vulva homologous to penis
__________9. absence of menstruation due to pregnancy
__________10. formed by tight junctions between Sertoli cells
__________11. stimulates anterior pituitary to release FSH and LH
__________12. fluid filled space in Graafian follicle
__________13. uterine layer shed during menstrual phase
__________14. coiled tube in which sperm mature
__________15. part of sperm containing digestive enzymes

II. For each condition indicate the effect on oogenesis or spermatogenesis.

Condition	Effect on Oogenesis	Effect on Spermatogenesis
1. decrease in testosterone		
2. absence of fertilization		
3. severing of hypothalamic-pituitary portal		
4. absence of Leydig cells		
5. absence of spermatogonia		
6. continuous presence of estrogen and/or progesterone		
7. increase in LH		
8. absence of androgen-binding protein		
9. excess of inhibin		
10. removal of prostate		

III. For each condition, indicate the effect on the production of the other hormones.

Condition	GnRH	FSH	LH	testosterone	estrogen
1. excess inhibin					
2. excess testosterone					
3. decrease in GnRH					
4. increase in FSH					
5. increase in LH					
6. increase in granulosa cells					
7. degeneration of corpus luteum					
8. presence of estrogen during follicular phase					
9. presence of estrogen during luteal phase					
10. presence of progesterone					

CHAPTER 31 PREGNANCY, FETAL DEVELOPMENT, AND LACTATION

Chapter Outline

I. The Process of Fertilization

A. Transport of the Ovum to the Fallopian Tube and Uterus
- * After ovulation, the ovum is drawn into the fallopian tube by the sweeping motion of cilia.
- * Fertilization normally occurs in the fallopian tube.

B. Transport of Sperm to the Fallopian Tube
- * Sperm released into the vagina are propelled to the fallopian tube by wavelength movements in their tails and by contractions of muscles in the uterus and fallopian tubes.

1. Cervical Mucus and Sperm Transport
   a. At ovulation cervical mucus is clear and watery. Glycoproteins in the mucus form elongated fibers thus allowing sperm to penetrate the mucus and pass upward through the cervix.
   b. Prior to and after ovulation cervical mucus is thick and sticky and lacks glycoprotein channels.

2. Sperm Loss in the Female
   a. An ejaculate contains an average of 100-500 million sperm but about 50% may be incapable of fertilization.
   b. Many sperm are lost in transit but only one is required for fertilization.

C. Capacitation and Activation of Sperm
- * In the epididymis sperm mature and acquire the ability to move but not to fertilize the ovum.
- * Sperm must undergo capacitation in the female reproductive tract before fusion of sperm and ovum.

D. The Fusion of Sperm and Ovum
- * The mature ovum is surrounded by three layers: the vitelline membrane, the zona pellucida, and the cumulus oophorus composed of several layers of granulosa cells.

1. The Acrosomal Reaction
   a. During this reaction the digestive enzymes in the acrosome are released and create a pathway for the sperm through the cumulus oophorus and zona pellucida.

2. The Incorporation of the Sperm by the Ovum
   a. When the sperm reaches the vitelline membrane, it is engulfed by the ovum.

E. Prevention of Polyspermy by the Ovum
- * Polyspermy is prevented firstly by an electrical change in the vitelline membrane immediately after one sperm has been engulfed and secondly by a chemical change involving the release of cortical granules into the space between the plasma membrane and zona pellucida.

F. Multiple Births: Fertilization of More than One Ovum
- * Fertilization of two or more ova released at ovulation results in dizygous twins, triplets or quadruplets.
- * Monozygous twins (triplets or quadruplets) result from the fertilization of a single ovum by a single sperm followed by a special type of cell division.

II. Cell Division and Implantation Following Fertilization

* Just after sperm entry, the chromosomes in the ovum nucleus and sperm head undergo changes and become pronuclei. The two sets of chromosomes align themselves to form a complete set of 46 chromosomes.

A. Stages in Early Embryonic Development

1. They Zygote
   a. The zygote, the fertilized ovum containing 46 chromosomes, begins to divide mitotically about 30 hours post-fertilization.
   b. The eight cell stage is called a morula. As cell division continues, a hollow area develops in the cell mass and the morula becomes a blastocyst.
   c. The cell divisions leading to the blastocyst occur while the cell mass is being moved down the fallopian tube toward the uterus.

2. The Blastocyst
   a. A blastocyst is composed of two types of cells:
      (1) trophoblast cells which play a role in implantation and later give rise to the placenta, and
      (2) embryoblasts which give rise to the embryo proper.

B. Implantation of the Blastocyst

1. Secretion of Enzymes and Hormones by the Blastocyst
   a. The blastocyst secretes estrogen and proteolytic enzymes which digest uterine endometrium to allow implantation.
   b. Estrogen induces localized permeability changes in the endometrium that are necessary for implantation, and stimulates the secretion of prostaglandins from the endometrium.

2. Formation of Embryonic Membranes
   a. After the trophoblasts penetrate the endometrium, they differentiate into two layers:
      (1) the outer layer which gives rise to membranes surrounding the embryo and the umbilical cord, and
      (2) the inner layer which gives rise to the chorion.

3. Secretion of Progesterone by the Corpus Luteum
   a. Implantation is completed around day 7 following ovulation.
   b. Progesterone stimulates uterine endometrium to receive and nourish the blastocyst and cell division of the fertilized ovum.

4. Abnormal Implantation
   a. Ectopic pregnancies result from abnormal ovum transport in the fallopian tube.

III. The Role of the Placenta

* The placenta delivers oxygen and nourishment, absorbs and removes waste products, supplies immunity and secretes hormone necessary for the maintenance of the pregnancy and expulsion of the fetus at term.

A. Development of the Placenta

* The placenta is formed from trophoblast cells and from membranes called decidua arising from the endometrium.

* Villi from the developing embryo invade pools of maternal blood in the endometrium. Capillaries in the villi serve as the route for exchange between mother and embryo.

B. Exchange of Materials Through the Placenta

1. Placental Exchange of Gases
    a. Fetal blood carries more oxygen than maternal blood because:
        (1) the concentration of hemoglobin is 50% higher, and
        (2) fetal hemoglobin can carry 20-30% more oxygen.

2. Placental Delivery of Nutrients
    a. Some nutrients like glucose, potassium and sodium diffuse across placental membranes while others like proteins, calcium, and iron are actively transported.

3. Placental Removal of Excretory Products
    a. Fetal wastes like urea pass by simple diffusion from fetal to maternal blood in the placenta.

4. Placental Transport of Drugs

5. Placental Transport of Antibodies
    a. The placenta actively and selectively transports large antibodies to the fetus.

C. Protection of the Placenta and Embryo from Immunological Reaction
* Rejection of the embryo by the mother does not occur because
    (1) the blastocyst does not express antigens,
    (2) the placenta secretes human chorionic gonadotropin which suppresses lymphocytes, and
    (3) the embryo is protected by membranes.

D. Hormones of the Placenta
* The placenta secretes hormones regulating the physiological changes associated with early pregnancy.
* Placental hormones are:
    (1) human chorionic gonadotropin (hCG),
    (2) estrogen and progesterone, and
    (3) human chorionic somatomammotropin (hCS).

1. Placental Secretion of Human Chorionic Gonadotropin (hCG)
    a. HCG produced first by trophoblast cells and later by the placenta stimulates the corpus luteum to continue secreting estrogen and progesterone in order to maintain the uterine endometrium.
    b. During the second month the placenta secretes estrogen and progesterone so the corpus luteum is no longer necessary.

2. Placental Secretion of Progesterone
    a. The placenta secretes ten times more progesterone than the corpus luteum.
    b. Progesterone
        (1) stimulates growth and secretion of nutrients from the endometrium, and the breast in preparation for lactation, and
        (2) inhibits uterine contractions.

3. Placental Secretion of Estrogen
    a. Estrogen stimulates enlargement of the uterus, and external genitalia, and breast growth, and relaxation of pelvic ligaments.

b. Estrogen synthesis involves the placenta and fetal adrenal glands which contain enzymes needed to convert cholesterol to androgens, specifically dehydroepiandrosterone-sulfate (DHEA-sulfate).

c. DHEA-sulfate is transported to the placenta where it is converted to estrogen.

4. Placental Secretion of Human Chorionic Somato-Mammotropin (hCS)

   a. HCS plays a role in metabolism and nutrition of both the pregnant woman and her fetus. It decreases maternal utilization of glucose and promotes the release of free fatty acids from maternal stores.

IV. Hormonal and Physical Changes in the Female During Pregnancy

A. Hormonal Changes in the Pregnanat Female

1. Inhibition of Pituitary Gonadotropins During Pregnancy

2. Stimulation of Prolactic During Pregnancy

   a. Prolactin is essential for synthesis of breast milk.

3. Stimulation of Relaxin During Pregnancy

   a. Relaxin is secreted first by the corpus luteum and later by the uterine endometrium. It relaxes pelvic ligaments and inhibits uterine contractions.

4. Stimulation of Insulin During Pregnancy

5. Stimulation of Aldosterone During Pregnancy

   a. Aldosterone maintains adequate sodium and hence water retention during pregnancy to maintain high maternal and fetal blood volumes.

6. Stimulation of Cortisol During Pregnancy

   a. Levels of free and protein-bound cortisol increase as a result of increased secretion by maternal adrenal glands and an increase in cortisol binding globulin (CBG) in maternal plasma.

   b. Increased cortisol contributes to development of the mammary glands.

7. Stimulation of Thyroxine (T_4) and Triiodothyronine (T_3) During Pregnancy.

   a. T_3 and T_4 stimulate maternal cardiopulmonary function which results in an increase in the rate of delivery of oxygen and nutrients to the fetus.

B. Physical Changes in the Pregnant Females

* Pregnancy is divided into three-month periods called trimesters.

1. Physical Changes During the First Trimester

   a. Morning sickness (tiredness, nausea, vomiting) may occur.

2. Physical Changes During the Second Trimester.

   a. Many women retain fluid which results in edema of hands and feet.

   b. The uterus and breasts grow rapidly.

3. Physical Changes During the Third Trimester

   a. A woman may gain much weight and experience frequent urination, muscle cramps and uterine contracting.

V. Growth and Development of the Fetus

* Prenatal development can be divided into three stages:
  (1) germinal stage from fertilization to two weeks,
  (2) embryonic stage from 2 to 8 weeks, and
  (3) fetal stage from 8 weeks to birth.

A. The Germinal Stage of Development (Weeks 1 and 2)

* The trophoblast cells give rise to the inner amnion and outer chorion. The amnion forms a thin sac of tissue surrounding the fetus and is filled with fluid.
* The inner cells of the blastocyst differentiate into three layers from which all body structures will develop.

B. The Embryonic Stage of Development (weeks 2 through 8)

* During this time all of the embryonic organs become partially formed.

C. The Fetal Stage of Development (week 8 to Birth)

* All primitive organs and structures become more differentiated.

VI. Parturition

A. Uterine Contractions During Parturition

* During labor the uterine myometrium contracts and the cervix dilates.
* The fetus is forced out first and then the placenta by the uterine contractions.

B. Hormonal Control of Parturition

1. Effect of Oxytocin on Parturition
   a. Oxytocin stimulates contraction of uterine muscles.

2. Effects of Protaglandins on Parturition
   a. Prostaglandins stimulate contractions of uterine smooth muscle.

3. Effects of Progesterone on Partuirtion
   a. The level of progesterone which inhibits uterine contractions drops just prior to delivery.

4. Effect of Relaxin on Parturition
   a. Relaxin increases the number of oxytocin receptors in the uterus, softens the cervix, and causes relaxation of pelvic ligaments.

VII. Lactation

A. Anatomy of the Breast

* The breast is composed of glandular epithelium and a ductal system embedded in interstitial tissue and fat. The alveoli, the milk secreting glands, are surrounded by myoepithelial cells.

B. Development of the Breast

* Breast development during pregnancy is stimulated by a number of hormones including estrogen, progesterone, hCG, hCS, prolactin and growth hormone.

C. Hormonal Control of Lactation

* Estrogen and progesterone stimulate breast development
* Prolactin and oxytocin control the production and release of milk following parturition.

1. Effects of Prolactin in Lactation
   a. Estrogen stimulates prolactin release during pregnancy
   b. After birth suckling of the breast stimulates release of prolactin via neural pathways to the hypothalamus. Prolactin levels rise and fall with every episode of nursing.
   c. Prolactin stimulates milk production.

2. Effects of Oxytocin on Lactation
   a. Oxytocin stimulates the release of milk from the breast by acting on the myoepithelial cells around alveoli.
   b. Suckling stimulates release of oxytocin via neural pathways to the hypothalamus.

D. The Composition of Breast Milk
   * Breast milk contains proteins, water, lactose, fat and a variety of vitamins and minerals.

Chapter Learning Objectives

1. Describe the transport of the ovum and sperm to the fallopian tubes.
2. Describe the barriers surrounding the ovum and how the sperm go through them.
3. Describe two methods by which polyspermy is prevented.
4. Describe the embryonic development from the time of fertilization to implantation.
5. Describe how implantation occurs.
6. Describe the formation of the placenta, how and what materials are exchanged through it.
7. Describe the hormones produced by the placenta and their effects on the mother and fetus.
8. Describe physical changes occurring in the mother during each trimester.
9. Describe embryonic and fetal development in general terms.
10. Describe the effects of oxytocin, prostaglandins, progesterone, and relaxin on parturition.
11. Describe the anatomy of the breast and the roles of estrogen, progesterone, prolactin and oxytocin and the effects of suckling on milk production and release.

Key Terms

acrosome
acrosome reaction
alveoli
amnion
areola
blastocyst
capacitation
cervical dilation
cervical mucus
chroion
cilia
colostrum
corpus luteum
cortical granule
cortisol binding globulin (CBG)
cumulus oophorus
decidua
dehydroepiandrosterone-sulfate (DHEA-sulfate)
dizygotic twins
ductal system
ectopic pregnancy
embryo
embryoblasts
embryonic stage
endometrium
fallopian tube
fimbriae
follicle stimulating hormone (FSH)
germinal stage
glandular epithelium
gonadotropin releasing hormone (GnRH)
human chorionic gonadotropin (hCG)
human chorionic somatomammotropin (hCS)
implantation
labor
lactation
lactose
lanugo
luteinizing hormone (LH)
monozygotic twins
morning sickness
morula
myoepithelial cells
oxytocin
placenta
polyspermy
progesterone
prolactin
pronucleus (female, male)
prostaglandin
relaxin
suckling
surfactant
trimester
trophoblast
umbilical cord
vitelline membrane
zona pellucida

Testing Your Understanding

I. Matching. Select the correct word from the Key Terms

_________ 1. released by ovum as a block to polyspermy
_________ 2. forms maternal part of placenta
_________ 3. results from abnormal implantation site
_________ 4. component of milk
_________ 5. released from posterior pituitary and stimulates uterine contractions
_________ 6. forms fluid-filled sac around fetus
_________ 7. process by which sperm attain ability to fertilize ovum
_________ 8. site of fertilization
_________ 9. physical change in mother occurring during first trimester
_________ 10. part of sperm containing digestive enzymes
_________ 11. individuals with exactly the same DNA
_________ 12. give rise to embryo proper
_________ 13. give rise to fetal part of placenta
_________ 14. interface between maternal and fetal circulatory systems
_________ 15. secreted by blastocyst and stimulates corpus leteum to continue producing its hormones.

II. Complete the Table. For each hormone, indicate the source and target tissues.

Hormone	Source(s)	Target tissue(s)	Effect
1. human chorionic gonadotropin (hCG)			
2. human chorionic somatomammotropin (hCS)			
3. estrogen			
4. progesterone			
5. oxytocin			
6. prolactin			
7. relaxin			
8. prostaglandins			

CHAPTER 32 SEXUAL PHYSIOLOGY

Chapter Outline

I. Sexual Determination and Differentiation

A. Sexual Determination: The Sex Chromosomes

1. Meiosis and the Sex Chromosomes
   a. Every cell except the sperm and ovum contains 23 pairs of chromosomes. One pair, the sex chromosomes, provide genetic information that directs the differentiation of gonadal tissues into testes or ovaries.
   b. The sex chromosomes are designated XX in the female and XY in the male.
   c. During meiosis each sperm and ovum receives one sex chromosome in addition to 22 chromosomes called autosomes. The sperm receives an X or Y while the ovum receives an X sex chromosome.
   d. The Y chromosome carries genes directing the gonad to differentiate as testes.

2. The Sex Chromosomes in Fertilization
   a. As a result of fertilization the zygote contains 46 chromosomes and its sex is determined.

3. The Role of the Y Chromosome and the H-Y Antigen
   a. The H-Y antigen is thought to be responsible for inducing testicular differentiation.
   b. The absence of the Y chromosome results in development of ovaries.

B. Differentiation of the Internal Genitalia

* During the first six weeks of embryonic development the gonads of a genetically male or female embryo are anatomically and morphologically identical.

1. The Embryonic Ductal Systems
   a. Two distinct ductal systems are present in the embryo.
   b. In the female the Mullerian duct system developed into the uterus, fallopian tubes and vagina and the Wolffian duct system degenerates.
   c. In the male the Mullerian duct system regresses and the Wolffian duct system develops into the epididymis, vas deferens, seminal vesicles, prostate and ejaculatory duct.

2. Differentiation of Internal Genitalia in the Male
   a. Differentiation of the testes begins at 6 to 7 weeks of gestation.
   b. The Sertoli cells secrete Mullerian Inhibiting Substance which induces regression of the Mullerian duct system.
   c. The Leydig cells secrete testosterone at 7 to 9 weeks of gestation which stimulates differentiation of the Wolffian duct.

3. Differentiation of Internal Genitalia in the Female
   a. Differentiation of the ovaries begins about 12 weeks of gestation.
   b. Differentiation of the Mullerian duct does not require the presence of hormones.

C. Differentiation of the External Genitalia

* The undifferentiated external genitalia consist of a urogenital slit, surrounded by urethral folds, labioscrotal swellings and a genital tubercle.

1. Differentiation of External Genitalia in the Female
   a. Differentiation occurs in the absence of hormones. The urethal folds and labioscrotal swellings become the labia minora and majora, respectively. The tubercle becomes the clitoris and the urogenital slit the vaginal opening and urethra.

2. Differentiation of External Genitalia in the Male
   a. In response to dihydrotestosterone the urethral folds fuse around the urethra to form the shaft of the penis. The labioscrotal swellings form the scrotum and the genital tubercle becomes the penis.

D. Abnormalities of Sexual Differentiation

* Normal patterns of sexual differentiation can be altered because of abnormalities at the level of chromosomal sex, gonadal sex, internal genital sex or external genital sex.

1. Chromosomal Abnormalities in the Female
   a. Both X chromosomes are necessary for development of the ovaries but only one X is needed for differentiation of the Mullerian duct system. Turner's syndrome results when one X is present.

2. Chromosomal Abnormalities in the Male
   a. Presence of an extra X in the male results in Klinefelter syndrome which is characterized by testicular dysfunction.

3. Enzyme Deficiencies in the Female
   a. Exposure of a genetically female embryo to androgens can result in masculinization particularly of external genitalia.

4. Enzyme and Receptor Deficiencies in the Male
   a. Genetic males who lack androgen receptors cannot respond to testosterone, which results in a condition known as testicular feminization syndrome. The testes develop but the Wolffian duct system doesn't.
   b. A deficiency of enzymes necessary for testosterone biosynthesis results in reduced masculization of external genitalia.

II. Human Sexual Response

A. Physiological Changes During the Sexual Response Cycle

* The physiology of the human sexual response in the male and female can be divided into four states: excitement, plateau, orgasm, and resolution.

1. Excitement Phase in the Male
   a. Physiological responses include
      (1) erection of the penis which results from vasocongestion,
      (2) increased blood flow to the testes, and
      (3) an increase in general muscle tone or myotonia.

2. Excitement Phase in the Female
   a. Physiological responses include
      (1) increased blood flow to the vagina and external genitalia,
      (2) vaginal lubrication occurring in response to vaso-congestion,
      (3) expansion of the vagina,
      (4) lifting of the uterus and cervix, and
      (5) increased myotonia.

3. Plateau Phase in the Male
   a. Physiological responses include
      (1) secretion from bulbourethral glands into urethra,
      (2) increased heart rate, blood pressure, respiration rate, and myotonia.

4. Plateau Phase in the Female
   a. Physiological responses include
      (1) tenting of the uterus,
      (2) retraction of the clitoris,
      (3) increased heart and respiration rates, blood pressure, and myotonia.

5. Orgasmic Phase in the Male
   a. Ejaculation involves two processes:
      (1) emission
      (2) expulsion

6. Orgasmic Phase in the Female
   a. Orgasm is characterized by rhythmic muscular contractions of the vagina and uterus and other muscles
   b. Orgasm is not essential for reproduction.

7. Resolution Phase in the Male
   a. The length of the refractory period is highly variable and is affected by age, fatigue and time since the last orgasm.
   b. During resolution the physiological responses return to pre-excitement levels.

8. Resolution Phase in the Female
   a. Females are multiorgasmic unlike males.
   b. During resolution the physiological responses return to pre-excitement levels.

B. Sexual Response During Infancy
   * Sexual arousal in response to physical stimulation occurs even before birth.

C. Sexual Response During Aging
   * Aging and the Female Sexual Response
      a. The breasts, clitoris and vagina remain sensitive to stimulation in old age.
      b. Physiological changes during aging include
         (1) deceased blood flow to the vagina resulting in decreased vaginal lubrication,
         (2) decrease in amount of myotonia previously occurring during excitement, and
         (3) decrease in vaginal elasticity.

2. Aging and the Male Sexual Response
   a. Physiological changes during aging include
      (1) decreased sperm production,
      (2) increase in time spent in refractory period,
      (3) increase in amount of time and stimulation required for erection, and
      (4) decrease in volume of ejaculatory fluid.

III. Sexual Dysfunction

* Sexual dysfunction refers to any condition in which normal physical responses to sexual stimulation are impaired.

A. Endocrine Factors in Sexual Dysfunction

1. Estrogen Deficiencies in the Female
   a. Inadequate estrogen results in atrophic vaginitis which is characterized by
      (1) dryness and thinning of vaginal mucosa,
      (2) decreased elasticity and muscle tone of the vagina.

2. Testosterone Deficiencies in the Male
   a. Low levels of testosterone negatively affect sexual desire and ejaculation.

B. Neural Disorders and Sexual Dysfunction

* Mechanical and disease-related injuries to the spinal cord or brain which interrupt afferent and efferent pathways can result in impairment of sexual arousal and orgasm in both males and females.

C. Drugs and Sexual Dysfunction

* Large amounts of alcohol, sedatives, narcotics, and tranquilizers can retard or inhibit sexual arousal and orgasm in both males and females.
* Other drugs can alter neural control of blood flow to genitalia.

D. Other Sources of Sexual Dysfunction

1. Anorgasmia, Infection, and Vaginismus
   a. Anorgasmia is due primarily to psychological factors.
   b. Nonatrophic vaginitis can be caused by infection, allergic reactions or chemical irritation.
   c. Endometriosus and pelvic inflammatory disease can both cause pain during arousal and intercourse.
   d. Vaginismus, or involuntary contractions and spasms of the vaginal muscles makes penetration very difficult.

2. Erectile Dysfunction, Premature Ejaculation, and Dyspareunea
   a. Erectile dysfunction or impotence, defined as the inability to achieve penile erection sufficient for vaginal penetration, may be classified as primary or secondary.
   b. Secondary dysfunction can occur in response to anxiety, illness, fatigue, lack of privacy, alcohol consumption, etc.
   c. Premature ejaculation occurs more often in younger males and after prolonged stimulation prior to vaginal penetration.
   d. Dyspareunea or painful erection, intromission, or ejaculation can result from balanitis or urethritis.

E. Infertility
   * Infertility can be due to anatomical, hormonal, chromosomal, immunological, or psychological factors.
   * Hormonal factors include:
     (1) inadequate secretion of gonadotropins, androgens or female sex hormones.
   * Infertility may result from low sperm count or abnormal sperm shape or structure.
   * Immunological factors include the production of antisperm antibodies in both males and females.

IV. Contraception

A. Barrier Methods
   * Barrier methods which prevent sperm transport include
     (1) condoms,
     (2) diaphragms,
     (3) cervical caps, and
     (4) contraceptive sponges.

B. Chemical Methods
   * Chemical methods include
     (1) spermicides which kill sperm, and
     (2) the birth control pill which blocks ovulation by interfering with the release of FSH and LH from the pituitary,
     (3) the morning after pill which prevents implantation.
   * The intrauterine device is believed to interfere with implantation.

C. Surgical Methods
   * Surgical methods include
     (1) vasectomy, and
     (2) tubal ligation.

D. Abstinence
   * Periodic abstinence during the time of ovulation is termed the rhythm method. The efficacy of this method depends on the accuracy of predicting ovulation.
   * Three methods to predict ovulation involve monitoring the:
     (1) length of the menstrual cycle.
     (2) daily basal body temperature, and
     (3) consistency of cervical mucus.

E. Future Trends

1. Female Contraception
   a. Future methods focus on the development of
      (1) long acting forms of estrogen and progesterone which can be administered by subcutaneous implantation or injection.
      (2) antagonists to gonadotropins.

2. Male Contraception

<u>Chpater Learning Objectives</u>

1. For each sex describe the chromosomal combination in the body cells and in the sex cells.
2. For each sex describe the differentiation of the internal and external genitalia.
3. Describe the chromosomal or hormonal abnormality, and characteristics associated with each of the following syndromes: Turner, Klinefelter, adrenogenital and testicular feminization.

4. For each sex describe the physiological responses for each of the four stages in the human sexual response.
5. Describe sexual response of infants and in an aging person.
6. Define sexual dysfunction and describe the effects of endocrine deficiencies, neural disorders, and drugs on sexual function.
7. Define and describe the causes of anorgasmia, vaginismus, erectile dysfunction, premature ejaculation, and dyspareunia.
8. Describe four factors contributing to infertility.
9. Compare various types of contraception as to efficacy, method of operation, and ease of use.

Key Terms

abstinence
adrenogenital syndrome
amenorrhea (primary, secondary)
anorgasmia
arousal
atrophic vaginitis
autosomes
birth control pill
contraception
dihydrotestosterone
dyspareunia
emission
endometriosis
erectile dysfunction
erection
excitement
expulsion
genetic sex (XX,XY)
genital tubercle
gonadal sex
H-Y antigen
infertility
intrauterine device
Klinefelter syndrome
labioscrotal swelling
masculinzation
meiosis
morning after pill
Mullerian duct system
Mullerian inhibiting substance
myotonia
nonatrophic vaginitis
orgasm
pelvic inflammatory disease
phenotypic sex
plateau
premature ejaculation
primitive gonads
resolution
rhythm method
sex chromosomes
sexual determination
sexual differentiation
sexual dysfunction
testicular feminization
testosterone
tubal ligation
Turner syndrome
urogenital folds, slit
vaginal lubrication
vaginismus
vasectomy
vasocongestion
Wolffian duct systems

Testing Your Understanding

I. Matching. Select the correct word from the Key Terms.

________ 1. sex chromosomes in female
________ 2. develops into clitoris or penis
________ 3. responsible for inducing testicular differentiation
________ 4. develops into uterus, vagina, cervix
________ 5. develops into vas deferens, epididymis
________ 6. becomes scrotum and labia majora
________ 7. stimulates differentiation of external genitalia
________ 8. abnormality in male with extra X chromosome
________ 9. syndrome with masculinization of external genitalia
________ 10. syndrome with absence of masculinization in external genitalia
________ 11. sexual response stage characterized by erection and vaginal lubrication
________ 12. sexual response stage characterized by ejaculation and decrease in myotonia
________ 13. dysfunction resulting from inadequate estrogen stimulation
________ 14. involuntary contractions and spasms of pubococcygeal muscles
________ 15. surgical procedure in which male transport duct is severed

II. Complete the Table

Embryonic Structure	Adult Structure: Male	Adult Structure: Female
genital tubercle		
labioscrotal swellings		
urogenital folds		
urogenital slit		
Mullerian duct system		
Wolffian duct system		
gonad		

III. Complete the Table. For each syndrome, indicate the cause and appearance of structure (if known).

Syndrome	Cause	external genitalia	gonad	internal genitalia
Turner				
Klinefelter				
adrenogenital				
testicular feminization				

IV. For each condition describe the effect on sexual differentiation for the stated sex.

Condition	Effect
1. exposure of female embryo to testosterone	
2. exposure of male embryo to estrogen and progesterone	
3. deficiency of alpha reductase in a male embryo	
4. deficiency of androgen receptors in a male embryo	
5. embryo with XX	
6. deficiency of 21-hydroxylase in a female embryo	

Answers to Questions in Part III

Chapter 16

I. Matching

1. tendon
2. antagonistic pair
3. sarcomere
4. actin
5. myosin
6. sarcolemma
7. sarcoplasmic reticulum
8. intercolated disks, gap junction
9. isometric
10. isotonic
11. power output
12. t-system
13. tetanus
14. lactic acid
15. white fiber

II.

1. c, thick filament
2. b, thin filament
3. b, thin filament
4. e, I band
5. a,e H zone, I band
6. d A band

IV.

1. contract
2. not contract - fatigue
3. continual contraction, cannot relax
4. keeps contracting
5. no contraction

Chapter 17

I. Matching

1. erythrocyte
2. erythropoiesis
3. viscosity
4. hemoglobin
5. hemolysis
6. anemia
7. neutrophil
8. eosinophil
9. cell-mediated
10. B-lymphocyte, plasma cell
11. leukemia
17. platelet
13. thrombin
14. complement
15. cytotoxic T

Chapter 18

I. Matching

1. atrium
2. ventricle
3. atrioventricular valve
4. pulmonary valve
5. myocardium
6. coronary vessels
7. sinoatrial node
8. Purkinje fibers
9. ECG
10. diastole
11. systole
12. diastole
13. stroke volume
14. tachycardia
15. cardiac output

Chapter 19

I. Matching

1. pulse pressure
2. systolic pressure
3. myogenic activity
4. autoregulation
5. vasodilation
6. vasoconstriction
7. vasodilation
8. oncotic pressure
9. Starling's hypothesis
10. filtration
11. absorption
12. veins
13. baroreceptors
14. lymphatic system
15. hypertension

II. Complete the Table

1, 2, 3, 4, 5, 6, 8 vasodilation
5, 7 vasoconstriction

III. Complete the Table

1, 3, 4, 6 arterial pressure increases
2, 5, 7, 8 arterial pressure decreases
1, 3, 4, 6, 8 cardiac output increases
2, 5, 7 cardiac output decreases

Chapter 20

I. Matching

1. alveolus
2. ventilation
3. turbulent air flow
4. tidal volume
5. forced vital capacity
6. residual volume
7. functional residual capacity
8. dead space volume
9. diaphragm
10. transpulmonic
11. pneumothorax
12. alveolar
13. thoracic cavity
14. compliance
15. pulmonary surfactant

II. Complete the Table

A. contact, increase size, decrease, decrease, increase, increase
B. relax, decrease size, increase, increase, decrease, decrease

III. Fill in the Table

1, 2, 3, 5 increase
4, 6 decrease

Chapter 21

I. Matching

1. pulmonary artery
2. pulmonary edema
3. angiotensin I
4. hypoxia
5. hypoxemia
6. pulmonary hypertension
7. bicarbonate ion
8. carbaminohemoglobin
9. embolus
10. foramen ovale

II. Fill in the Table

1, 2, 3, 5 right, unloading
4 left, loading

Chapter 22

I. Matching

1. analgesia
2. carboxyhemoglobin
3. atelectasia
4. retrolental fibrous
5. redout
6. anoxic
7. free radicals
8. hyperventilation
9. polycythemia
10. bends

Chapter 23

I. Matching

1. muscosa
2. portal circulation
3. mucin
4. short
5. long
6. gastrin
7. secretin
8. lower esophageal sphincter
9. peristalsis
10. pyloric sphincter
11. chief cells
12. acini
13. lipose, bile salts
14. microvilli
15. small intestine

Chapter 24

I. Matching

1. glomerulus
2. proximal convoluted tubule
3. ureter
4. juxtamedullary nephron
5. luminal membrane
6. peritubular capillary
7. juxtaglomerular apparatus
8. glomerular hydrostatic pressure
9. fenestra
10. tubular transport maximum (Tm)
11. loops of Henle
12. vasa recta
13. colloid osmotic pressure
14. ADH
15. urea

II. Complete the Table

1, 4, 5 none
2, 3, 6, 7 decrease
8 increase

Chapter 25

I. Matching

1. positive balance
2. osmoreceptor
3. baroreceptor
4. hyponatremia
5. ADH
6. micturition
7. urethra
8. aldosterone
9. atrial natriuretic factor
10. diuretic
11. hypokalemia
12. hypertension
13. azotemia
14. hemodialysis
15. detrusor

II. Complete the Table

1. increase, increase
2. decrease, increase
3. increase, decrease
4. increase, increase
5. decrease, decrease
6. increase, increase
7. increase, increase
8. increase, increase
9. increase, -
10. increase, increase

III. Complete the Table

1. increase
2. increase
3. increase
4. increase
5. decrease
6. decrease
7. increase
8. increase
9. increase
10. decrease
11. decrease
12. decrease
13. decrease
14. -

Chapter 26

I. Matching

1. acid
2. base
3. amphoteric
4. dissociation
5. association
6. buffer
7. chemoreceptor
8. respiratory acidosis
9. respiratory alkalosis
10. metabolic acidosis

II. Complete the Table

1, 4, 6, 8 all decrease
2, 3, 5, 7 all increase

Chapter 27

I. Matching

1. filtered calcium
2. tetany
3. hydroxyapatite crystals
4. osteoid
5. osteoblast
6. osteoclasts
7. epiphyseal plate
8. chondrocyte
9. PTH
10. calcitonin
11. 1, 25-dihydroxy-vitamin D_3
12. proteoglycan, collagen
13. phosphaturia
14. osteoporosis
15. rickets, osteomalacia

II. Complete the Table

1. increase, increase, decrease
2. all decrease
3. all increase
4. decrease, decrease, increase
5. all decrease

Chapter 28

I. Matching

1. poikilotherm
2. rectal
3. mean skin temperature
4. thermography
5. mean body temperature
6. metabolic rate
7. thermal homeostasis
8. human calorimeter
9. respirometer
10. radiation
11. evaporation
12. convection
13. antirise response
14. heat exhaustion
15. hypothermia

II. Complete the Table

1, 3, 4, 5, 7, 9 increase
2, 6, 8 decrease

Chapter 29

I. Matching

1. phosphagen energy system
2. static
3. VO_2 max
4. alactacid oxygen debt
5. diffusing capacity of lung

II. Complete the Table

1, 3, 5 increase
2, 4 decrease

Chapter 30

I. Matching

1. Leydig cells
2. corpus luteum
3. corpus luteum, granulosa cells
4. seminiferous tubules
5. LH
6. FSH
7. prostate
8. clitoris
9. secondary amenorrhea
10. blood-testis barrier
11. estrogen or GnRH
12. antrum
13. endometrium
14. epididymis
15. acrosome

II. Complete the Table

1. none, decrease
2. stops, none
3. stops, stops
4. none, stops
5. none, stops
6. stops, none
7. continues, continues
8. none, stops
9. none, stops
10. none, none

Chapter 31

I. Matching

1. cortical granule
2. decidua
3. ectopic pregnancy
4. lactose
5. oxytocin
6. amnion
7. capacitation
8. fallopian tube
9. morning sickness
10. acrosome
11. monozygous twins
12. embryoblasts
13. trophoblasts
14. placenta
15. hCG

Chapter 32

I. Matching

1. XX
2. genital tubercle
3. H-Y antigen
4. Mullerian duct system
5. Wolffian duct system
6. labioscrotal swellings
7. dihydrotestosterone
8. Klinefelter syndrome
9. adrenogenital syndrome
10. testicular feminization
11. excitement
12. orgasm
13. atrophic vaginitis
14. vaginismus
15. vasectomy